Study Guide
with Worked Examples

for use with

essentials of
international economics
second edition

Robert C. Feenstra   Alan M. Taylor

D1569774

Stephen Ross Yeaple
University of Colorado at Boulder

WORTH PUBLISHERS

Study Guide with Worked Examples
by Stephen Ross Yeaple
for use with **Feenstra/Taylor:** *Essentials of International Economics, Second Edition*

© 2011, 2008 by Worth Publishers

ISBN 13: 978-1-4292-7934-5
ISBN 10: 1-4292-7934-6

First Printing 2011

Printed in the United States of America

Worth Publishers
41 Madison Avenue
New York, NY 10010
www.worthpublishers.com

CONTENTS

PREFACE

Robert Feenstra and Alan Taylor have written an excellent textbook that identifies the important issues in international economics and presents and explains a wide range of microeconomic and macroeconomic models that can be used to analyze these issues. This *Study Guide with Worked Examples* complements the textbook by providing students additional opportunities to develop their knowledge of international economics through active learning. Active learning strategies are useful not only in academics but also in sports, music, or the arts. A good coach or teacher (1) *identifies* an important skill for a player or student to develop, (2) *demonstrates* that skill to the player or student, (3) *confirms* that the player or student is executing the technique properly, and finally (4) *drills* the player or student until the skill becomes second nature. In most higher education settings, materials are made available to you that can take you through these steps, but it is up to you to take those steps.

The strategy employed in the *Study Guide with Worked Examples* has two components. First, for each section of each chapter in the textbook, the essential concepts are reviewed and key terms are presented in order to make students aware of what material they need to know. In places, fundamental economic principles from introductory microeconomic and macroeconomics courses are reviewed. Students are also invited to provide the definition of the key terms that form the basic vocabulary of international economics.

The second component involves problem solving. For each section of each chapter questions are asked (1) that test students' knowledge of essential concepts and (2) that help reinforce the logical structure of economic analysis. The problems vary considerably in difficulty, occasionally asking students to extend the uses of economic principles beyond the applications discussed in the textbook. Although space is provided for answers directly after each question, students are encouraged to use additional space to provide careful explanations because most of the value created from answering stimulating questions is in the practice of writing detailed answers. Tips are provided immediately following questions that delve into particularly important or difficult topics to identify common mistakes and demonstrate common features of different types of economic problems. Finally, detailed answers for every study guide question are provided at the end of the book.

The more time and effort that you put into your studies, the more rewarding your experience will be and the more you will appreciate the quality of the textbook that Robert Feenstra and Alan Taylor have written.

ACKNOWLEDGMENTS

I would like to thank Rob Feenstra, Alan Taylor, and Sarah Dorger, Acquisitions Editor at Worth Publishers, for encouraging me to write this study guide. I thank all of the people at Worth Publishers who gave me direction and helped in putting this book together, especially Marie McHale, Development Editor; Edgar Bonilla, Project Editor; and Stacey Alexander, Production Manager. I am deeply grateful to my wife, Katherine, for proofreading much of the book. Thanks also to the students in my International Trade class at Princeton University for commenting on the earliest drafts of the manuscript. Finally, I thank my children for their enthusiasm.

Stephen Ross Yeaple
University of Colorado at Boulder

1

The Global Economy

Overview

The term "globalization" means many things: the flow of goods and services across borders; the movement of people and firms; the spread of culture and ideas between countries; and the tight integration of financial markets around the world. In this book we analyze the flows of goods and services, people, and capital between countries and the policies that governments use to influence these flows. The volume of these flows is huge and is growing very rapidly. In addition to attempting to understand the forces that drive these flows, we will also delve deeply into the impact of these flows on welfare. How does trade affect a nation's material well-being? Does international trade increase the gap between the rich and the poor? What is the impact of immigration on workers?

This chapter presents a broad view of the flows in goods and services, people, and capital across borders. We will see that these flows are complex and difficult to summarize, but there are patterns in these flows that can be explained. The second half of this chapter provides a brief overview of international macroeconomics. The topics are organized into three categories. Because the exchange rate is the most important price in the economy, affecting the well-being of all of a country's citizens, the structure of the foreign exchange market and the theory of the exchange rate come first. The causes and implications of financial globalization are next on the agenda. The ability to borrow and lend on international financial markets is shown to improve a country's well-being, but there are limits to a country's activities on international markets and dramatic consequences when countries cannot fulfill their international obligations. Finally, as in virtually every chapter, there is some analysis of the policy decisions facing governments. These policies span the mundane, such as fiscal policy, through very intricate decisions, such as whether a country would be well served by joining the Eurozone.

1 International Trade

ESSENTIAL CONCEPTS

International trade occurs when the residents of one country sell *merchandise goods* or *services* to residents of another country. The volume of international trade between countries is huge. In 2005 the total value of exports of goods was $10.2 trillion and the total volume of exports of services was $2.4 trillion. This chapter presents a large amount of information on the size and direction of international trade flows that may be hard to digest. We attempt to boil down some patterns in the international trade data.

- Countries with large *gross domestic product* (GDP) account for most international trade.
- Small countries engage in proportionately more trade relative to their GDP than do large countries.
- The volume of trade between two countries falls off rapidly in the distance between the two countries.
- Trade occurs between very similar countries and between very different countries.
- Two-way trade between countries is common; for example, the largest market for U.S. exports is Canada, and Canada is the largest source country for U.S. imports.
- Trade volumes have increased more rapidly than gross domestic product since the 1950s.
- Tariffs have fallen steadily since the 1950s.
- Technological progress in shipping has dramatically reduced international trade costs.

Why do countries engage in international trade? What affect does international trade have on the wealth of nations? What impact do these trade volumes have on the distribution of income? These are the big questions within the field of international trade, and various answers to these questions are given in Chapters 2 through 7. Chapters 2 to 4 and Chapter 7 present models that explain the motive for trade between countries with different characteristics, such as access to technology and natural resource abundances. Chapter 6 presents a model that explains why very similar countries, perhaps even identical countries, can gain from engaging in international trade and why most international trade between countries occurs between large developed countries that are in close proximity to each other.

Government policies toward trade have a big impact on the volume of trade. During periods when trade barriers, such as tariffs and quotas, have been low, international trade has flourished, whereas during periods of high trade barriers, such as the years between World War I and World War II, trade volumes have contracted. The effect of trade policies on the volume of international trade and on welfare are the subject of Chapters 8 through 11. Throughout this section of the book, we discuss the role of an important international institution, the World Trade Organization (WTO), in coordinating trade policies among its member countries and facilitating the growth of international trade.

KEY TERMS

Use the space provided to record your notes on the following key terms.

Exports _____

_____

_____

Imports _____

_____

_____

Merchandise goods _____

_____

_____

Service exports _____

_____

_____

Trade balance _____

_____

_____

Trade surplus _____

_____

_____

Trade deficit _____

_____

_____

Bilateral trade balance _____

_____

_____

Gross domestic product _____

_____

_____

Value-added _____

_____

_____

Offshoring _____

_____

_____

Trade barriers _____

_____

_____

Import tariffs _____

_____

_____

Import quota _____

_____

_____

REVIEW QUESTIONS

Problem 1: Why is a bilateral trade balance often a misleading measure? Explain.

_____

_____

_____

Problem 2: Table 1-2 in the textbook shows the share of trade in gross domestic product. What characteristics appear to be important in explaining how reliant a country is on international trade?

_____

_____

_____

Problem 3: According to Table 1-2 in the textbook, the international trade volumes of Hong Kong and Malaysia exceed their GDP. How is this possible?

_____

_____

_____

Problem 4: Consider the following assertion: "Globalization is an irresistible force drawing countries together." Does the historical record support this assertion?

_____

_____

_____

TIPS

The statistics presented in the chapter are "aggregate" volumes, lacking any detail about the types of goods and services traded. The actual motives for trade are obscured. In later chapters we will see that there are patterns in the composition of trade between countries.

Problem 4 is meant to point out that trade barriers between countries affect the volume of international trade. Historically, tariffs and quotas have occasionally increased rather than decreased. This is one reason for the fact that the two "golden eras" of globalization are separated by many years.

2 Migration and Foreign Direct Investment

ESSENTIAL CONCEPTS

International _migration_ is a contentious topic in many countries. Many concerns raised by immigration are economic in nature. How does immigration affect wages? Do immigrants take jobs away from native-born residents? Given these fears, it is not surprising that all countries have restrictions on inward migration, and it is a safe bet that in the absence of these restrictions there would be substantially more international migration of labor. Chapter 5 presents an economic analysis of the effects of migration and shows that from the perspective of theory, immigration's effect on wages is primarily a short-run phenomenon. In the long run, the economy can absorb an increase in labor force without major changes in wages. The trade models presented in Chapter 4 also demonstrate that international trade acts as a substitute for immigration: A worker may not be able to enter the U.S. labor market, but the goods produced by the worker can.

Foreign direct investment occurs when a firm in one country owns a company in another country. Flows of foreign direct investment (FDI) between countries are substantial. A common perception is that multinational companies primarily invest in low-wage countries in order to reduce their costs of production. Although this type of foreign direct investment does occur, most foreign direct investment is between developed countries. A key example is the vast network of assembly plants in the United States owned by the Japanese firm Toyota. This type of foreign direct investment is often called *horizontal FDI* because it involves replicating the same production activity in many locations. The motive for this type of FDI is typically explained by the desire of firms to produce near their customers. *Vertical FDI* occurs when a multinational opens a plant in a low-wage country. Much of the vertical FDI of U.S. multinationals is in Mexico. Although the numbers for vertical FDI are considerably smaller than the numbers for horizontal FDI, vertical FDI is more controversial. Reverse-vertical FDI is where a multinational from a low-wage country opens or acquires a plant in a high-wage country, such as the recent takeover of the formerly Swedish company Volvo by the Chinese automaker Geely.

KEY TERMS

Use the space provided to record your notes on the following key terms.

Migration _____

_____

_____

Foreign direct investment _____

_____

_____

Horizontal FDI _____

_____

_____

Vertical FDI _____

_____

_____

REVIEW QUESTIONS

Problem 5: Worker migration between countries is almost entirely from the lowest-wage countries to the highest-wage countries. True or false? Explain.

_____

_____

_____

Problem 6: Why might a multinational produce the same good in many different countries? Explain.

_____

_____

_____

Problem 7: Foreign direct investment can affect the volume of trade. Would you expect that vertical and horizontal FDI have a different or similar impact on trade volumes? Explain.

_____

_____

_____

The book measures migration by the number of foreign-born people in a country, and it measures foreign direct investment by the change in the level of foreign ownership of companies in a given time period. The first is a "stock"; the second is a "flow." The actual sales of the foreign companies owned by multinationals are much larger than the flow of new investments.

Problem 7 points out that the flows of trade and foreign direct investment are interrelated.

3 International Macroeconomics

FOREIGN EXCHANGE: CURRENCIES AND CRISES

The exchange rate is the price of one country's currency in terms of another. It is the single most important price in an open economy because its level determines how expensive foreign goods and services are relative to domestic goods and services and because changes in the exchange rate affect the relative return on foreign assets. The foreign exchange market, where currencies are traded, is the largest market in the world. The structure and operation of the market are laid out in Chapter 13 and a theory of the monetary forces that determine the exchange rate is laid out in Chapters 14 and 15.

Movements in the exchange rate can have a big impact on an economy's performance because the exchange rate affects demand for a country's goods and services and can directly alter a country's wealth. A sudden sharp drop in the exchange rate, known as an _exchange rate crisis,_ can have serious economic implications, including a large drop in economic output, a rise in poverty, and widespread bank failures. The economic dislocation caused by such crises occasionally spills over into the political arena in the form of riots and government failures. The _International Monetary Fund_ is the international institution charged with helping countries in crisis. The tools to understand the links between countries are developed in Chapter 13, whereas the effect of exchange rate movements on the economy is the subject of Chapter 14.

To avoid the effects of a changing exchange rate, some governments choose to have a _fixed_ exchange rate. To do so, they must be prepared to buy and sell their currency for foreign currency. Other countries prefer to let their exchange rate _float,_ allowing market forces to determine the exchange rate. Some countries group together and adopt a common currency. The relative merits of different exchange rate regimes is the focus of Chapter 19, whereas the euro, the common currency of many European countries, is discussed in detail in Chapter 21.

KEY TERMS

Use the space provided to record your notes on the following key terms.

Fixed exchange rate _____

_____

_____

Floating exchange rate _____

_____

_____

Exchange rate crisis _____

_____

_____

Default _____

_____

International Monetary Fund (IMF) _____

_____

_____

World Bank _____

_____

REVIEW QUESTIONS

Problem 8: Why do economists call the exchange rate "the single most important price in the economy"? _____

_____

Problem 9: How can a movement in the exchange rate affect a country's exporters?

_____

_____

GLOBALIZATION OF FINANCE: OF DEBTS AND DEFICITS

Essential Concepts

When a household spends more than it earns, it must either draw down its savings or sell assets (borrow). Countries find themselves in the same situation. A country whose *expenditure* exceeds its *income* is running a current account *deficit* and must sell assets to another country that is running a current account *surplus.* Countries that persistently spend less than their income build up their external *wealth,* whereas countries that run current account deficits run down their wealth. As is the case with households, *capital gains* and losses also affect a country's wealth. The *balance of payments* is an elaborate accounting system designed to follow international transactions and the evolution of its external wealth. The balance of payments accounts is closely integrated with a country's national accounts, which follow the flow of spending within a country. The national accounts and balance of payments are explained in Chapter 13.

Financial globalization allows countries to separate their savings from their investment, thereby helping countries that are experiencing bad times or that have high investment needs. The downside is that countries occasionally find themselves unwilling to repay their debts to international creditors. Countries considered likely to default on their foreign debts pay higher interest rates due to their *country risk.*

KEY TERMS

Use the space below to record your notes on the following key terms.

Income _____

_____

_____

Expenditure _____

_____

_____

Surplus _____

_____

_____

Deficit _____

_____

_____

Wealth _____

_____

_____

Capital gains _____

_____

_____

Country risk _____

_____

_____

Balance of payments _____

_____

_____

REVIEW QUESTIONS

Problem 10: Suppose that it costs Brazil 10% interest to borrow and in the United States only 4%. What is the level of Brazilian country risk? _____

_____

_____

Problem 11: Suppose that Home runs a current account deficit.

11a. What should happen to Home's external wealth, *ceteris paribus?* _____

_____

_____

11b. What phenomenon could make Home's external wealth move in an unexpected direction?

_____

_____

_____

GOVERNMENTS AND INSTITUTIONS: OF POLICIES AND PERFORMANCE

Essential Concepts

The implications of various *policies* are discussed throughout the half of the book devoted to international macroeconomics. Some of these policies are more fundamental than others. *Regimes* are sets of rules that define the parameters within which policy is implemented. Even more fundamentally, *institutions* cover the most basic legal, political, and social structures that influence economic behavior.

The process of globalization is driven in large part by governments reducing their restrictions on the economic integration of their country with other nations. Countries have reduced their barriers to trade in goods and services and have increasingly removed restrictions on capital flows in and out of the country. A definite pattern arises across countries in terms of the extent of liberalization, with the *advanced countries* liberalizing the most, *emerging markets* liberalizing some, and *developing countries* still largely outside the global economy.

One of the most important policies facing a country is its choice of exchange rate regime. A country that fixes its exchange rate avoids the uncertainties created by exchange rate fluctuation but limits its ability to carry out an independent monetary policy. Moreover, it may become more susceptible to exchange rate crises. Some countries have starkly integrated their economy with those of others by adopting a *common currency* or by engaging in *dollarization*. The monetary implications of a fixed exchange rate are addressed in Chapter 12, and the criteria for preferring a fixed exchange rate over a flexible system are elaborated in Chapter 15.

KEY TERMS

Use the space below to record your notes on the following key terms.

Policies _____

_____

_____

Regimes _____

_____

_____

Institutions _____

_____

_____

Advanced countries _____

_____

_____

Emerging markets _____

_____

_____

Common currency _____

_____

_____

Dollarization _____

_____

_____

The Great Divergence _____

_____

_____

Income per person _____

_____

_____

Income volatility _____

_____

_____

Developing countries _____

_____

_____

REVIEW QUESTIONS

Problem 12: What forces propel globalization?

_____

_____

TIPS   If this chapter has been a bit of blur, do not worry too much. You will get the opportunity to work through it all carefully in the next 10 chapters.

2

Trade and Technology: The Ricardian Model

Overview

Trade patterns between countries display regularities that can be explained using economic theory. Different facts suggest different economic mechanisms. This chapter introduces a model developed by the nineteenth-century economist David Ricardo that relates a particular country characteristic, its technology, to its trade pattern. Ricardo showed that a country could be technologically "backward" in every industry and still gain from trading with more productive countries. The analysis of Ricardo's model illustrates the principle of *comparative advantage,* one of the most fundamental concepts in economics. Many of the economic mechanisms found in Ricardo's model are also to be found in the more complicated models discussed later in the book. For this reason, it will pay to be especially vigilant in your study of this chapter!

The next four chapters explore various other models that offer explanations for particular regularities in the pattern of trade across countries. In addition to providing some explanation for these trade patterns, the models can also be used to understand the impact of international trade on welfare.

1 Reasons for Trade

ESSENTIAL CONCEPTS

The pattern of trade between countries, both in the aggregate statistics presented in Chapter 1 and in the example of U.S. imports of snowboards presented at the beginning of this chapter, suggests that there are a range of explanations for why countries trade with each other. Many of these explanations involve differences across countries in terms of the characteristics of their economies. For instance, countries may differ in their access to *technology* or in their supply of productive *resources*. Differences in technology will lead some countries to have *absolute advantages* in the production of some goods. That is, in the production of some goods they may be the world's productivity leaders. The actual explanation for trading patterns lies not in a country's absolute advantage, however, but rather in its *comparative advantage*. A country has a comparative advantage in the good that it is relatively better able to produce. Comparative advantage can be due to differences in technology, but it can also stem from a country's endowment of *resources,* be those resources natural (such as arable land or coal) or artificially created (such as capital).

Finally, geography matters for the structure of trade in many ways. Aside from geography's impact on a country's endowments of natural resources, geography also determines the distances between countries. A key regularity in the data is that the amount of trade between two countries falls in the distance between them. Trading relationships that are fostered by *proximity* are often strengthened by government policy. Canada, Mexico, and the United States have traditionally traded a great deal with each other because of the ease of transport and communication. A *free trade area* agreed to by these countries has also deepened their trading ties.

KEY TERMS

Use the space provided to record your notes on the following key terms.

Exports _____

_____

_____

Imports _____

_____

_____

Proximity _____

_____

_____

Resources _____

_____

_____

Natural resources _____

_____

_____

Labor resources _____

_____

_____

Capital _____

_____

_____

Factors of production _____

_____

_____

Absolute advantage _____

_____

_____

Comparative advantage _____

_____

_____

Technology _____

_____

_____

Free trade area _____

_____

_____

Foreign direct investment _____

_____

_____

Offshoring _____

_____

_____

2 The Ricardian Model

ESSENTIAL CONCEPTS

This chapter uses a simple general equilibrium model developed by David Ricardo to illustrate the principle of *comparative advantage*. In a general equilibrium model, an economy has a supply of *factors,* or resources used to produce goods. *Technology* determines how factors are turned into goods. Demand for these goods is determined by consumers' income, which depends on the economy's output; by consumers' preferences, which are represented by *indifference curves;* and by *relative prices.* Finally, a general equilibrium model specifies how people and firms compete. In this chapter, perfect competition prevails in every market.

The economy's *production possibility frontier* (PPF) summarizes what the economy can produce given its technology and factor endowment. In Ricardo's model, the marginal product of labor (MPL) in each industry is constant so that an industry's output is just its marginal product of labor multiplied by the number of workers employed in the industry. By moving labor between industries, we can trace out a country's PPF. The slope of this PPF tells us the *opportunity cost* of expanding the output of the good on the X axis in terms of the good on the Y axis. A country has a comparative advantage in a good if its opportunity cost of production of that good is lower than the opportunity cost of that good in other countries.

The level of consumer demand for goods depends on (1) consumers' budget constraints, (2) consumers' tastes, and (3) relative prices. Because these concepts are used in many of the book's chapters, it is worth reviewing them. Suppose a consumer has income I to spend on apples and shirts. The number of apples she demands is D_A and the number of shirts she demands is D_S. The price of apples is P_A and the price of shirts is P_S. If she spends all her income, then

$$I = P_A \cdot D_A + P_S \cdot D_S \Rightarrow D_S = \frac{I}{P_S} - \frac{P_A}{P_S} \cdot D_A.$$

Note that P_A / P_S is called the *relative price* of apples. The relative price tells us the *opportunity cost* of an apple to a consumer given the prices of the two goods, or how many shirts need to be given up to buy an additional apple. For simplicity, the country is treated as one consumer that has its own budget constraint. Where on the budget constraint a consumer chooses to purchase depends on her preferences, which are represented by *indifference curves* as shown in Figure 2-1.

There are two assumptions behind the way that indifference curves are drawn: (1) consumers want *more* of all goods, and (2) *ceteris paribus* (all other things equal) consumers get diminishing returns out of consuming more of the same good. From these assumptions it follows that indifference curves are convex (as shown) and higher indifference curves imply greater utility. Changes in income and relative prices change a consumer's budget constraint but have no impact on the consumer's tastes. That is, the map of indifference curves never changes; all that changes is which curve we can reach. The tastes of the entire country are represented using a single set of indifference curves that tells us which bundle on their budget constraint consumers choose and how well-off they are.

Finally, we assume that there is perfect competition. Because firms take prices and wages as given in making their hiring decisions, the relative prices that they charge ex-

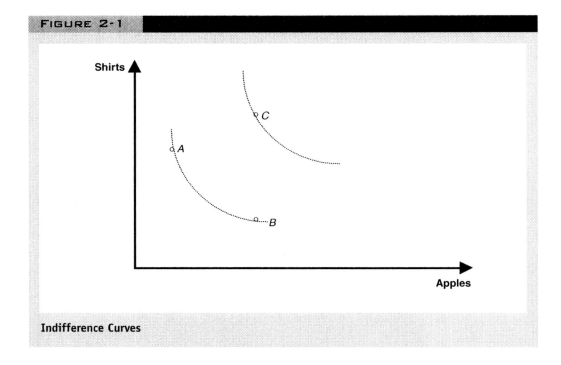

FIGURE 2-1

Shirts

C

A

B

Apples

Indifference Curves

actly reflect the opportunity cost of production facing the economy. Because firms make zero profits, their earnings are passed on to workers so that workers can consume what is produced.

An equilibrium occurs when firms supply goods and hire workers to maximize their profits, consumers demand goods to maximize their utility, and supply equals demand. In a "no-trade equilibrium" there is only domestic demand, so the level of domestic production must equal the level of domestic demand. When international trade is allowed, foreign demand and supply must be taken into account.

KEY TERMS

Use the space provided to record your notes on the following key terms.

Factors _____

_____

_____

Marginal product of labor _____

_____

_____

Production possibilities frontier _____

_____

_____

Opportunity cost _____

_____

_____

Relative price _____

_____

_____

Indifference curves _____

_____

_____

Utility _____

_____

_____

REVIEW QUESTIONS

Problem 1: Home is endowed with 100 workers who can produce two goods: shirts and apples. Workers' *marginal product* of labor in shirts (MPL_S) is 2. (One worker can produce 2 shirts.) The marginal product of labor in apples is 5.

1a. Graph Home's PPF with output of shirts (Q_S) on the Y axis and apples (Q_A) on the X axis; label the intercepts and the slope.

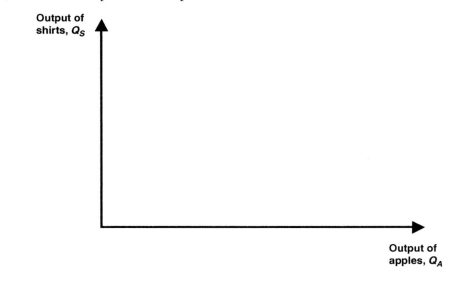

1b. Explain why the PPF is a straight line. _____

_____

_____

1c. What is the opportunity cost of apples in terms of shirts? _____

_____

1d. What is the opportunity cost of shirts in terms of apples? _____

_____

1e. How would you change the graph that was the answer to 1a if the number of workers in the country fell to 50? Show in the axes provided below.

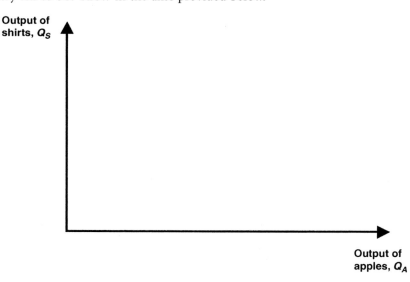

1f. Does this change the opportunity costs of the goods? _____

_____

1g. Suppose that the workers wake up feeling sick one day and their marginal product in both goods is half as much as it was before ($MPL_S = 1$ and $MPL_A = 5/2$). How would this change the PPF relative to your answer in 1a? Show in the axes provided below.

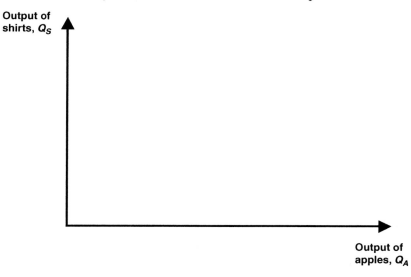

1h. Now suppose that the bumblebees in Home become depressed and so are less able to pollinate the apple trees. As a result, the MPL_A falls from 5 to 2. How does this change affect Home's PPF? Show the "before" and "after" cases in the axes provided below.

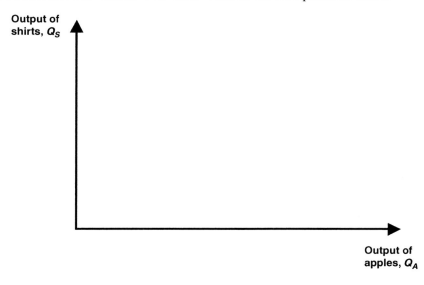

1i. How does "the great bee depression" affect the opportunity cost of apples in terms of shirts? _____

_____

_____

TIPS

In the Ricardian model the PPF is always straight, never curved. This is because there is only one factor and its marginal product in each industry is assumed to be constant. Later we will see models with "curved" PPFs.

The opportunity cost of good A in terms of good B is only equal to the slope of the PPF if good A is on the X axis.

The problems above can be used as a "cookbook" for other problems. Experiment with different numbers for stock of factors and for technology to get more practice.

Problem 2: Home is endowed with 100 workers. The marginal product of labor in shirts (MPL_S) is 2. The marginal product of labor in apples is 5. Suppose the price of a shirt is $5 and the price of an apple is $2.

2a. Given the information provided in problem 2, where on the PPF will the economy produce?

_____

_____

2b. Suppose the price of an apple rises to $4. What will firms produce?

_____

_____

TIPS

There is perfect competition. Given prices, firms adjust output to maximize their profits and in the process generate demand for factors. Prices of factors then adjust to guarantee that firms make zero profits.

Because marginal products are constant in Ricardo's model, firms are willing to supply *any* level of output along the PPF as long as relative prices are equal to the slope of the PPF.

For any other relative price, the economy *must* specialize in one good.

Problem 3: An apple costs 20¢ ($P_A = \$1 / 5$), a shirt costs 50¢ ($P_S = \$1 / 2$), and the consumer's income is $100.

3a. What is the equation for the budget constraint? Graph this budget constraint, being careful to label all the relevant information.

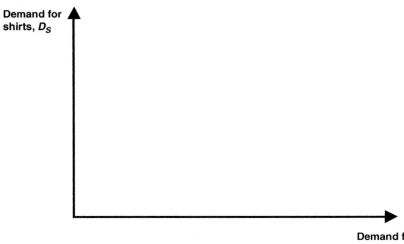

3b. How would your graph change if income is $200, the price of apples is 40¢, and the price of a shirt is $1?

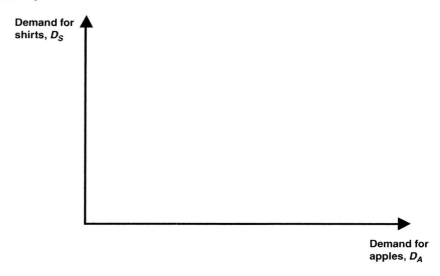

3c. Starting from the case in which income is $200, the price of apples is 40¢, and the price of shirts is $1, show how the graph changes when the price of shirts falls to 50¢ and everything else stays the same. How has the opportunity cost of apples been affected by the change in the dollar price of shirts? _____

_____

_____

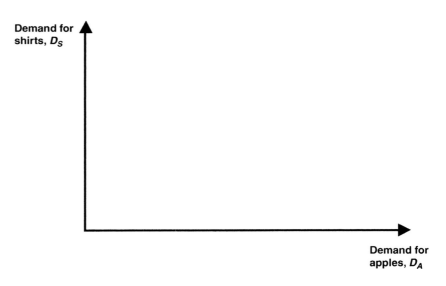

3d. Show how the graph changes when the price of shirts is $1 and the price of apples falls to 20¢. How has the opportunity cost of shirts been affected by the change in the price of apples? _____

_____

_____

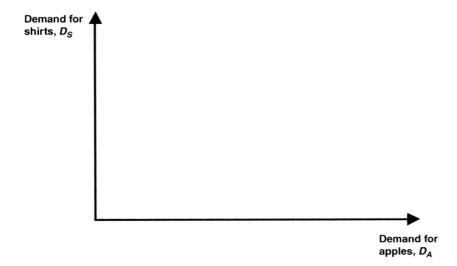

It is important to remember that the slope of the budget constraint is the price of the good on the *X* axis divided by the price of the good on the *Y* axis.

Relative prices do *not* involve dollar signs! They are "real" in the sense that they tell us the tradeoff facing consumers in actual goods.

In the Ricardian model, international trade will be like a change in relative prices as shown in problems 3c and 3d. Consumers can afford more of both goods as long as the consumer spends his income on both goods.

Problem 4: Consider the information in Figure 2-1. The dotted lines are indifference curves, and *A*, *B*, and *C* are three different bundles of goods.

4a. Given the choice of *A*, *B*, or *C*, which bundle would the consumer select? _____

_____

_____

4b. Given the choice of *A* or *B*, which bundle would the consumer select? _____

_____

_____

4c. A consumer's income is $200, the price of apples is 40¢, and the price of a shirt is $1. Graph the consumer's budget constraint. Draw an indifference curve that determines the consumer's demand. Label this demand.

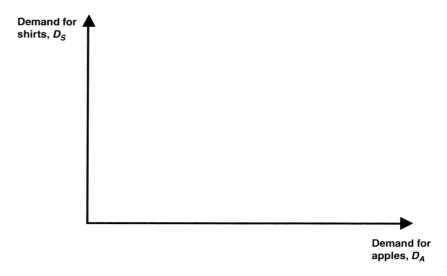

4d. Show how the graph changes when the price of shirts falls to 50¢ and everything else stays the same. Show the new indifference curve and demand levels.

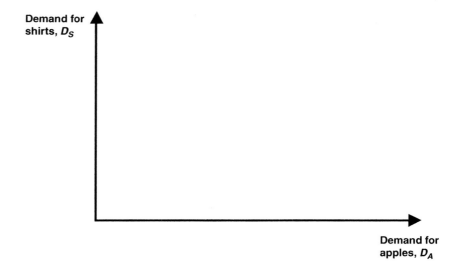

It is imperative not to draw indifference curves so that they appear to cross. Indifference curves *cannot* cross because otherwise they could not involve different levels of "utility."

We often draw two indifference curves, one representing utility before a change and one representing utility after a change. In principle, there are an infinite number of indifference curves corresponding to all other possible levels of utility, but we don't draw them to avoid cluttering up the picture.

TIPS

Problem 5: Home's stock of factors is 100 workers. Two goods are produced: shirts and apples. Workers' marginal product of labor in shirts is 2, and the marginal product of labor in apples is 5.

5a. Graph a no-trade equilibrium for this economy that shows the country's PPF (with axes labeled) and an indifference curve that shows demand levels. Indicate the relative prices.

5b. Suppose that a technology improvement leads to an increase in the marginal product of labor in apples to 10. Show how the equilibrium changes.

5c. Going back to the initial information, suppose the economy is given the opportunity to trade as much as it wants with the outside world at the *fixed* international relative price of apples of 1. On the next page, draw a figure showing how producers and consumers respond to this opportunity.

....

Problem 5c demonstrates a general feature of the Ricardian model. Being allowed to trade with the outside world at *any* relative price that is different than the no-trade equilibrium price must make the country better off.

    You should notice a similarity in the answers to problems 5b and 5c. Technical progress and the ability to trade at fixed world prices have the same effect: They shift out the consumption possibilities frontier.

TIPS

....

3   Determining the Pattern of International Trade

ESSENTIAL CONCEPTS

To analyze how different technologies across countries affect the trading pattern, the model includes two countries. One of these countries will have an *absolute advantage* in both goods. That is, it will have a better technology for producing both goods. A country has an *absolute advantage* in a good if its marginal product of producing that good is higher than in another country. A country has a *comparative advantage* in a good when it has a lower opportunity cost of producing it than does another country. Because the relative price of a good in a no-trade equilibrium reflects the opportunity cost of producing that good, the country with a lower relative price for a good in a no-trade equilibrium has a comparative advantage in that good.

    Consider the following example. Suppose that Home workers' *marginal product* of labor in shirts (MPL_S) is 2, and the marginal product of labor in apples is 5. Foreign workers' marginal product of labor in shirts is 8, and the marginal product of labor in apples is 8. Hence, Foreign has an absolute advantage in the production of both goods. The opportunity cost of apples in Home is 2 / 5 shirts, whereas the opportunity cost of apples in Foreign is 1 shirt. By definition, then, Home has a comparative advantage in apples and Foreign has a comparative advantage in shirts.

    By reorganizing production toward their comparative advantage, countries increase the quantity of world output. To see this, suppose that the two countries are producing both goods. If Home expands production of apples by 1 unit, it has to cut shirt production by 2 / 5 units. If Foreign cuts apple production by 1 unit, it will free enough labor to produce another shirt. Apple output is unchanged, while shirt output has *risen* by 1 − 2 / 5 = 3 / 5 units. Reorganizing production toward countries' comparative advantage and allowing international trade give rise to *gains from trade* due to the more efficient use of the world's resources. The distribution of these gains between countries depends on the *terms of trade* on world markets.

KEY TERMS

Use the space provided to record your notes on the following key terms.

Absolute advantage _____

_____

_____

Comparative advantage _____

_____

_____

International trade equilibrium _____

_____

_____

Gains from trade _____

_____

_____

World price line _____

_____

_____

REVIEW QUESTIONS

Problem 6: Suppose that Home has a marginal product of labor of 4 making apples and a marginal product of labor of 4 making shirts.

6a. Foreign has a marginal product of labor of 6 making apples. Choose a number for the marginal product of labor in Foreign for shirts that gives Foreign a comparative advantage in apples. _____

_____

_____

6b. Choose numbers for the marginal product of labor in apples and in shirts in Foreign so that the wage rate is twice as high in Foreign, but there are no gains from trade. _____

_____

_____

Problem 7: Explain why a country will export the good in which it has a comparative advantage and import the other good if trade is balanced. _____

_____

_____

Problem 8: Suppose that Home has 100 workers, a marginal product of labor of 4 making apples, and a marginal product of labor of 4 making shirts. Foreign has 100 workers, a marginal product of labor of 8 making apples, and a marginal product of labor of 6 in shirts.

8a. What range of relative prices could be observed in a trading equilibrium? Explain.

_____

_____

8b. Draw the production possibilities frontier, world price line, and indifference curves for each country for a trading equilibrium when the relative price on world markets is halfway between their autarky relative prices. Label the intercepts of the world price line and PPF.

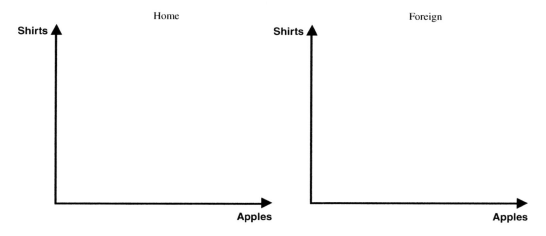

....

Gains from trade have nothing to do with wage differences between countries. Wage differences are due to absolute advantage, but it is comparative advantage that creates gains from trade.

From your work with production and budget constraint you should notice that the greater the difference between world relative prices and relative prices in a no-trade equilibrium, the more the country gains from trade.

....

4 Solving for International Prices

ESSENTIAL CONCEPTS

International prices are determined by international supply and demand for goods. The model includes two goods, but it is sufficient to think about just one good for determining the *one* relative price. If trade is balanced, then the value of Home's exports is equal to the value of its imports of the other good *and* to the value of Foreign's imports. Exports are domestic production minus domestic consumption. By varying the relative price of the good, we observe how a country's production and consumption change and so predict how the country's desire to trade is affected. The relative price that makes one country's export supply equal the other country's import demand is the equilibrium international price, or the *terms of trade*.

KEY TERMS

Use the space provided to record your notes on the following key terms.

Export supply curve _____

_____

_____

Import demand curve _____

_____

_____

Terms of trade _____

_____

_____

REVIEW QUESTIONS

Problem 9: Suppose that Home has 100 units of labor with a marginal product of 4 making apples and a marginal product of 4 making shirts. In the no-trade equilibrium, suppose that consumers in Home demand 175 apples. Foreign has 100 units of labor with a marginal product of 8 making apples and a marginal product of 6 in shirts. In a no-trade equilibrium Foreign consumes 400 apples. It may help you to consult your answers to problem 8 for the following problems.

9a. Draw Home's export supply curve.

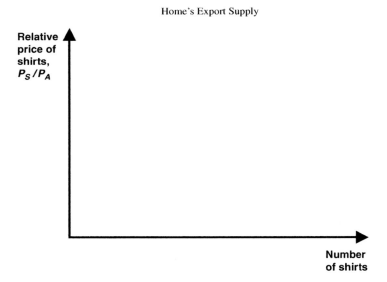

Home's Export Supply

9b. Add Foreign's import demand curve to the diagram so that the world relative price of shirts is between the two countries' no-trade relative prices.

9c. Suppose the number of workers in Home were to double. How would this change shift Home's export supply curve? Show in your original diagram.

If instead the problem had asked about Foreign's export supply and Home's import demand, the graph would have looked different but the information would be the same!

The answer to 9c displays a general result in trade models: Larger countries are less likely to gain from trade. Relative prices in the international trade equilibrium are not much different for the large country than in a no-trade equilibrium. This is because Foreign demand is small relative to Home supply. As we saw in earlier problems, countries gain more the bigger the difference is between no-trade and trade relative prices.

3

Gains and Losses from Trade in the Specific-Factors Model

Overview

Chapter 2 demonstrated that there are gains from trade in the sense that international trade allows a country as a whole to consume more of all goods. This chapter analyzes the way that international trade affects the actual spending power, or real income, of individuals rather than countries. As the title of the chapter suggests, it is possible for a country to gain from trade while some (but not all!) individuals living in that country are made poorer by international trade.

International trade affects the welfare of individuals through its effects on the real earnings of the factors that they own. Some people get most of their income by working, whereas others get income from their ownership of land or of capital. International trade increases the earnings of some factors and lowers the real earnings of other factors. As a result, some individuals will gain from international trade and others will lose. To get at these issues, it is critical to use a model that has more than one type of factor.

The *specific-factors model* that is introduced in this chapter features three factors. This model shows that there are clear winners and clear losers from international trade. The idea that a country gains from trade has a very specific meaning: The gains to those that benefit from international trade exceed the losses of those that are harmed by international trade.

1 Specific-Factors Model

ESSENTIAL CONCEPTS

The model assumes that one industry (agriculture) uses labor and land and the other industry (manufacturing) uses labor and capital. This model is called the specific-factors model because land is *specific* to the agriculture sector and capital is *specific* to the manufacturing sector; labor is used in both sectors, so it is not specific to either one. Labor is sometimes referred to as the mobile factor because it can move freely between the two industries.

Adding a specific factor to production in each industry gives rise to the key feature of the specific-factors model: *diminishing returns*. To produce agricultural products, a firm needs land and labor. Land is in fixed supply, so output can only be expanded by adding labor (i.e., moving it out of manufacturing). As more workers are put to work using the same amount of land, the marginal product of labor in agriculture decreases. In the manufacturing industry the same assumption applies. Because the amount of capital is fixed, the marginal product of labor in manufacturing is decreasing in the level of manufacturing employment because as the number of workers in manufacturing rises there are fewer machines for each worker to use.

One important implication of diminishing returns is that it causes a country's PPF to be bowed out (or concave). This means that when the country goes to trade with the outside world, it will increase the output of the good whose relative price has risen and decrease the output of the other good, but it will not completely specialize in the production of either good. This is because moving labor from one industry to another causes the marginal product of labor to fall in the expanding industry and rise in the contracting industry. For example, if the relative price of manufacturing goods rises because of international trade, the opportunity cost of manufacturing goods will also rise as the country expands the production of manufacturing goods (falling MPL_M) and contracts the production of agricultural goods (rising MPL_A).

When countries are not engaged in international trade, the opportunity costs of production differ across countries. Trade allows the countries to expand the production of the goods in which they have a lower opportunity cost in the no-trade equilibrium and contract production of the goods in which they have a higher opportunity cost. Hence, there are gains from trade.

KEY TERMS

Use the space provided to record your notes on the following key terms.

Specific-factors model _____

_____

_____

Diminishing returns _____

_____

_____

Embargo _____

_____

_____

Autarky _____

_____

_____

REVIEW QUESTIONS

Problem 1: Suppose that the technology for creating manufacturing goods is $Q_M = \sqrt{\overline{K} \cdot L_M}$, where Q_M is manufacturing output; $\overline{K}$ is the country's endowment of capital, the factor specific to manufacturing; and L_M is the amount of the mobile factor, labor, used in manufacturing.

1a. How much does Q_M rise if both inputs $(\overline{K}, L_M)$ are doubled? _____

1b. Now suppose that $\overline{K}$ is fixed at 100. How much does Q_M rise if L_M is doubled? _____

_____

1c. Is the cost of lost manufacturing output associated with reducing manufacturing employment by one employee larger or smaller when the initial level of employment is 100 or 10? _____

_____

_____

Problem 2: Suppose that there are two goods: Agriculture (A) and Manufacturing (M). Agriculture is produced with Land and Labor and Manufacturing is produced with Capital and Labor. Labor is mobile between industries. The next two questions refer to Figure 3-1.

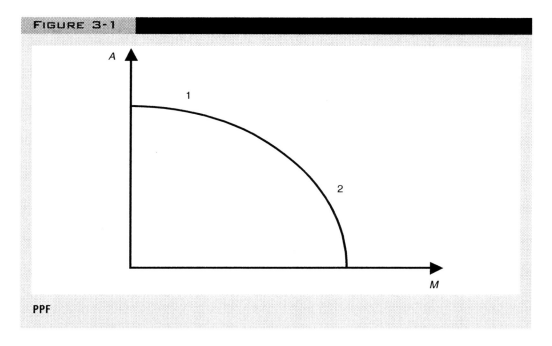

FIGURE 3-1

PPF

2a. Is the opportunity cost of M in terms of A higher at point 1 or point 2 in Figure 3-1?

_____

2b. Provide an intuitive explanation for why the PPF is "bowed out" in Figure 3-1.

_____

_____

2c. If the price of a manufactured good is $P_M = \$10/$unit and the marginal product of labor in manufacturing is 2 units per worker, what must the wage paid to a unit of labor be?

_____

_____

2d. If $P_M > P_A$, in which industry is the marginal product of labor higher? _____

_____

_____

2e. Suppose you own a manufacturing firm. If $P_M = \$10/\text{unit}$, the wage is $25, and the marginal product of labor is 4 units per worker, are you hiring too many, too few, or the right amount of labor? _____

_____

_____

2f. Suppose the price of manufactured goods in terms of agricultural products falls. What would we expect to happen to the marginal product of labor in agriculture?

_____

_____

Problem 1 explores the fundamental concept of diminishing marginal product. Do not go into an exam until you are completely comfortable with this concept!

An important implication of the diminishing marginal product of labor in the specific-factors model is that the PPF displays increasing opportunity costs. That is, the more of a good that is produced, the higher the opportunity cost of producing more.

Problem 3: An economy called Home makes autos from capital and labor and bananas from land and labor. Labor is mobile between the two industries. Home is in a no-trade equilibrium, but it is considering opening to international trade with the rest of the world. The relative price of autos in terms of bananas is higher in Home than the fixed price on world markets.

3a. Create a diagram with a PPF, indifference curves, and an international price line showing how production and consumption in Home changes from its no-trade levels to its post-trade levels. Indicate the trade pattern on the diagram.

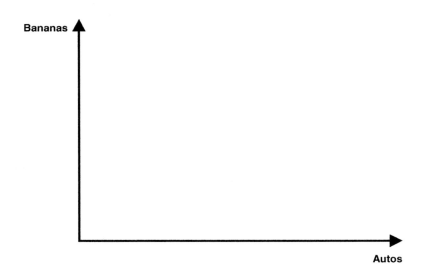

3b. Explain how your diagram shows how the country as a whole is better or worse off with trade than without trade. _____

_____

_____

3c. Now suppose that there are two countries in the world, Home and Foreign. The countries are not initially engaged in international trade and the relative price of autos is higher in Foreign than in Home. If the countries engaged in international trade, which country would export bananas? _____

_____

_____

3d. Once the two countries are engaged in trade, in which country is the opportunity cost of producing autos higher in terms of bananas? _____

_____

_____

_____

TIPS

Make sure that you can correctly identify production and consumption on a PPF-indifference curve diagram. This is fundamental!

Study carefully how the indifference curves are drawn in the answer to problem 3a. Trade allows the country to get to a higher indifference curve. It is *not* shifting indifference curves.

Care must be taken in drawing the diagram to avoid the suggestion that the indifference curves would ever cross.

The answers to problems 3c and 3d illustrate an important point. Without trade, the opportunity cost of production is different in the two countries, whereas with trade it is the same. When the opportunity cost of production is the same in both locations, world resources are being used efficiently: No country is "low cost" or "high cost."

2 Earnings of Labor

ESSENTIAL CONCEPTS

How does trade affect the livelihoods of people who get their income from their labor? To answer this question, one needs to understand how trade affects the buying power of a worker's wage (W). This is known as the *real wage*. There are two ways to measure the buying power of the wage. If the two goods being produced are agricultural products and manufacturing products, we can measure the buying power of the wage in terms of agricultural products (W/P_A) or in terms of the buying power of the wage in terms of manufacturing products (W/P_M).

To see this, consider a worker's budget constraint. The worker earns nominal income (in dollars) W and pays P_A for autos and P_B for bananas. Her budget constraint is then

$$W = P_A D_A + P_B D_B,$$

which is plotted in panel (a) of Figure 3–2. If both W/P_A and W/P_B were to increase, then the worker's budget constraint shifts out and the worker can afford more of both

Figure 3-2

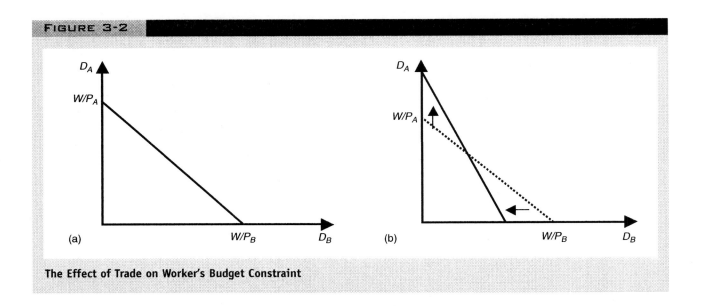

The Effect of Trade on Worker's Budget Constraint

goods. The opposite is true if W/P_A and W/P_B were to decrease. The case where these two measures of welfare do not move in the same direction creates complications. This case is shown in panel (b) of Figure 3-2, where W/P_A increases but W/P_B decreases.

The dotted line is the budget constraint before the price change, and the solid line is the budget constraint after the change. If the worker spends all her income on autos, she is better off. If the worker spends all her income on bananas, she is worse off. The actual impact depends on how much the consumer values autos relative to bananas.

The effect of international trade on the real income of a worker can be determined by the profit-maximizing equation for firms and the knowledge of how labor moves from one industry to another. For instance, the hiring equation for agriculture is $P_A \cdot MPL_A = W$, which can be rewritten $W/P_A = MPL_A$. If employment in agriculture went up, then MPL_A went down and so too did the earnings of a worker relative to the price of agricultural goods. If employment in agriculture went down, then the opposite conclusion is reached. The real wage in terms of manufacturing goods can be analyzed in the same way.

KEY TERMS

Use the space provided to record your notes on the following key terms.

Real wage _____

_____

_____

Trade adjustment assistance _____

_____

_____

Services _____

_____

_____

REVIEW QUESTIONS

Problem 4: A country called Home makes autos from capital and labor and bananas from land and labor. Labor is mobile between the two industries. The country is in a no-trade equilibrium, but it is considering opening to international trade with the rest of the world. The relative price of autos in terms of bananas is higher in Home than the (fixed) price on world markets.

4a. The diagram below shows the real wage in terms of bananas (how many bananas a unit of labor can buy) and the allocation of labor across industries in the no-trade equilibrium. Use this diagram to show how these variables change in a trading equilibrium.

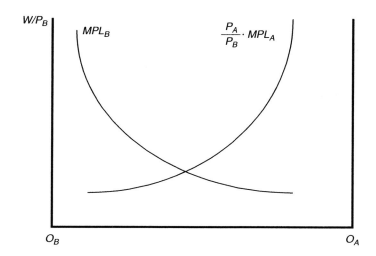

4b. If workers spend all their income on autos, does trade make workers better off or worse off? _____

_____

4c. If workers spend all their income on bananas, does trade make workers better off or worse off? _____

_____

4d. If workers spend their income on both goods, what can you say about the effect of trade on workers' well-being? _____

_____

....

The effect of trade on the real income of the mobile factor (labor) must always be ambiguous in the specific-factors model because the movement of labor between industries raises the marginal product in the contracting industry and lowers it in the expanding industry.

    Notice that the marginal products diagram in problem 4 has been reformulated by dividing all the nominal variables (wage, value of marginal products, etc.) by P_B. A change in the relative price has exactly the same effect on real variables as a change in the nominal price of one, holding fixed the other price. In other words, an increase in P_A holding P_B fixed has the same consequences as a decrease in P_B holding P_A fixed. The key difference is in how the diagram works when drawn this way. Either type of price change affects only the curve that is "attached" to the relative price P_A/P_B. A good exercise would be to redo problem 4 with all prices in terms of autos.

TIPS

....

Problem 5: Consider the following questions concerning worker mobility.

5a. Suppose that wages in a country were $15 per hour in one industry and $12 per hour in another. Is labor perfectly mobile in this country? Explain. _____

_____

_____

5b. Provide an explanation for why it is often the case that displaced workers earn less in their new jobs than they did in their previous job. _____

_____

_____

Problem 6: Suppose a country makes computers with capital and labor and tulips with land and labor. When the country goes from a no-trade equilibrium to a trade equilibrium, the price of computers rises while the price of tulips stays the same. Suppose that labor is not allowed to move between industries.

6a. What is the effect of trade on the real income of computer workers? _____

_____

_____

6b. What is the effect of trade on the real income of tulip workers? _____

_____

_____

TIPS　Both problems 5 and 6 illustrate the role that labor mobility plays in the specific-factors model. It is important to understand that there is only one wage because workers can move freely between industries. If there were some reason labor couldn't move, such as a trade union or government-imposed barrier to entry, then there would be two wages.

3　Earnings of Capital and Land

ESSENTIAL CONCEPTS

Although the specific-factor model makes "wishy-washy" predictions about the effect of international trade on the real income of the mobile factor, it makes strong predictions about the effect of international trade on the real income of specific factors. International trade increases the real income of the factor specific to the export industry and decreases the real income of the factor specific to the import industry. This has a very intuitive explanation. Trade induces the export sector to expand and the import sector to contract. Because the amount of the specific factor is fixed in the export sector, the only way to expand production is to increase the amount of labor in that sector. As more labor enters the export sector and there are more workers using the fixed quantity of the specific factor, the specific factor becomes more valuable. As labor leaves the import sector, the specific factor has fewer workers using it and that factor becomes less valuable. In terms of the marginal product of a specific factor, an increase in the amount of labor using that fixed factor increases the marginal product of that factor. The higher the marginal product of the factor, the greater the real income of that factor when measured in terms of the output of that sector.

KEY TERMS

Use the space provided to record your notes on the following key terms.

Rental on capital _____

_____

_____

Rental on land _____

_____

_____

REVIEW QUESTIONS

Problem 7: Two countries, Home and Foreign, produce autos from capital and labor and ba-nanas from land and labor. Labor is mobile between the two industries. The no-trade equi-librium in the two countries is illustrated in the diagram below.

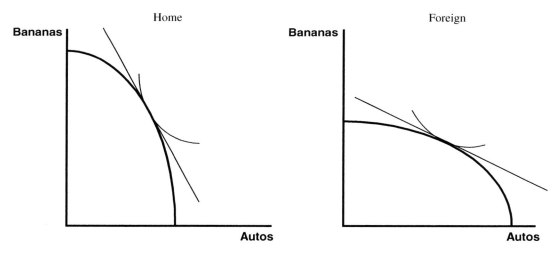

7a. In the diagram above, show a candidate equilibrium if the two countries are trading with each other. Indicate how production and consumption have changed in the two countries.

7b. How has the real rental to capital changed in Home? Explain. _____

_____

_____

7c. How has the real rental to capital changed in Foreign? _____

_____

_____

7d. What happens to the demand for land in Home? _____

_____

_____

7e. If the winners could without cost compensate the losers, would the countries engage in free trade?

_____

_____

TIPS

When the ratio of factors used in production changes, it means (1) that the marginal products of each factor has changed and (2) that the change of the marginal product of one factor moves in exactly the opposite direction as the marginal product of the other factor. If capital and labor are used in production and the capital/labor ratio increases, then the marginal product of labor goes up (more machines per worker) and the marginal product of capital goes down (fewer workers per machines).

Because the marginal products of different factors used in production move in opposite directions in response to changes in the price of goods, the incomes of factors move in opposite directions. Trade is always controversial in the specific-factors world.

A specific factor is just an input into production that is used only in that industry. In the textbook, land is specific to agriculture and capital is specific to manufacturing. In reality, there are many inputs into production that are specific to an industry. Machines are designed for uses that are specific to an industry. Worker skills can also be industry specific (pastry cooks have skills that do not translate well into law enforcement).

4

Trade and Resources:
The Heckscher-Ohlin Model

Overview

This chapter outlines the structure of a "long-run" model of international trade that relates a country's factor endowment to its trade pattern. This model is called the Heckscher-Ohlin model after the economists Eli Heckscher and Bertil Ohlin, who sought to understand the rapid increase in international trade in the late nineteenth century. The model predicts a country's trade pattern on the basis of its endowments, and it predicts how international trade affects the real income of the owners of a country's capital and labor. As in the specific-factors model, a country gains from trade in the sense that it can consume more goods, but some (perhaps many!) individuals within the country will find that their real income has fallen.

1 Heckscher-Ohlin Model

ESSENTIAL CONCEPTS

The classic *Heckscher-Ohlin model* is a world in which there are two countries, two goods, and two factors. For convenience we call the factors capital and labor and the countries Home and Foreign. Both goods use capital and labor in their production and both factors are free to move from one industry to another. This is the sense in which this is a "long-run" model. (In the short run it is easy to imagine that factors are stuck in their industry.) The key way that the two goods are different from each other (aside from how consumers use them) is in their *factor intensity*.

Factor intensity is a key concept that merits some review. Suppose that computers and shoes both use capital (K) and labor (L) in their production. The going market rate for a unit of capital is R and the going rate for a unit of labor is W. The relative demands for labor in the computer and shoe industry are shown in Figure 4-1.

The technology used to produce these goods allows producers some degree of substitutability between these factors. Hence, as W rises relative to R, firms in both industries

FIGURE 4-1

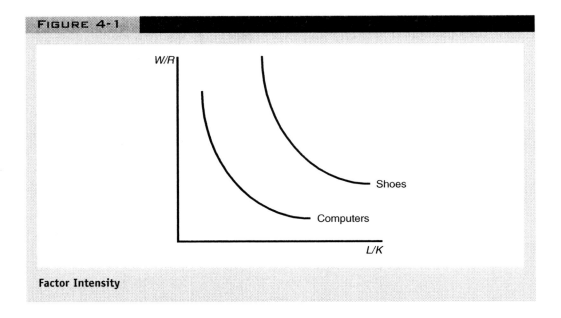

Factor Intensity

use a mix of inputs that features relatively less *L* and relatively more *K,* as Figure 4-1 shows. We say that shoes are labor-intensive compared with computers because whatever level of W / R prevails in factor markets, the firms that produce shoes use a higher ratio of labor to capital than the firms that produce computers. Alternatively, we could say that computers are capital-intensive relative to shoes.

The assumption that goods differ in their factor intensity is important because it tells us something about the shape of a country's PPF. First, because goods differ in their factor intensity, the PPF is concave (or bowed out), as shown in Figure 4-2.

To see why the PPF is concave, consider the effect of reallocating capital and labor across industries. At a point such as 1 in Figure 4-2, nearly all the country's factors are be-

FIGURE 4-2

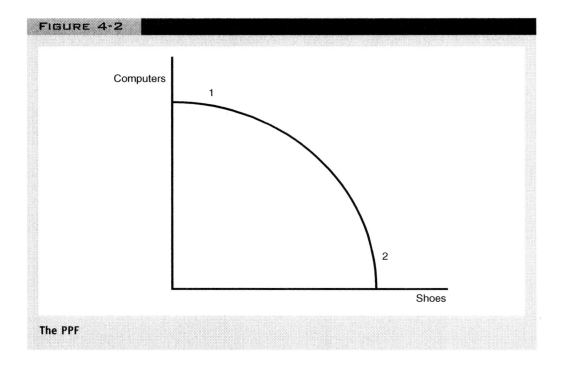

The PPF

ing used to make the capital-intensive good, computers. The opportunity cost of shoe production is very low at point 1 because a lot of labor and a little capital can be pulled out of computer production to produce a substantial quantity of shoes with only a little reduction in computer production. As we move from point 1 to point 2, most of the labor has been extracted from the production of computers so that the expansion of shoe production can only be accomplished by extracting a lot of capital and a little labor from computer industry. This results in a small increase in the output of the labor-intensive shoe industry and a large drop in the output of the capital-intensive computer industry.

The second important implication of goods that differ in their factor intensity is the effect on the shape of the PPF of changing a country's endowment. Suppose that we were to add capital to a country's endowment. Because the country has a larger stock of factors and because both goods use both factors, the PPF shifts outward: More of both goods can be produced. However, because computers are capital intensive and shoes are labor intensive, the PPF shifts out in favor of computers, as shown in Figure 4-3.

The two countries are identical in every dimension except in terms of their endowments. They have identical tastes and technologies, but they have different *factor abundances*. Factor abundance is measured as the ratio of capital to labor (or its inverse). The *capital-abundant* country has a higher ratio of capital to labor in its endowment than the *labor-abundant* country, which has a higher ratio of labor to capital. From our discussion in the previous paragraph, this means that the two countries have systematically different PPFs: The capital-abundant country has a PPF skewed out toward the capital-intensive good, whereas the labor-abundant country has its PPF skewed out toward the labor-intensive good. Faced with the same relative price of computers, the capital-abundant country will supply relatively more computers and fewer shoes than the labor-abundant country, which will supply relatively more shoes than computers. Because the two countries have the same tastes, they will consume the two goods in the same ratio. This means that in a trading equilibrium, the capital-abundant country will export the capital-intensive good and the labor-abundant country will export the labor-intensive good. This is the *Heckscher-Ohlin theorem*.

FIGURE 4-3

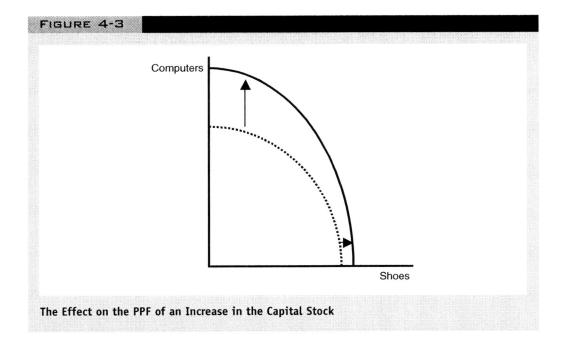

The Effect on the PPF of an Increase in the Capital Stock

KEY TERMS

Use the space provided to record your notes on the following key terms.

Heckscher-Ohlin model _____

_____

_____

Free-trade equilibrium _____

_____

_____

Factor intensity reversal _____

_____

_____

Factor abundance _____

_____

_____

Factor scarcity _____

_____

_____

Heckscher-Ohlin theorem _____

_____

_____

_____

REVIEW QUESTIONS

Problem 1: The two countries are Home and Foreign, the two factors are capital and labor, and the two goods are shoes and computers.

1a. Shoes and computers are produced using capital and labor. Using the following diagram, draw a *factor intensity reversal* between shoes and computers.

1b. Home is endowed with 200 units of capital and 100 units of labor. Foreign is endowed with 100 units of capital and 40 units of labor. Which country is capital-abundant? _____

_____

_____

_____

· ·

It is very easy to accidentally say (or write on an exam) *factor intensity* when *factor abundance* is meant or vice versa. This slip up will likely result in a lower grade, so don't do it!

TIPS

· ·

Problem 2: There is a world with two countries called Home and Foreign. Home and Foreign produce computers and shoes using capital and labor. Computers are capital intensive relative to shoes. It is unknown what the factor endowments of each country are, but it is known that the relative price of computers is higher in Home than Foreign in a no-trade equilibrium.

2a. Which country is capital-abundant? _____

_____

_____

_____

2b. Which country is producing a higher ratio of computers to shoes in a no-trade equilibrium? _____

_____

_____

_____

Problem 3: There is a world with two countries called Home and Foreign. Home and Foreign produce airplanes and shirts using capital and labor. Airplanes are capital intensive relative to shirts and Foreign is capital-abundant relative to Home. All the Heckscher-Ohlin assumptions hold.

3a. In free-trade equilibrium, which country is exporting shirts? _____

_____

_____

_____

3b. In free-trade equilibrium, the consumers in Home are buying twice as many shirts as airplanes. What is the ratio of shirt to airplane consumption in Foreign? _____

_____

_____

_____

_____

3c. Suppose that Foreign's endowment of capital is increased. What happens to the relative price of airplanes in terms of shirts on world markets? Use the diagrams below in answering the question. _____

_____

_____

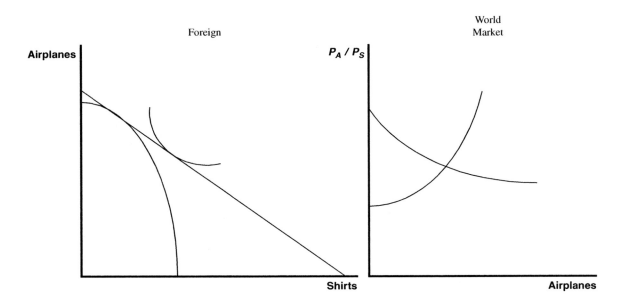

3d. Suppose that Foreign's endowment of capital is increased. What happens to the level of national welfare in Home (can it reach a higher indifference curve)? Use the diagram below in answering the question. _____

_____

_____

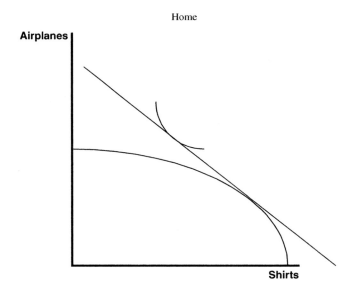

Problem 4: An important assumption in the Heckscher-Ohlin model is that the tastes are the same in both countries. Suppose that tastes are different in the Home and Foreign. Is it

possible for a capital-abundant country (Foreign) to export the labor-intensive good (shirts) if tastes are different? If so, draw a PPF-indifference curve diagram for Home and a PPF-indifference curve diagram for Foreign that illustrates this case in the following space.

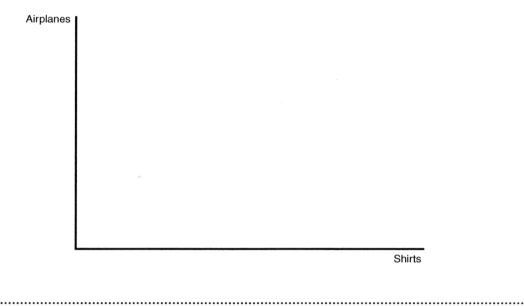

Problem 4 illustrates the importance of assumptions in a model. Change an assumption and you change the model's predictions.

2 Testing the Heckscher-Ohlin Model

ESSENTIAL CONCEPTS

As intuitively sensible as the prediction of the Heckscher–Ohlin model sounds, it actually has some difficulty explaining trade patterns. When Wassily Leontief measured the *factor content of exports* and the *factor content of imports* for the United States, he found that the U.S imports appeared to be more capital-intensive than U.S. exports for the year 1947. As it is widely believed that the United States was capital-abundant relative to the rest of the world, this rejection of the Heckscher–Ohlin model has been dubbed the *Leontief Paradox*.

The apparent failure of the simple Heckscher–Ohlin model to explain the world has been attributed by many to be due to two simplifying assumptions. First, considering a world with only two goods and two factors is too simple. For instance, a category called "labor" lumps together scientists, lawyers, and assembly line workers. Second, the assumption that technology is everywhere the same, although useful for isolating factor endowment differences across countries in the context of an abstract model, it is unrealistic in practice.

Fortunately, it is not hard to adjust the Heckscher–Ohlin model in order to accommodate many different factors and technologies that differ across countries. To do so, we define a new concept of factor abundance. To determine whether a country is abundant in a certain factor, we compare the country's share of that factor with its share of world GDP. If its share of a factor exceeds its share of world GDP, then we conclude that the country is *abundant in that factor,* and if its share in a certain factor is less than its share of world GDP, then we conclude that the country is *scarce in that factor.* This definition allows us to calculate factor abundance in a setting with as many factors and countries as we want.

For example, if the United States has 26.6% of the world's GDP, it should consume 26.6% of all of the services of capital (i.e., the time the capital was used to make goods), and 26.6% of all the services of land, and so on. If the United States has 50.7% of the world's research and development (R&D) scientists, then the goods that the United States exports to the rest of the world should have more R&D services embodied in them than the goods that the United States imports from the rest of the world.

To accommodate the fact that the productivity of factors varies across the world, an additional adjustment has to be made. For instance, if the workers from country B are twice as productive as workers from country A, then we count each worker in B twice relative to each worker from country A so as to measure accurately each country's *effective labor force.* By correcting each factor for its productivity, we can then measure each country's *effective factor endowment.* If its share of a factor measured in effective terms exceeds its share of world GDP, then we conclude that the country is *abundant in that effective factor,* and if its share in a certain effective factor is less than its share of world GDP, then we conclude that the country is *scarce in that effective factor.*

KEY TERMS

Factor content of exports _____

_____

Factor content of imports _____

_____

Abundant in that factor _____

_____

Scarce in that factor _____

_____

Leontief Paradox _____

_____

Effective labor force _____

_____

Effective factor endowment _____

_____

Abundant in that effective factor _____

_____

Scarce in that effective factor _____

_____

REVIEW QUESTIONS

Problem 5: Consider the assumptions of the Heckscher-Ohlin model. What three failures of these assumptions could explain the Leontief Paradox? _____

_____

_____

Problem 6: What kind of result could Leontief have found that would not have been called a paradox? _____

_____

_____

Problem 7: Suppose that Home has 15% of the world's capital, 7% of the world's labor, 5% of the world's arable land, and 10% of the world's GDP.

7a. What does the Heckscher-Ohlin model predict about the labor content of Home's net exports? _____

_____

_____

7b. Suppose that Home's workers are much better paid than workers in the rest of the world. What additional adjustment must be met before predicting the factor content of Home's net exports? _____

_____

_____

7c. Suppose that factor endowments have not been corrected for their effectiveness. Is it possible for a country to appear to be scarce in all factors?

_____

_____

_____

3 Effects of Trade on Factor Prices

ESSENTIAL CONCEPTS

We now consider the effect of changes in goods prices induced by international trade on the prices of factors in the long-run Heckscher-Ohlin model. As in the specific-factors model, international trade causes the real incomes of factor owners to change, with some factors seeing their real incomes rise and others seeing their real incomes fall. The types of predictions are very different in the long-run Heckscher-Ohlin model than in the specific-factors model. In the specific-factors model, we see that there is a divide across industries in the effect of international trade on real income: The factor specific to the export industry sees its real income rise with trade, whereas the factor specific to the import industry sees its real income fall. In the Heckscher-Ohlin model there is no specific factor. Instead, the *Stolper-Samuelson theorem* has the key implication that the owners of the factor in which the country is abundant gain from international trade, whereas the owners of the factor in which the country is scarce are hurt by international trade. It becomes possible then that an individual could see her real income fall in the short run (factor specific to import industry) and rise in the long run (abundant factor).

To think about the economics of the Stolper-Samuelson theorem, consider Figure 4-2. An increase in the relative price of shoes shifts production away from point 1 and toward point 2. An increase in shoe production requires a decrease in computer production. But because shoe producers demand a lot of labor and a little capital and computer producers demand a lot of capital and a little labor, shutting down computer output releases "too much" capital and "too little" labor. This is why W/R has to rise to get firms to use less labor and more capital. Because firms in both industries increase the ratio of capital to labor that they use in production, the marginal product of labor rises and the marginal product of capital falls in *both* industries. A decrease in the relative price of shoes has exactly the opposite effect.

KEY TERMS

Use the space provided to record your notes on the following key term.

Stolper-Samuelson theorem _____

_____

_____

REVIEW QUESTIONS

Problem 8: Consider the relative demand curve for a country shown in Figure 4-4. *RD* stands for relative demand and *RS* stands for relative supply. The two industries are computers and shoes.

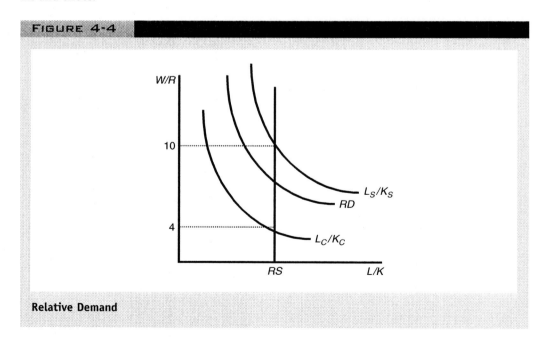

FIGURE 4-4

Relative Demand

8a. What is the highest relative wage that we could observe in this economy? _____

_____

_____

8b. What causes the relative demand curve for labor in a country to shift up? _____

_____

_____

8c. Suppose there is an upward shift in the relative demand curve for labor. What happens to the ratio of labor to capital used in production in each industry? _____

_____

_____

Problem 9: Consider the real-sounding but fictional country of Ubetcha. Ubetcha produces two goods, autos and hats, using capital and labor. Autos are capital intensive relative to hats. The country has long enjoyed its isolation from the world but is now considering free trade. The top Ubetchan economist traveled abroad and noticed that the relative price of autos is lower on world markets than it is in Ubetcha. All Heckscher-Ohlin assumptions hold.

9a. Suppose the country were to institute free trade with the rest of the world. How would the capital/labor ratio used by Ubetcha's producers of autos and hats change? _____

_____

_____

9b. If Ubetcha engages in free trade with the rest of the world, how will the marginal product of capital change in the auto and hat industries? _____

_____

_____

9c. Suppose there is an organization in Ubetcha, the Union of Ubetchan Capitalists, or UUC for short, that represents the interests of capital owners in the country. Would that organization support or lobby against the free-trade idea? Explain. _____

_____

_____

Problem 10: The National Election Study (NES) survey in the United States in 1992 found that workers with higher levels of education were more likely to support free trade than less educated workers.

10a. Assuming that the United States is a relatively skill-abundant country, is this result consistent with the Heckscher–Ohlin model? Explain. _____

_____

_____

10b. Suppose that the same questions were asked in a skill-scarce country. What would the Heckscher-Ohlin model predict about the responses of workers? _____

_____

_____

Problem 11: Suppose that the world was one large, happy country that produced doughnuts and sofas using capital and labor. Sofas are capital-intensive relative to doughnuts. International trade is _not_ allowed. The following questions build on one another.

11a. Suppose that the world is divided into two identical countries (Home and Foreign); that is, they receive the same amount of labor and capital. Would there be any motive for immigration (i.e., would laborers want to move) between the two countries? Explain. _____

_____

_____

_____

11b. Now suppose that some of the capital is moved from Foreign to Home so that Home is capital-abundant relative to Foreign. Trade is still not allowed. What happens to the real income of labor in each of the two countries? _____

_____

_____

11c. If laborers are free to move internationally, which way do they move?

_____

_____

11d. What does the migration do to real incomes of laborers in Home and Foreign?

_____

_____

11e. If you were a capitalist in Home, would you be in favor of immigration? Explain.

_____

_____

_____

TIPS Note that in problem 11, international trade is not allowed but immigration is. The problem shows that trade and immigration have similar effects on income distribution.

Problem 12: Your well-meaning but excessively enthusiastic relative, Bob, wants you to sign a petition to ban trade with a developing country. He claims that trade will encourage the expansion of labor-intensive "sweatshop" industries in the developing country and so will reduce the welfare of workers (the abundant factor) in that developing country. Does the Heckscher-Ohlin model necessarily imply that developing country workers will be hurt by trade? _____

_____

_____

_____

5

Movement of Labor and Capital between Countries

Overview

This chapter analyzes the effects that movements in factors between countries have on (1) factor rewards (wages, rental, etc.), (2) the pattern of production across countries, and (3) the size of global output. Two kinds of factor flows are considered: immigration (the movement of labor) and foreign direct investment (movement of capital). To analyze the short-run effects of immigration and foreign direct investment we use the specific-factors model introduced in Chapter 3. To analyze the long-run effect of factor movements we use the Heckscher-Ohlin model introduced in Chapter 4. To keep the analysis simple, we assume that in both the short run and the long run the international prices of goods are fixed.

A key point made in this chapter is that the short-run and long-run effects of factor movements on factor rewards are very different. Immigration and FDI alter the distribution of income across factors in the short run but have no effect on real income in the long run. The effects of factor flows on the pattern of production are also very different in the short run than in the long run. The chapter concludes by considering the gains from factor flows. Both immigration and foreign direct investment lead to a more efficient use of the world's resources and therefore to greater output given the same world resources.

1 Movement of Labor between Countries

ESSENTIAL CONCEPTS

Immigration causes the supply of labor to fall in one location and to rise in another. Hence, the effects of immigration on the real incomes of different factors and the output of each industry are treated as changes in countries' endowments of labor. How does the economy absorb the new workers, and what effect does it have on the people living in that country? The answer to this question depends on whether one considers the short run, when factors are limited in their ability to move across industries, or the long run, when factors are perfectly mobile across industries.

Because the specific-factors model is built upon the assumption of limited factor mobility across industries, it is appropriate for analyzing the short-run effects of immigration. To be consistent with Chapter 3, the specific factors are called land and capital and the mobile factor is called labor. (Of course, the specific factors could be different types of capital or labor.) To keep things as simple as possible, we assume that the country is trading freely with the rest of the world at fixed prices.

In the specific-factors model, new workers must be absorbed into both industries. When a worker is hired in an industry, the marginal product of labor in that industry must fall because there is now less of the specific factor per worker. Because prices are fixed, the decline in the marginal product of labor must be accompanied by a decline in the real wage in that industry. If workers were to enter only one industry, then the wage in that industry would fall below the wage level in the other industry. Hence, labor must be absorbed in both industries. Changes in the remaining economic variables are driven by the increase in labor employed in both industries. First, output of both industries must increase because there are more factors being used in production. Second, because there is more labor and the same amount of specific factor, the marginal products of both specific factors must rise. Hence, immigration increases the real income of the specific factors.

How does a country absorb an increase in its labor endowment in the long run? There are two possible channels that we will discuss in the context of a specific example. Suppose there are two industries, A and B. Industry A is labor-intensive relative to industry B. The country is endowed with $\overline{K}$ units of capital and $\overline{L}$ units of labor. Because all factors are used, we have $\overline{K} = K_A + K_B$ and $\overline{L} = L_A + L_B$. In Chapter 4, we learned that the condition that the relative supply of labor $\overline{L}/\overline{K}$ must be equal to the relative demand for labor (a weighted average of relative demand in each industry) can be written

$$\frac{\overline{L}}{\overline{K}} = \left(\frac{K_A}{\overline{K}}\right)\left(\frac{L_A}{K_A}\right) + \left(\frac{K_B}{\overline{K}}\right)\left(\frac{L_B}{K_B}\right).$$

From this expression, we see that an increase in the endowment of labor $\overline{L}$ due to immigration can be absorbed either (1) by increasing the labor-to-capital ratio in each industry (L_A / K_A and L_B / K_B) or (2) by increasing the weight of the labor-intensive industry A (with its higher labor/capital ratio) in relative demand (increasing $K_A / \overline{K}$ and decreasing $K_B / \overline{K}$).

It turns out that the first channel plays *no* role in absorbing new workers in the long run. The labor/capital ratios used in each industry cannot change as long as the prices of goods are held fixed. This is hard to show formally, but we provide some intuition. The key insight follows from the fact that for a fixed set of goods prices, there is only *one capital-to-labor ratio* for each industry that makes (1) the value of the marginal product of labor the same in both industries, and (2) the value of the marginal product of capital the same in both industries. In the short run, the rental on capital can be different across industries (think specific-factors model) so that employment can increase in both industries. This is not so in the long run. In the long run labor is absorbed into the economy exclusively through an increase in the output of the labor-intensive good and a decrease in the output of the capital-intensive good.

To see how changing the mix of output can absorb the increase in labor, consider the following numerical example as an alternative to the *box diagram*. Suppose that the production of good A requires 1 unit of labor and 1 unit of capital, whereas the production of good B requires 1 unit of labor and 5 units of capital. If Q_A is the output of good A and Q_B is the output of good B, then if all factors are being used we have

$$\overline{K} = 5 \cdot Q_B + 1 \cdot Q_A$$

and

$$\overline{L} = 1 \cdot Q_B + 1 \cdot Q_A.$$

Doing a little algebra, we find that

$$Q_A = \frac{5\bar{L} - \bar{K}}{4} \text{ and } Q_B = \frac{\bar{K} - \bar{L}}{4}.$$

From these two expressions, it is clear that an increase in the labor endowment, $\bar{L}$, increases the output of the labor-intensive good A and decreases the output of the capital-intensive good B. This example illustrates the *Rybczynski theorem* and the *Factor price insensitivity result*. A change in endowments for whatever reason leads to a change in the mix of the country's outputs rather than a change in the country's factor prices when the prices of goods are held fixed.

KEY TERMS

Use the space provided to record your notes on the following key terms.

Specific-factors model _____

_____

Rybczynski theorem _____

_____

Factor price insensitivity _____

_____

Real value-added _____

_____

REVIEW QUESTIONS

Problem 1: Consider a country called Home that produces manufactured goods (*M*) and agricultural products (*A*). *M* is produced using capital and labor. *A* is produced using land and labor. (Hence, this is a short-run problem.) Labor is perfectly mobile between industries. Suppose that the country is trading with the rest of the world at fixed prices (P_M and P_A). Initially, the country has the same wages as the rest of the world.

1a. Suppose that the country's endowment of land expands. What impact does this expansion of land have on the wage (*W*)? Use the diagram provided below to support your answer.

_____

_____

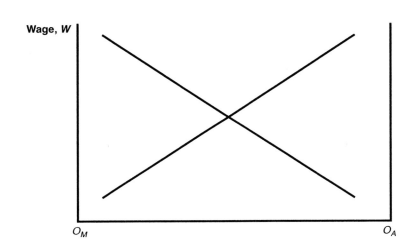

1b. Suppose that the wage is higher in Home than in the rest of the world so that Foreign labor will move to Home. What is the impact of the increase in labor for the wage in Home? Use the diagram provided below to support your answer. _____

_____

_____

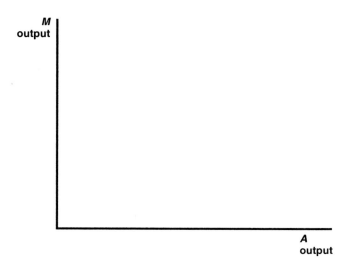

1c. What is the impact of the immigration to Home on the real earnings of a unit of capital in Home and on the real earnings of a unit of land in Home? _____

_____

_____

1d. Using the axes below, show how the output of both goods is affected by the immigration into the country. Explain your diagram. _____

_____

_____

TIPS

It is important to understand why adding more of a specific factor shifts up the marginal product of labor in the industry using that factor.

When the stock of the endowment of the mobile factor changes, it is always the case that in the short run the output of both goods and the real return to both specific factors must change in the same direction. It is not possible without additional information, however, to say which industry is affected the most.

It does not matter whether one shifts the axes O_M or O_A when increasing the size of the labor force.

To convince yourself that you know the material well, run all the questions in problem 1 in reverse (consider an outflow of labor). All the answers should be reversed.

Problem 2: Consider a country that produces two goods: airplanes and shirts. The country is trading with the rest of the world at fixed goods prices. Airplane producers are using 5 units of capital and 3 units of labor to produce one unit of airplanes and shirt producers are using 2 units of capital and 2 units of labor to produce one shirt. Both factors are mobile between industries.

2a. Which good is capital-intensive? _____

_____

_____

2b. Suppose there is a sudden emigration (outflow of labor). What happens to the level of employment in the airplane industry in the long run? Show using the box diagram below.

_____

_____

_____

2c. Can you derive an equation that relates the country's output to its endowments? _____

_____

_____

2d. Use the axes below to show how the emigration of labor alters the shape of the production possibilities frontier in the long run. Indicate the level of production of both goods before and after the outflow of labor.

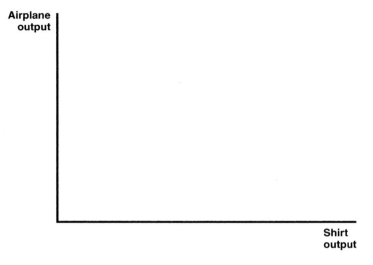

....

TIPS The Rybczynski theorem can be used to explain why a country's PPF is skewed toward the good that is intensive in the country's relatively abundant factor. It would be helpful to convince yourself that this is so.

....

Problem 3: Consider a country that produces two goods, computers and shirts, using capital and labor. In the short run, labor is specific to its sector because workers need particular skills to be productive in the industry. In the long run, labor is perfectly mobile between industries. Capital is perfectly mobile in both the short and long run. The country is engaged in free trade at fixed world prices.

3a. Suppose there is an inward flow of computer workers into the country. What is the short-run impact of the immigration on the real incomes of both computer and shirt workers already in the country? Explain using the axes below. _____

_____

_____

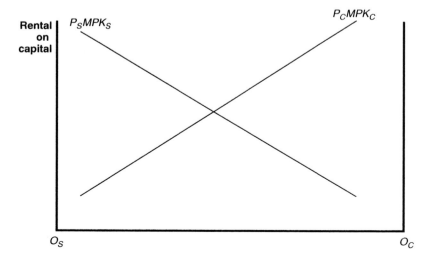

3b. What is the impact of the influx of computer workers on real wage in the long run (i.e., when workers are free to move between industries)? _____

_____

_____

3c. What is the effect of the immigration in the short and long run on the real income of capital? _____

_____

_____

···

The assumptions that economists make regarding the nature of technology have important implications for how they perceive the effects of immigration. To answer any problem correctly, you must identify what factors are assumed to be mobile.

The contrast between the short-run and the long-run implications of immigration on factor prices is important. Any calculation of the impact of immigration on factor prices depends on the assumptions that were made to generate those estimates!

In the example considered here, workers have skills that are specific to particular industries. This is probably closer to truth than assuming that workers are perfectly mobile between sectors. By giving factors different names, we can use the same framework to think about other real-world cases.

TIPS

···

Problem 4: Answer the following questions "true," "false," or "uncertain," and **explain** your answer.

4a. Most immigrants into the United States enter the country legally. _____

_____

_____

4b. Almost all immigrants (both legal and illegal) into the United States are very low skilled.

_____

_____

4c. The response of Miami's output to the Mariel boat lift is consistent with the Rybczynski theorem. _____

_____

_____

2 Foreign Direct Investment

ESSENTIAL CONCEPTS

Foreign direct investment (FDI) occurs when a company from one country obtains a production plant in a foreign country. If the plant is built from scratch, it is a greenfield investment. If instead the plant already existed under a different firm's ownership, the investment is called acquisition FDI. The chapter focuses mostly on greenfield investment because this type of FDI better fits the way FDI is modeled. In the short run, FDI is modeled as an increase in a country's endowment of one of the specific factors, capital. The key result is that an increase in the endowment of one of the specific factors drives up the demand for labor and its real wage. The real rental to both specific factors must fall. With respect to the outputs of goods, in the short run an increase in the stock of one specific factor increases the output of that specific factor and reduces the output of the other industry. The reduction in the output of the other industry occurs because the growth in the industry receiving FDI attracts workers out of agriculture.

In the long run, we assume that all factors are perfectly mobile between industries and that industries are characterized by their factor intensity; therefore, the effect of an inflow of capital is symmetrical to the case of an inflow of labor. Both the Rybczynski theorem and the factor price insensitivity result are still valid. FDI changes the country's total output and composition of that output between industries but has no impact on its factor prices in the long run.

KEY TERMS

Use the space provided to record your notes on the following key term.

Foreign direct investment _____

_____

_____

REVIEW QUESTIONS

Problem 5: Agricultural products (*A*) are produced with land and labor, and manufacturing products (*M*) are produced using capital and labor. Labor is perfectly mobile between industries but cannot move internationally.

5a. Suppose there are two countries, Home and Foreign, that are identical except that Home has a larger endowment of labor than Foreign. The two countries are engaged in free trade. Given this scenario, is there any motive for capital to move internationally? If so, which direction would it move? _____

_____

_____

5b. Assume that the international prices of *A* and *M* do not change and that capital moves from Foreign to Home. What will FDI do to Home's level of production of *M* and of *A*? Show using the following diagram. _____

_____

_____

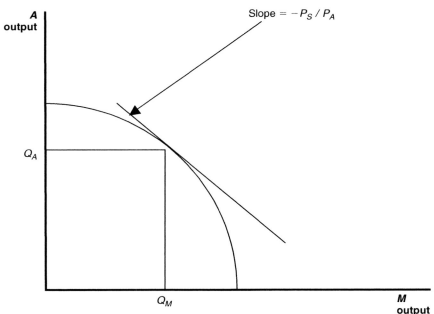

5c. What is the impact of this inward FDI on the real wage of labor, the real rental of capital, and the real rental of land in Home? _____

_____

_____

5d. How does the outward investment affect the real earnings of labor in Foreign? _____

_____

_____

....

Note the difference in the answers to problems 5c and 5d. The factors that are helped in Home are the factors that are hurt in Foreign and vice versa.

TIPS

....

Problem 6: Consider a country that produces airplanes and shirts using capital and labor. Shirts are labor-intensive relative to airplanes. Labor and capital are perfectly mobile between industries. The country is engaged in free trade at fixed world prices. Suppose that some of the capital used to make shirts is transferred abroad via outward foreign direct investment.

6a. What is the impact of the transfer of capital abroad on the production of shirts in the long run? _____

_____

_____

6b. What is the long-run impact of the outward foreign direct investment on the real wage?

_____

_____

_____

3 Gains from Labor and Capital Flows

ESSENTIALS CONCEPTS

Thus far, the analysis has highlighted how changes in endowments due to labor and capital flows alter real incomes of various factors and the output of different goods. How do these flows affect the national welfare of the country that is the source of these flows and the national welfare of the country that is the destination for these flows? To answer this question, keep in mind that labor moves from the low-wage country to the high-wage country and capital moves from the low- to the high-rental country. In an *equilibrium with full migration*, the wages in both countries, and hence the marginal product of labor in both countries, are equalized. Because factor prices reflect the value of the marginal product, factors move from countries with low marginal products to countries with high marginal products. This means that factor flows increase world output: There are gains from factor movement. In general, both source and destination countries share in the gains, but the disruptive effect of the change in income distribution can be very large relative to the total welfare gain.

KEY TERMS

Use the space provided to record your notes on the following key term.

Equilibrium with full migration _____

_____

_____

REVIEW QUESTIONS

Problem 7: There are two countries, Home and Foreign. The two countries are identical except that Home has a labor force of 100 and Foreign has a labor force of 200. Given this allocation of labor across Home and Foreign, the value of the marginal product of labor in Home

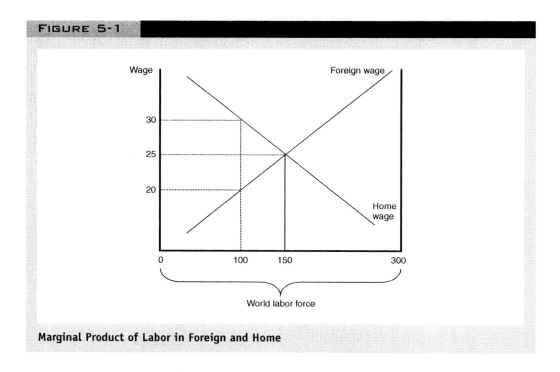

FIGURE 5-1

Marginal Product of Labor in Foreign and Home

is 30 and the value of the marginal product of labor in Foreign is 20. If labor were to be free to move, the wage in both countries would be 25. Figure 5-1 summarizes this situation.

7a. If immigration were free between countries, how much would the value of output change in Home? _____

_____

_____

7b. What is Home's national gain in allowing immigration? _____

_____

_____

7c. Who benefits from this immigration in Home and how much? _____

_____

_____

The analysis of the gains from FDI is conceptually identical to that of immigration. The marginal product of capital and the rental are considered instead of the marginal product of labor and the wage. One could repeat problem 7 for FDI renaming all the variables appropriately.

TIPS

Problem 8: Why are younger people more likely to immigrate than older people?

_____

_____

_____

6

Increasing Returns to Scale and Monopolistic Competition

Overview

This chapter begins with an example of actual trading patterns, U.S. imports and exports of golf clubs. Two aspects of this trading pattern cannot be explained by the models of comparative advantage presented in earlier chapters. First, the United States simultaneously imports golf clubs from a wide range of countries at very different prices. Second, the United States exports golf clubs to many of the same countries from which it is also importing golf clubs! This kind of *intra-industry trade,* or "two-way" trade in the same good between countries, is pervasive, occurring between many trading partners in many goods.

This chapter shows that models built on the assumption of *imperfect competition* improve our understanding of trade patterns and provide additional insight into the gains from trade. The centerpiece of the chapter is the model of trade under *monopolistic competition.* Firms in a monopolistically competitive industry have a monopoly over their own particular brand or "variety" of a *differentiated* good. There is an element of competition, however, in the sense that the demand for a firm's variety depends on the actions of other firms. Firms produce their variety using an *increasing returns to scale* technology. Firms face fixed product development cost and constant marginal costs of production, so their average cost falls as they produce larger volumes of output.

The monopolistic competition model makes predictions that are distinct from those of a comparative-advantage–based model. With respect to trade patterns, the model predicts intra-industry trade between similar countries and gives rise to the *gravity equation,* which is an accurate predictor of the volume of trade between countries. With respect to the gains from trade, the model identifies two channels through which trade affects welfare. International trade expands the range of variety available to consumers and allows firms to take advantage of increasing returns to scale, by expanding the size of their operations.

1 Basics of Imperfect Competition

ESSENTIAL CONCEPTS

The first section is designed (1) to review the theory of monopoly and (2) to introduce the concept of *product differentiation* in the context of a *duopoly.* A monopolist faces a downward-sloping demand curve and chooses its output (and hence the price of its product) to maximize its *monopoly profits*. A firm's profit is equal to the difference between its sales revenue and its total costs of production. By choosing to sell one more unit, the firm increases its revenue by the value of its *marginal revenue* and increases its total cost by its marginal cost. Suppose a firm is selling Q units at a price of P. The additional revenue raised by this firm if it sells one more unit is

$$P - \Delta P \cdot Q.$$

The firm earns P from selling one more unit but because the firm has to cut its price by ΔP on all the units it had been selling, it loses $\Delta P \cdot Q$. If the marginal revenue exceeds marginal cost, then the firm can increase its revenue by more than its cost by selling one more unit. If the marginal revenue is less than marginal cost, a firm can raise its profits by selling one less unit of its good because cutting production by one unit lowers revenue by less than it lowers total cost. Hence, a profit-maximizing firm chooses output so that marginal revenue is equal to marginal cost.

In the case of duopoly with differentiated products, there is a single demand curve for an industry's output, D, but each firm faces a demand curve that is specific to its variety of that industry's good. When the two firms charge the same price, industry demand is divided equally among varieties so that each firm sells $D / 2$. Because products are differentiated, a firm cannot grab the entire market by lowering its price below that of its competitor. Instead, a firm that reduces its price attracts new customers to its product, some of whom would have chosen to purchase the product of the firm's competitor. The demand curve for the firm, d, is flatter than the demand curve $D / 2$, because the firm can steal some of its competitor's customers by lowering its price.

KEY TERMS

Use the space provided to record your notes on the following key terms.

Imperfect competition _____

_____

_____

Duopoly _____

_____

_____

Marginal revenue _____

_____

_____

Marginal cost _____

_____

_____

Differentiated goods _____

_____

_____

Monopoly profits _____

_____

_____

REVIEW QUESTIONS

Problem 1: After extensive market research a firm discovers that it faces the demand curve recorded in the following table.

Quantity Sold	Price, $	Revenue, $	Marginal Revenue, $
1	7		
2	6		
3	5		
4	4		
5	3		
6	2		
7	1		

1a. Calculate the revenue and the marginal revenue associated with each output level and fill in the columns in the table.

1b. If the marginal cost is $2.5 per unit, what level of production should the firm choose to maximize its profits? Explain. _____

_____

_____

1c. Calculate the profits associated with this level of output. _____

_____

_____

Problem 2: A firm faces the demand curve, marginal revenue curve, and marginal cost curve shown in the following diagram. Add to this diagram the optimal level of output and show geometrically on this diagram the level of a firm's profits.

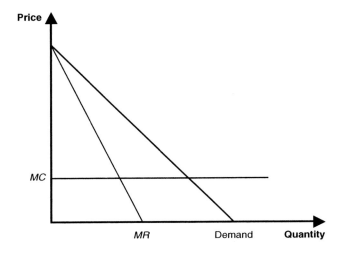

Problem 3: Consider a duopoly. In the diagram below, $D / 2$ is industry demand divided by the two differentiated varieties in the market when each variety has the same price and d is the demand curve specific to each firm.

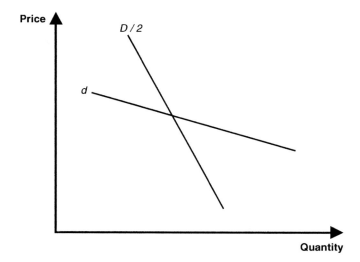

Why is the d curve flatter than the $D / 2$ curve? _____

_____

_____

2 Trade under Monopolistic Competition

ESSENTIAL CONCEPTS

The model of monopolistic competition is based on four assumptions. First, each firm produces a good that is similar to but differentiated from the goods that other firms in the industry produce. Because each firm's product is somewhat different from the goods of the other firms, a firm can raise its price without losing all its customers to other firms; that is, each firm faces a downward-sloping demand curve for its product. Second, there are many firms in the industry. Third, firms produce using a technology with increasing returns to scale: average costs of production fall as the quantity produced increases. Fourth, firms can enter and exit the industry freely, so that monopoly profits are zero in the long run. In monopolistic competition, firms have some monopoly power, and yet in a long-run equilibrium each firm's profits are zero.

The model neatly captures two gains from trade that are very different than those due to comparative advantage: International trade results in (1) a wider variety of goods available and (2) lower prices due to the better exploitation of increasing returns to scale. Opening to trade induces a rationalization effect: Some firms close when exposed to the increased competition in a larger global market, but the ones that remain produce at a larger scale. Increasing returns to scale mean that as a firm expands its output, its average costs are falling. The drop in average cost is passed on to consumers in the form of lower prices.

The model also allows us to better understand trade patterns between countries. Each variety is produced in one location but is demanded in all trading countries. Hence, there is one-way trade in each variety. Because each country produces distinct varieties, there is two-way or *intra-industry trade* within goods in an existing national market.

KEY TERMS

Use the space provided to record your notes on the following key terms.

Increasing returns to scale _____

_____

_____

Monopolistic competition _____

_____

_____

Intra-industry trade _____

_____

_____

REVIEW QUESTIONS

Problem 4: A firm faces a fixed cost of $100 and a marginal cost of $2 per unit of output. If the firm is planning to sell 10 units, what is the lowest price that the firm can charge that will allow it to break even?

_____

_____

Problem 5: In the following diagram, D / N is industry demand divided by the number of differentiated goods when each good has the same price and d is the demand curve facing each individual producer of a differentiated good in an existing national market.

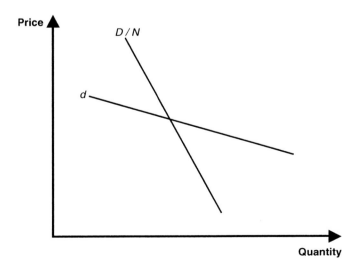

5a. Draw in the diagram the effect on d and D / N of an increase in N, the number of competing varieties within the existing market.

5b. Explain why you drew the demand curves as you did. _____

_____

_____

TIPS Understanding the response of demand curves D / N and d is critical to understanding many of the key implications of the monopolistic competition model.

Problem 6: The marginal and average cost curves facing a firm are drawn in the following diagram.

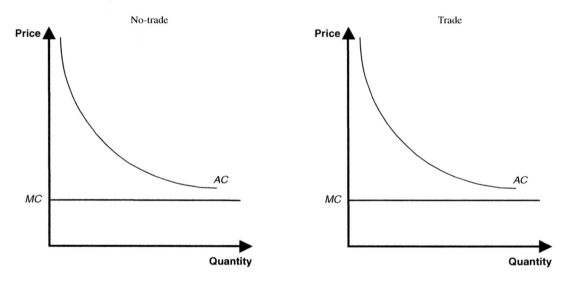

6a. In the left-hand panel, draw demand curves D / N and d, a marginal revenue curve, and the level of the optimal price and quantity for a firm in a long-run no-trade equilibrium.

6b. In the right-hand panel, draw demand curves D / N and d, a marginal revenue curve, and the level of the price and quantity for a firm in a long-run trading equilibrium for the case of two identical countries.

6c. Explain *how* the two panels are drawn differently. _____

_____

_____

6d. Explain *why* the two panels are different. _____

_____

_____

6e. What are the gains from trade, and how can they appear in the difference in the way the two panels were drawn? _____

_____

6f. What are the adjustment costs associated with international trade, and how do they appear in the way the two panels were drawn in the previous diagram? _____

_____

_____

Problem 7: Consider a world with two countries. One of the countries is large and the other is small. There is one monopolistically competitive industry that uses labor as the only input.

7a. In autarky, which country has the highest real wage? Explain. _____

_____

_____

7b. Which country gains the most from international trade? Explain. _____

_____

_____

Problem 8: Essentially only two producers in the world make wide-bodied aircraft. Would monopolistic competition be an appropriate model for this industry? Why or why not?

_____

_____

···

TIPS

The monopolistic competition model is popular among economists because it is neat and tidy. Because the number of firms is large, we abstract from messy "strategic behavior" across firms. When the number of firms is small, however, we can no longer avoid thinking about strategic behavior.

A key observation is that the gains from trade are essentially gains to market size. Large markets allow for more variety at lower prices. The gains from trade come from consolidating two small markets into one large global market.

···

3 The North American Free Trade Agreement

ESSENTIAL CONCEPTS

This section uses the experience of the North American Free Trade Agreement (NAFTA) to assess the predictions of the monopolistic competition model. The monopolistic competition model predicts that a reduction to trade barriers between countries should have disruptive effects in the short run and gains from trade in the long run. The disruptive effects in the short run include employment losses as some firms go out of business. In the long run, however, employment should recover as surviving firms expand into foreign markets. As firms expand into foreign markets, consumers gain access to increased variety, and the larger size of surviving firms allows them to better exploit increasing returns to scale. This latter effect should appear in the data as an increase in productivity and an increase in real wages as the prices charged by firms fall.

Many of the model's predictions are supported by the experience of the three countries that participated in NAFTA. This *free-trade agreement* eliminated most tariffs and other barriers to trade among the countries of Canada, Mexico, and the United States. As expected, the short-run effects of the free-trade agreement proved to be quite disruptive. For instance, NAFTA led to a sharp decrease in Canadian employment in manufacturing. This job loss was followed by a sharp increase in Canadian manufacturing productivity as firms expanded their exports to the American market, and the increase in productivity also appears to have increased real wages in Canada. The productivity effects were also substantial in Mexico, although many of the positive effects of NAFTA appear to have been obscured by a deep recession caused by a financial crisis.

In the United States, NAFTA was associated with a modest loss of jobs in certain industries that was offset in part by the expansion of the *trade adjustment assistance* program for those workers whose jobs disappeared due to NAFTA. This program is specially designed for exactly the disruptive effects of trade. In the long run, American consumers have benefited from NAFTA as the number of varieties made available as trade with Mexico expanded. On net, the gains from free trade with Mexico are calculated to exceed the losses.

KEY TERMS

Free-Trade Agreement _____

_____

_____

Trade adjustment assistance (TAA) _____

_____

_____

REVIEW QUESTIONS

Problem 9: Would you expect the effects of NAFTA to be most pronounced for the United States or Canada and Mexico? _____

_____

_____

Problem 10: Why is it difficult to establish the effects of NAFTA on the Mexican economy?

_____

_____

Problem 11: How were displaced workers in the United States partially shielded from the disruptive effects of NAFTA? _____

_____

_____

Problem 12: How has NAFTA affected the range of product variety available in the United States?

_____

_____

_____

_____

4 Intra-industry Trade and the Gravity Equation

ESSENTIAL CONCEPTS

This section shows that the monopolistic competition model is helpful in understanding key parts of international trading patterns. For instance, the monopolistic competition model predicts that intra-industry trade should be highest in industries in which there is a high degree of product differentiation. The *index of intra-industry trade* measures the extent to which trade is two-way between countries. As predicted by the monopolistic competition model, the index is high for goods that also exhibit a high degree of product differentiation.

The monopolistic competition model predicts that international trade patterns should be well predicted by a *gravity equation,* which is given by

$$TRADE = \frac{GDP_1 \cdot GDP_2}{DIST^n}.$$

The gravity equation predicts that the volume of trade between two countries (here Countries 1 and 2) is increasing in the gross domestic product of either country and is decreasing in their distance from each other. This relationship comes from the fact that each country produces a distinct set of varieties that are demanded in each country. The share of a country's GDP (the value of the output of its varieties) that is sold to a given foreign country is increasing in the foreign country's income or GDP and decreasing in distance between the two countries because transport costs rise with distance. The gravity equation is an accurate predictor of the volume of trade between countries.

KEY TERMS

Use the space provided to record your notes on the following key terms.

Index of intra-industry trade _____

_____

_____

Gravity equation _____

_____

_____

Border effects _____

_____

_____

Tariffs _____

_____

_____

Quotas _____

_____

_____

REVIEW QUESTIONS

Problem 13: Different soil conditions generate variation in the character of grapes and the wine that is made from them. Is it possible that intra-industry trade can be high in certain industries even in the absence of imperfect competition? _____

_____

_____

Problem 14: Consider a country that opens to trade with a neighboring country. The immediate effect of this opening is an increase in unemployment. Workers eventually find jobs, but most workers find themselves employed in a different industry. Is the main motive for trade between these two countries most likely to be monopolistic competition or comparative advantage? Explain. _____

_____

_____

Problem 15: Would you expect the gravity equation to explain trade patterns best between a set of countries that are similar in terms of their endowments or a set of countries that are different in their endowments? Explain. _____

_____

_____

Problem 16: How could you use data on international trade flows to assess which industries display a high degree of product differentiation and which ones do not? _____

_____

_____

....

TIPS

As indicated in the answer to problem 13, product differentiation alone can give rise to high levels of intra-industry trade.

Problems 14 to 16 demonstrate that there are many things at work in trading patterns between countries. Because different models have different implications, it is important to know which model is appropriate for which phenomenon.

....

7

Import Tariffs and Quotas under Perfect Competition

Overview

As trade creates gains between countries and winners and losers within countries, a country's *trade policy* affects the welfare of other nations and redistributes income within its borders. Because one country's policies can negatively affect other countries, the *World Trade Organization* acts as a forum for countries to come to a collective agreement on trade policies and resolves disputes between countries when they arise. The structure and history of the WTO affect all relevant aspects of trade policy.

The chapter introduces a perfectly competitive, partial equilibrium model to analyze the welfare impact of two types of trade policies: the import *tariff* and the import *quota*. The tariff, which is a tax on imports, is the most common way that countries reduce the volume of their imports. The analysis suggests that import tariffs lower the welfare of *small* importing countries but can actually improve the welfare of *large* importing countries. Large countries' gain is at the expense of their trading partners, however, explaining some of the conflicts that arise between countries. The import quota is a direct restriction on the number of imports allowed into a country. In the perfectly competitive model, the welfare effects associated with import *quotas* are much like those of the import tariff. Like tariffs, quotas raise domestic prices above world price and so aid producers and harm consumers. Governments typically enforce quotas in a way that ensures that they lower national welfare.

1 A Brief History of the World Trade Organization

ESSENTIAL CONCEPTS

Prior to World War II the world was in a major economic slump commonly referred to as the Great Depression. During this period, countries used trade policies to aid domestic producers, but the collective effect of a simultaneous rise in tariffs across all major countries was to reduce the volume of trade for all countries. The loss of the gains from trade is generally thought to have contributed to the seriousness of the Depression.

In 1947, the General Agreement on Tariffs and Trade (GATT) was established, with the goal of reducing trade barriers. In addition to providing a forum for negotiating the reduction of trade barriers, the GATT contained 24 articles that regulated countries' use of trade policies. Under the GATT, countries met periodically for negotiations, called *rounds,* with the purpose of lowering trade barriers and introducing rules for the conduct of trade policy.

In 1995 the GATT was replaced by the World Trade Organization. The articles of the GATT were written into the WTO agreement. Unlike the GATT, the WTO is a formal institution that has a mechanism, or procedure, for settling disputes that arise when countries are accused of violating the rules. This subsection introduces some of the key rules of the WTO and the GATT before it.

KEY TERMS

Use the space provided to record your notes on the following key terms.

Trade policy _____

_____

_____

Import tariff _____

_____

_____

Dumping _____

_____

_____

Import quota _____

_____

_____

Export subsidies _____

_____

_____

Regional trade agreements _____

_____

_____

Free-trade areas _____

_____

_____

Customs unions _____

_____

_____

Safeguard provision _____

_____

_____

Escape clause _____

_____

_____

REVIEW QUESTIONS

Problem 1: The following questions test your knowledge of the WTO's rules.

1a. How would you know if a foreign firm was dumping its product in your domestic market? _____

_____

_____

1b. Suppose that several countries decided to reduce tariffs exclusively on each others' products but maintain their tariffs on other countries' products. Would this agreement violate the WTO's "most favored nation" principle? Why or why not? _____

_____

_____

1c. Why is "most favored nation status" called "normal trade relations" in the United States?

_____

_____

Memorize the appropriate article in GATT for each of the relevant key terms.
   Be patient. Each of the articles highlighted in this section will be featured at some point in the next several chapters.

TIPS

2 The Gains from Trade

ESSENTIAL CONCEPTS

A simple partial equilibrium framework is introduced to analyze the effect of Home's trade policy on its welfare. There are two types of actors in Home, consumers and producers. In Figure 7-1, Home's consumers are represented by a demand curve (D) and Home's producers are represented by a supply curve (S). When Home is in autarky, the price (P^A) and quantity (Q_0) in this market is determined by the intersection of supply and demand. Now suppose that the country could trade with the outside world at fixed world prices. If the price on the world market is below the price in Home in autarky, then Home's consumers will expand their demand and its producers will contract their supply. When Home's demand exceeds its domestic supply, the country must import the difference. Home's import demand curve is shown on the right-hand panel of Figure 7-1. Given a world price P^W, a country imports M_1, which is equal to $D_1 - S_1$.

FIGURE 7-1

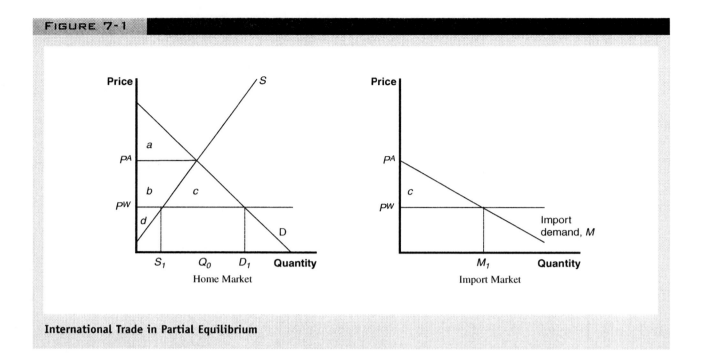

International Trade in Partial Equilibrium

To measure welfare in this framework, we rely on the concepts of *consumer surplus* and *producer surplus.* The surplus that accrues to a consumer who buys D_1 units of a good when the price is P^W is equal to the area under the demand curve up to D_1 (the total utility of consuming that much of the good), less the amount that the consumer had to pay, or price P^W multiplied by D_1 (the forgone utility of consuming other goods). In Figure 7-1, given a price of P^W, the consumer surplus is equal to the sum of the areas *a, b,* and *c.* Because international trade lowers the price of the import good, trade improves the well-being of consumers by the area $b + c$, as shown in the left-hand panel of Figure 7-1.

The producer surplus associated with selling S_1 units at a price P^W is the revenue earned $(P^W \cdot S_1)$ less the total payments to variable factors (the area under the supply curve up to S_1). In Figure 7-1, the producer surplus given a price of P^W is the area *d.* International trade lowers the price in an import industry relative to autarky and so harms producers whose revenues fall by more than their variable costs. In Figure 7-1, the loss imposed on producers by international trade is the area *b.*

International trade creates winners and losers in this model, but the gains to the winners exceed the losses to losers. In Figure 7-1, the gains from trade are measured by the area *c.* Notice that this welfare effect is measured by the area of a triangle. The area of a triangle is easy to calculate: It is one half of the product of the base and height of the triangle. Finally, notice that the gains from trade can also be measured by triangles in either diagram.

KEY TERMS

Use the space provided to record your notes on the following key terms.

Consumer surplus _____

_____

_____

Producer surplus _____

_____

_____

Import demand curve _____

_____

_____

Small country _____

_____

_____

REVIEW QUESTIONS

Problem 2: Anne is willing to buy one tomato if the price of tomatoes is $3 and two tomatoes if the price of tomatoes is $2. If the price of tomatoes is $2, what is Anne's consumer surplus?

_____

_____

Problem 3: Suppose tomatoes are grown using land (a specific factor) and labor (a mobile factor). If the revenue of tomato growers is $100 and the wage bill (amount paid to the mobile factor) is $60, what is the producer surplus in the tomato industry? _____

_____

Problem 4: Figure 7-2 shows the trading equilibrium for a small country with import demand M facing a fixed world price for a good.

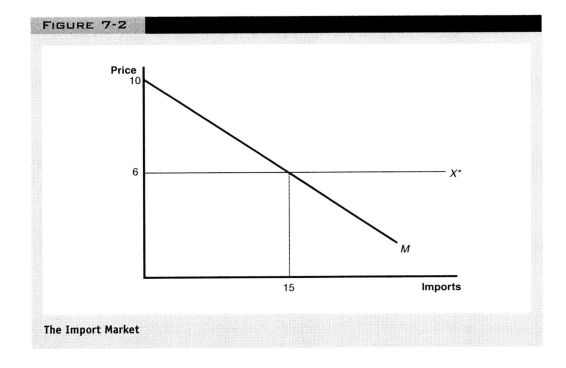

FIGURE 7-2

The Import Market

4a. What is the autarky price in this small country? _____

4b. What are the national welfare gains from trade for this economy compared with national welfare in autarky? _____

_____

_____

4c. The following Home Market diagram shows Home's domestic supply and demand for the good. Fill in the information from Figure 7-2 (prices and imports) and your answer to problem 4b (gains from trade) in this diagram.

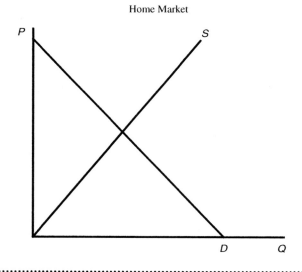

Home Market

TIPS   When a country goes from autarky to free trade, the price on the world market becomes the price in the importing country. Home's producers would not be able to sell any goods for a price higher than the world level.

The diagrams used in the book have linear supply and demand curves. This means that the measurement of deadweight losses always involves calculating the area of triangles. The area of a triangle is one half of the product of the triangle's base and its height.

----

3 Import Tariffs for a Small Country

ESSENTIAL CONCEPTS

A *small country* faces a horizontal export supply curve. It cannot affect the world price of its imports by changing its behavior. When Home puts a tariff of size t into place, the price facing home consumers and producers is equal to the fixed world price P^W plus the tariff t. As shown in Figure 7-3, consumers reduce their demand and producers increase their supply and imports fall.

The increase in the price in the home market lowers consumer surplus by the area $a + b + c + d$. At the same time, the increase in price in Home increases its producer surplus by the area a. Because the country is an importer, the loss of consumer surplus is always greater than the gain in producer surplus because consumption in Home is greater than production in Home. The tariff also raises revenue for the government, however, and this revenue has value equal to $t + M_t$, where t is the tariff rate and M_t is the amount of

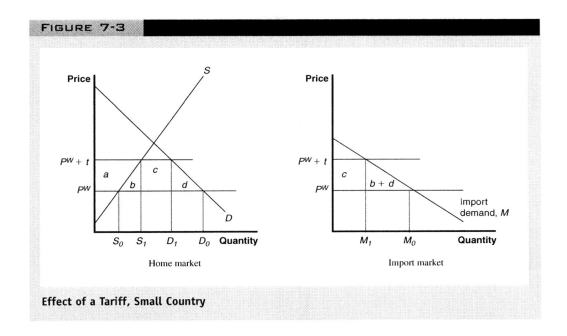

FIGURE 7-3

Effect of a Tariff, Small Country

the good imported. In Figure 7-3 (both panels) this is the area *c*. On net, a tariff imposed by a small country must reduce the welfare of that country by the area *b* + *d*. These welfare losses are called the *deadweight loss* of the tariff and are equal to the sum of the *production loss* (area *b*) and *consumption loss* (area *d*). The deadweight loss appears in both the Home Market and Import Market diagrams and can be easily calculated using the formula for the area of a triangle.

KEY TERMS

Use the space provided to record your notes on the following key terms.

Deadweight loss _____

_____

_____

Production loss _____

_____

_____

Consumption loss _____

_____

_____

Dispute settlement procedure _____

_____

_____

Tariff war _____

_____

_____

REVIEW QUESTIONS

Problem 5: Consider the information in Figure 7-2. Now suppose that this country puts in a tariff of $2 per unit imported. Suppose that the country's imports fall from 15 units to 7.5 units.

5a. What is the effect of the tariff on the domestic price? _____

5b. What is the value of tariff revenue raised by this tariff? _____

5c. What is the effect of the tariff on national welfare (provide a number)? _____

_____

Now suppose that the tariff causes the revenue of domestic firms to rise by $9 and the payments to variable factors of production to rise by $4.

5d. What is the effect of the tariff on producer surplus? _____

5e. Given your answers to questions 5b through 5d, what is the effect of the tariff on consumer surplus? _____

_____

5f. Fill in as much of the information as possible in the following domestic supply and demand diagram.

Home Market

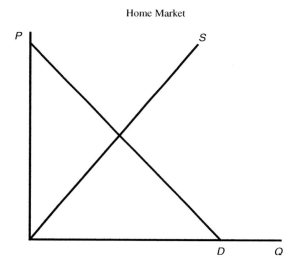

TIPS You should be comfortable understanding the relationships between the information in the Home Market diagram and the Import Market diagram.

Problem 6: Home has a tariff of $2 on the import of a pair of shoes. Home is small, and the price of shoes on the world market is $15. Home had been producing 100 pairs of shoes and consuming 300 pairs of shoes. Now suppose that Home gets rid of its tariff entirely. As a result, consumption of shoes rises by 25 pairs and production of shoes falls by 25 pairs. Assume that Home's supply and demand curves are linear.

6a. What is the impact of the tariff removal on producer surplus? (Provide a number.)

_____

6b. What is the impact of the tariff removal on consumer surplus? (Provide a number.)

_____

6c. What is the impact of the tariff removal on government revenue? (Provide a number.)

_____

6d. Is the country better or worse off after the tariff is removed and by how much? _____

_____

6e. Use the following diagram to illustrate the information provided in the questions and answers to the other parts of the problem.

Home Market

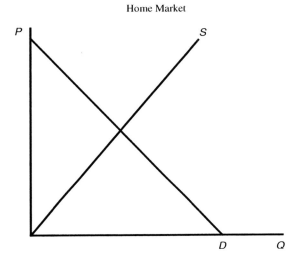

4 Import Tariff for a Large Country

ESSENTIAL CONCEPTS

If Home is a *large country,* it can alter world prices by changing its demand on the world market. To model a large country, we assume that the country faces an export supply curve that has a positive slope, as shown in the right-hand panel of Figure 7-4. By imposing a tariff, the government raises the price in Home, inducing producers to supply more and consumers to demand less so that imports contract for any given world price. This reduction in demand pushes down the world price in Import Market, shown in Figure 7-4 as the decrease in the world price P_0^W to P_1^W. Meanwhile, the domestic price rises from P_0^W to $P_1^W + t$.

The reduction in the world price is called the *terms-of-trade gain* for Home, and it represents an increase in Home's welfare. The gain occurs because Home has pushed some of the incidence of the tariff onto foreign producers. Total tariff revenue accruing to the government is shown in both panels of Figure 7-4 as the area $c + e$, of which the area e is paid by foreign producers. The remainder of the welfare analysis for Home is similar to the case of the small country. Because the price rises in Home (P_0^W to $P_1^W + t$), consumer surplus falls by the area $a + b + c + d$ and producer surplus rises by the area a. The total impact of the tariff on national welfare is then $e - (b + d)$. The key result is that if the government chooses its tariff carefully, then the terms-of-trade gain exceeds the dead-

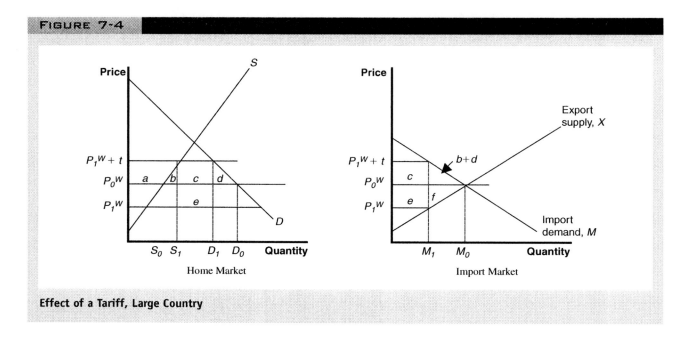

Figure 7-4

Effect of a Tariff, Large Country

weight loss and Home is better off with a tariff than it is with free trade. The tariff rate that maximizes the welfare gain for Home is called the *optimal tariff.*

Home's welfare gain comes at the expense of its trading partner, where producer surplus falls by more than consumer surplus rises in response to the lower world price (because the foreign country is an exporter of the good and hence produces more than it consumes). Total losses to the exporting country are shown as the area $e + f$ in the Import Market in Figure 7-4. By imposing a tariff, Home might precipitate a *trade war* by inducing its trading partner to impose *retaliatory* tariffs on Home products as punishment. Finally, because free trade maximizes global efficiency, a tariff necessarily leads to welfare losses through production and consumption losses, which are equal to $-(b + d + f)$.

KEY TERMS

Use the space provided to record your notes on the following key terms.

Large country _____

_____

_____

Terms of trade _____

_____

_____

Terms-of-trade gain _____

_____

_____

Optimal tariff _____

_____

_____

REVIEW QUESTIONS

Problem 7: Suppose Home is importing 100 units of a good at a world price of $10/unit. Home then puts in a tariff of $2 per unit. As a result of the tariff, the price paid in Home rises to $11 per unit and imports fall to 50 units.

7a. What impact has the tariff had on the world price? _____

_____

7b. What tariff revenue is raised by this tariff? _____

7c. Assuming that the country's import demand curve is linear, what is the deadweight loss in Home caused by this tariff? _____

7d. By how much did this tariff raise or lower Home's welfare?

_____

7e. By how much did this tariff raise or lower Foreign welfare?

_____

7f. What is the effect of the tariff on world welfare? _____

7g. Use the following domestic supply and demand diagram for the exporting country to illustrate the welfare impact of Home's tariff on consumer surplus, producer surplus, and national welfare. Where possible, provide numbers.

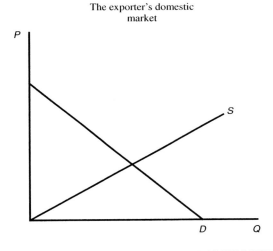

The exporter's domestic
market

- -

When Home imposes a tariff, its consumers and producers react to a price that exceeds the world price by the size of the tariff. When the tariff is imposed, the price in Home increases by *t*, causing consumers to demand less and producers to supply more. The demand for imports then falls, pushing down the price on the world market. The new equilibrium occurs when at the new world price plus the tariff, Home consumers want to import the same quantity that Foreign producers want to sell at the new world price.

TIPS

- -

Problem 8: The optimal tariff formula states that the tariff that raises national welfare the most is inversely related to the elasticity of the export supply curve. Provide an intuitive explanation for why this is so. _____

_____

_____

TIPS

A tariff is just a tax on imports. As we know from introductory economics, the incidence of a tax falls on both suppliers and consumers. If we think of the importing country as the consumer and the exporting country as the supplier, then it makes sense that the steeper (more inelastic) the supply curve, the more the effect of a tax (tariff) is borne by the exporting country.

5 Import Quotas

ESSENTIAL CONCEPTS

A quota is a limit on the number of imports allowed into a country. If Home imposes a quota, its government requires anyone importing the good to have a *quota license.* In the presence of a quota, the price in Home rises above the world price in order to make Home's excess demand (equal to domestic demand minus domestic supply) equal the amount of the quota. As in the case of the tariff, a higher domestic price reduces consumer surplus by more than it increases producer surplus. The fact that the price in Home exceeds the world price means that quota licenses have value as they give their owner the right to buy low at the world price and sell high at the domestic price. The total value of quota licenses is called the *quota rent.*

Who gets the quota rents? There are several possibilities. First, if the government auctions the quota licenses in a perfectly competitive market, then the quota rents accrue to the government. In this case, the welfare effect of a quota is *equivalent* to a tariff that restricts imports by the same amount. The diagrams for a quota would be drawn in exactly the same way that they would be for a tariff. Second, the quota rents could be given away. One potential problem with giving the quota licenses away is that people engage in *rent-seeking* behavior: They use real resources to lobby the government in order to obtain quota licenses. In fact, quota rents are often given to the governments of the exporting countries to distribute as they please. When quota rents are given to foreigners, the effect of the quota on national welfare is unambiguously negative in both the small- and large-country cases.

KEY TERMS

Use the space provided to record your notes on the following key terms.

Quota licenses _____

_____

_____

Quota rents _____

_____

_____

Equivalent import tariff _____

_____

_____

Rent seeking _____

_____

_____

Voluntary export restraint (VER) _____

_____

_____

Voluntary restraint agreement (VRA) _____

_____

_____

Multifiber arrangement (MFA) _____

_____

_____

REVIEW QUESTIONS

Problem 9: Consider two scenarios for a small country. In one case, the government imposes a tariff on the import of a good. In the second case, the government imposes a quota that restricts imports by the same amount as the tariff and distributes the quota licenses by selling them on a perfectly competitive market.

9a. Compare and contrast the welfare effects of these two policies given the fixed world price. _____

_____

_____

9b. Now suppose that the protected good's price falls on world markets after the tariff and quota are in place. If you were a producer in the protected market, would you rather be protected by the tariff or by the quota? Explain. _____

_____

_____

Problem 10: Consider a large country that is importing 100 units of a good at $10 a piece. The government of the importing country puts in a quota of 50 units, which is enforced by having the government of the importing country distribute these licenses. As a result of this quota the Home price rises to $13 and the price on the world market drops to $8.

10a. What is the value of the quota rent? _____

10b. What is the effect on the export country's total welfare (provide a number)? _____

_____

_____

10c. What is the effect on the import country's total welfare (provide a number)? _____

_____

_____

10d. Illustrate the welfare effects on the importer and exporter countries in the following export–import diagram.

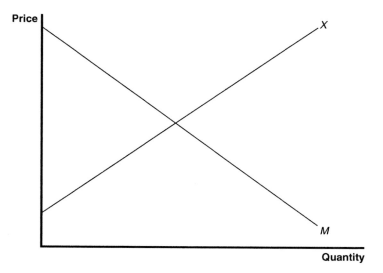

10e. If instead the importing country allowed the exporting country to sell the import licenses, what would be the welfare effect of the quota on the two countries? _____

_____

_____

_____

Problem 11: Why would a country give the quota rents to the exporting country? _____

_____

_____

· ·

TIPS The effect of a quota on national welfare depends on how the quota rents are distributed. Read problems on quotas carefully.

· ·

8

Import Tariffs and Quotas under Imperfect Competition

Overview

Perfect competition is a useful abstraction that economists use as a starting point in their analyses. No market is perfectly competitive, however, so it is important to consider the affects of trade policies when markets are imperfectly competitive. This chapter considers two broad types of imperfect competition. The first type occurs when firms, either domestic or foreign, have *market power*. Firms with market power have some control over the prices that they receive for their output. The second type occurs when there are *market failures*, such as *imperfect capital markets* or the existence of *externalities*. Market failures often justify government intervention.

Trade policy can have very different welfare effects when firms have market power. Government policies that alter the behavior of firms in an imperfectly competitive environment are often referred to as strategic trade policies. One benefit of international trade is that imports limit the ability of domestic firms to exploit their market power. These pro-competitive effects of international trade remain even when the government implements a tariff, but they are largely eliminated when the government implements an import quota. The differential effect of the two policies arises because a tariff continues to allow imports to respond to price changes in the home market, whereas a quota does not.

When a country is served by a single foreign monopolist, a country's tariff policy interacts with the price-setting behavior of the foreign firm. Home is always large in the sense that its tariff policy alters the price received by the foreign firm, but terms-of-trade gains only arise when the demand curve has a particular shape. Finally, the nature of a government's tariff policy also matters in the welfare implications. An *antidumping* policy threatens foreign firms with tariffs if they set a price in the home market that is below some measure of "fair value." When foreign firms raise their price in the home market to avoid these tariffs, the home market's consumer surplus falls and no tariff revenue is collected.

Market failures that are distinct from the existence of the market power of firms also have important implications for trade policy. When capital markets are imperfect and it takes time for firms to learn how to produce efficiently, potentially prosperous industries may never come into being because firms have no way to cover short-term losses. When there are positive externalities across firms, such as *knowledge spillovers,* industries may only be viable if they reach a certain size. Market failures of these sorts justify *infant industry protection:* Temporary trade barriers give new industries time to become internationally competitive.

1 Tariffs and Quotas with Home Monopoly

ESSENTIAL CONCEPTS

To analyze the effect of trade policies when the Home industry is imperfectly competitive, we adjust the partial equilibrium model by assuming that Home has only one firm with an upward-sloping marginal cost curve. In autarky, the Home firm is a monopolist and so faces a downward-sloping *marginal revenue* curve. The firm maximizes its profits by choosing the quantity that sets marginal revenue equal to marginal cost. As a result, the price facing Home consumers is greater than the firm's marginal cost. We assume that Home is small in the sense that there is a fixed world price for the good. With free trade, the Home price becomes the fixed world price and so the monopolist becomes a price taker. Because the Home firm has no incentive to restrict output, competition from imports can lead to an increase in the amount that the Home firm is willing to sell!

Tariffs and import quotas have different effects on welfare because they affect the *market power* of the Home firm differently. With a tariff, the Home firm would lose all its sales if it raised its price above the world price plus the tariff. Hence, the Home firm continues to be a price taker. As long as the Home firm is a price taker, the welfare effect of a tariff is the same as in the case of many Home firms. With a quota, imports cannot respond to price increases by the Home firm. The quota reduces the demand facing the domestic firm, but the firm still faces a downward-sloping demand curve for its output and so has an incentive to restrict output to raise the price. Hence, the quota leads to a higher price and less consumption than does a tariff.

KEY TERMS

Use the space provided to record your notes on the following key terms.

Market power _____

_____

_____

Marginal revenue _____

_____

_____

REVIEW QUESTIONS

Problem 1: Consider an industry in which Home (a small country) has a single firm with an upward sloping marginal cost curve. The price on world markets is P^W.

1a. In the following diagram, show the quantity sold and price charged by the monopolist if international trade is not allowed.

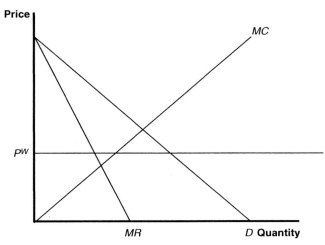

1b. What price is charged by Home's single firm if international trade is allowed? _____

_____

_____

1c. How does international trade affect the quantity sold by Home's single firm? Illustrate your answer in the previous diagram. _____

_____

1d. How does going from autarky to free trade affect the welfare of the monopolist? _____

_____

_____

1e. How does going from free trade to autarky affect consumers' welfare? _____

_____

_____

1f. How does going from autarky to free trade affect national welfare? _____

_____

1g. Suppose the world price was very low (below the intersection of *MR* and *MC*). In this case, how would the monopolist's output react to being exposed to free trade? _____

_____

_____

⋯⋯

Although producer surplus and profit are different concepts, the producer surplus here continues to be the excess of revenue (price times quantity sold) over the payments to variable factors of production (the area under the marginal cost curve). The difference here is that we are no longer measuring producer surplus with a triangle but with a trapezoid.

TIPS

⋯⋯

Problem 2: Could free trade increase consumer surplus relative to autarky even if it did not lead to any imports? Explain. _____

_____

_____

Problem 3: Consider an industry in which Home (a small country) has a single firm with an upward sloping marginal cost curve. The price on world markets is P^W. The country is originally engaged in free trade and it imposes a (nonprohibitive) tariff of size t.

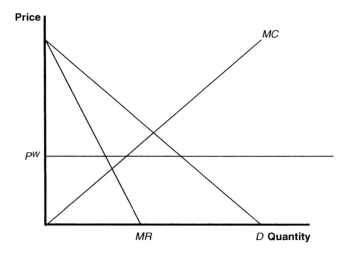

3a. Use the previous diagram to show the effects of this tariff on producer surplus, consumer surplus, and government revenue.

Now suppose instead that the government imposed a quota that yielded the same level of imports as the tariff t.

3b. Which policy (the quota or the tariff) has a larger effect on consumer surplus? Explain.

_____

_____

3c. Would the quota rent created by this quota be bigger than, smaller than, or exactly the same as the revenue generated by the tariff? Explain. _____

_____

··

TIPS

With a tariff the Home firm continues to be a price taker, whereas with a quota the firm has market power. The difference is that with a quota imports cannot respond to a higher price charged by the Home firm.

··

2 Tariffs with Foreign Monopoly

ESSENTIAL CONCEPTS

When a foreign monopolist supplies the Home market, Home can influence the price charged for its imports. A monopolist chooses to supply the level of output that sets its marginal revenue equal to its marginal cost, and in turn this level of output determines the price in the market. A tariff on a foreign monopolist increases the marginal cost of serving the market and so influences both the level of output supplied by that monopolist and the implied price.

Home can increase its welfare by applying a tariff if the marginal revenue curve facing the monopolist is steeper than the demand curve (as is the case with linear demand). The reason for this is that the monopolist optimally chooses not to pass on all of the tariff increase to consumers, creating a terms-of-trade–like gain for the country. That is, the monopolist bears some of the cost of the tariff. If this gain outweighs the consumer surplus loss (remember, there are no producers in Home!), then the country will be better off. The example of the tariff on Japanese trucks illustrates this effect. When the tariff on Japanese trucks was raised from 4% to 25%, the price of a truck to U.S. consumers rose by 12%.

REVIEW QUESTIONS

Problem 4: The demand in Home for a good produced by a foreign monopolist is given by the equation $P = 100 - Q$, where P is the price and Q is the quantity sold. The marginal revenue curve facing the foreign monopolist is then $MR = 100 - 2Q$. Suppose that the foreign monopolist has a constant marginal cost of $10 per unit.

4a. What price does the foreign monopolist charge if there is no tariff? _____

_____

_____

4b. Now suppose that Home puts a $10 per unit tariff on imports of the good. What price does the foreign monopolist charge? _____

_____

_____

4c. What is the impact of the tariff on Home's welfare? _____

_____

_____

_____

Problem 5: Consider the demand and marginal revenue curves in Figure 8-1. These curves are drawn so that the marginal revenue curve is "flatter" than the demand curve ("constant elasticity," for those who care).

5a. Use the following diagram to confirm that a tariff will raise domestic prices by more than the amount of the tariff.

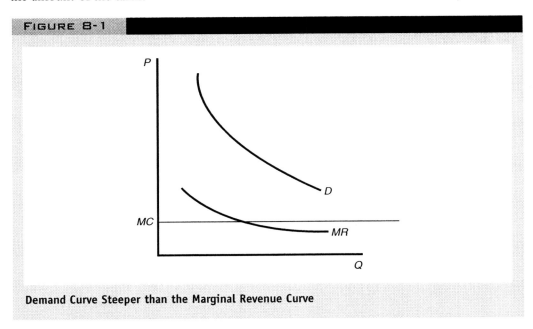

FIGURE 8-1

Demand Curve Steeper than the Marginal Revenue Curve

5b. In this case, can a tariff on the foreign monopolist raise national welfare? Explain. _____

_____

_____

....

TIPS Home can always affect the price charged by the foreign firm, but whether there is a terms-of-trade gain from the tariff depends on the shape of the demand curve.

   The equation for marginal revenue for a linear demand curve was derived in Chapter 6. Review that discussion.

....

3 Dumping

ESSENTIAL CONCEPTS

This section shows that imperfect competition can explain the common phenomenon of *dumping*. Dumping occurs when a firm sells a product abroad at a price that is either less than the price it charges in its local market, or less than its average cost of production. Firms with some degree of market power may choose to charge different prices in different countries depending on differences in demand conditions in those countries. Such a firm is known as a *discriminating monopolist* that is engaging in international *price discrimination*. In the example given in the text, a firm has monopoly power in its home market but can also sell on international markets at the world price. The firm finds it optimal to exploit its market power at home, keeping the price there high, and still sell on world markets at the lower world price because the marginal revenue of selling one more unit in each market is equal.

   Many governments actively seek to discourage dumping by charging an *antidumping duty* on firms that have been found to be dumping. As we will see in the next section, antidumping policy is highly controversial and is the source of substantial friction between countries.

KEY TERMS

Price discrimination _____

_____

Discriminating monopoly _____

_____

Dumping _____

_____

Antidumping duty _____

_____

REVIEW QUESTIONS

Problem 6: Suppose a monopolist located in Home has a constant marginal cost of $2 and can sell its good in two countries, Home and Foreign. Consumers are assumed to be unable to arbitrage any price difference across countries. Demand at Home is given by P = 10 – Q and demand in Foreign is P = 6 – Q.

6a. What is the equation for the marginal revenue curve facing the monopolist in the Home and Foreign markets? _____

_____

_____

6b. At what price is the firm selling its product in the two markets? _____

_____

_____

6c. In the diagrams below, draw demand and marginal revenue curves in Home (its domestic market) and Foreign (its export market) so that the firm chooses to "dump" its product abroad.

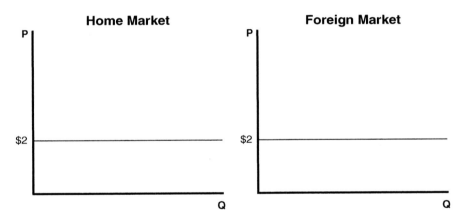

It is important to know how to derive the marginal revenue equation from a linear demand curve. If you get stuck at this step, then you cannot answer fully any subsequent question! For a linear demand curve, the marginal revenue curve always has the same Y-intercept and a slope that is twice as large (in absolute value) as the demand curve.

Problem 7: Suppose that a firm charges $10 for a good in its home market and $10 in its export market. Could this firm be accused of dumping? Explain. _____

_____

_____

Problem 8: A firm located in country H produces the sleep medication, Beddybuy. The firm faces a downward sloping (linear) demand curve in its home market. In the neighboring country F, the government imposes prices controls so that there is a ceiling on the price that the firm can charge for Beddybuy.

8a. Uses the axes provided below to show the case where the firm is willing to sell Beddybuy in country F and charges a higher price for Beddybuy in H.

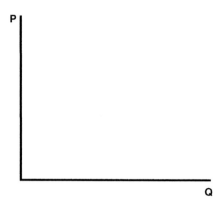

8b. Suppose some sleep-deprived consumers in country H learn that they can get Beddybuy in country F for the lower price from Internet pharmacies. Is it possible that this would cause the firm to stop selling its product in F? Explain. _____

_____

_____

4 Policy Response to Dumping

ESSENTIAL CONCEPTS

As discussed in detail in the previous section, the phenomenon of "dumping" naturally arises in models of imperfect competition. An imported product is being dumped (a) if its price is below the price that the exporter charges in its own local market or (b) if the exporter's local price is not available; then dumping is determined by comparing the import price with (1) a price charged for the product in a third market or (2) the exporter's average costs of production. Under the rules of the WTO, an importing country is entitled to apply an *antidumping duty* when a foreign firm is dumping its product and this dumping has caused "material injury" to domestic firms.

Unlike other trade policies, such as the *safeguard tariff,* a foreign firm can influence the level of a tariff that it faces in a market by changing the price that it charges for its good. The antidumping duty (the tariff) that is actually applied will be equal to the difference between the price charged by the firm and its "fair value." By raising its price to the "fair value," the foreign firm can avoid a tariff on its product altogether. It is for this reason that antidumping policy creates a situation in which the home country loses from the mere existence of the policy. Prices are high because of the threat of the antidumping duty, but the antidumping duty is never applied so there is no tariff revenue.

The application that is presented in the chapter is crucial reading because it illustrates the excessive usage of antidumping policy. Evidence that antidumping policy often leads to a change in the behavior of foreign firms is the high percentage of antidumping cases that are withdrawn and settled. U.S. antidumping law actually permits U.S. firms to withdraw their case and agree with foreign firms on the level of prices and market shares. That is, the law encourages collusion between domestic and foreign firms in the U.S. market.

KEY TERMS

Use the space provided to record your notes on the following key terms.

Dumping _____

_____

_____

Antidumping duty _____

_____

_____

Safeguard tariff _____

_____

REVIEW QUESTIONS

Problem 9: Consider the following (fictional) claim of a government official. "Since we implemented our antidumping policy, we have not applied antidumping duties to any foreign products. Therefore, the policy could not have had any effect on foreign producers." Discuss.

_____

_____

_____

Problem 10: Why do firms make claims of dumping so often? _____

_____

_____

Problem 11: Under the antidumping procedure in the United States, can antidumping duties be applied if there is no domestic competitor? _____

_____

_____

There was a time when antidumping was justified by the fear of "predatory pricing." Modern treatments of dumping rarely mention this possibility because the way that antidumping laws are applied tends to reduce rather than increase competition.

TIPS

5 Infant Industry Protection

ESSENTIAL CONCEPTS

This section addresses different kinds of *market failure* that are sometimes used to justify policies that restrict imports. A key assumption of the model considered in this section is that there is some form of increasing returns to scale over time. Domestic firms have high costs in the short run, but they could have low costs in the long run if they expand their output. Market failures can keep these kinds of increasing returns from being exploited. Two types of market failures, (1) imperfect capital markets and (2) positive *externalities,* are considered. To analyze the effect of imperfect capital markets, we suppose that there is a single firm that has high costs because it has little experience. This firm would make negative profits in the short run because of its high costs, but over time its costs would fall if it were to gain sufficient experience. The firm might be viable in the long run but still fail if it cannot get loans to cover its losses in the short run. A tariff would reduce the firm's losses in the short run (at the expense of lower consumer surplus) but would no longer be needed in the long run once the firm's costs fell to internationally competitive levels. To understand the role of externalities, consider the example of *knowledge spillovers.* Suppose that (1) firms learn from experience so that the knowledge created by one firm is increasing in its output; (2) knowledge from one firm is learned by another (i.e., it spills over); and (3) knowledge lowers a firm's costs. In this setting, firms do not produce enough knowledge and so industry-wide costs are high.

A tariff that expands industry output lowers industry cost, and so firms in the industry can then become competitive on world markets. A tariff that is intended to give firms "time to grow" is called *infant industry protection.* Under the right circumstances, the tariff will help the industry lower its costs so that it will no longer need to be supported by tariffs in the future. A government contemplating this type of policy needs to weigh the short-run cost to consumer surplus induced by a tariff against the long-run benefit of increased producer surplus. This type of argument can also be used to justify protecting existing firms that have fallen behind their international competitors. If a firm has good prospects but is currently struggling and cannot obtain loans from banks, then the government can protect the industry temporarily. An example of such an experience is discussed in the Harley-Davidson case study in the textbook.

KEY TERMS

Use the space provided to record your notes on the following key terms.

Infant industry _____

_____

Externality _____

_____

_____

Market failure _____

_____

_____

Knowledge spillover _____

_____

_____

Problem 12: Suppose you are a government official in charge of tariff policy. A businessperson approaches your office and argues that she could establish a world-class cucumber operation if only a tariff were applied to cucumber imports for next 5 years.

12a. What costs would the proposed policy have on the country? _____

_____

12b. If the world price of cucumbers were P, what would have to be true about the cost of production in cucumbers now and in 5 years to make this a reasonable policy? _____

_____

_____

12c. If capital markets in the country were perfect, would that change your opinion about the validity of this proposal? _____

_____

_____

12d. What other considerations could you suggest that would serve to justify supporting an infant industry such as this one? _____

_____

Problem 13: A foreign multinational opens an affiliate in Home. The multinational is the only firm in the industry, and it lobbies the government for infant industry protection.

13a. If the multinational's argument for protection were that capital markets were imperfect, would it be in Home's best interest to follow a policy of infant industry protection in this industry? Explain. _____

_____

_____

13b. If the argument were that there are knowledge spillovers in this industry, would it be in Home's best interest to follow a policy of infant industry protection? Explain. _____

_____

_____

Problem 14: What kind of market failure would justify the protection of Harley-Davidson?

_____

_____

_____

....

For infant industry protection to make sense, a government must be able to identify a real market failure. How would the government know that the industry will eventually become competitive?

TIPS

....

Safeguard tariff _____

_____

_____

9

International Agreements:
Trade, Labor, and the Environment

Overview

International agreements impose restrictions on the policies of their signatories. Countries allow their own policy options to be restricted by an agreement because the agreement also restricts the policies of the other participating countries. For instance, countries that belong to the WTO are expected to adhere to a set of obligations, such as the most favored nation principle. This chapter discusses international agreements that influence policies in areas that are relevant to international trade, including trade policy, labor standards, and environmental regulation.

The World Trade Organization is the result of a *multilateral trade agreement* that is designed to overcome a particular *prisoner's dilemma* between countries. Countries have an incentive to protect domestic industries, but tariffs and quotas have a negative impact on their trading partners. If everyone has an incentive to protect, then the outcome can result in collectively small gains from trade. Each party would be better off with free trade but, given the protection offered by other countries, sees it in its best interest to offer protection as well.

A *regional trade agreement* (RTA) requires its adherents to allow free trade to its signatories while maintaining tariffs on countries outside the agreement. These agreements can create trade between participating countries, but they can also divert trade from countries outside the agreement. Regional trade agreements often include *side agreements* on *labor standards*. These standards involve regulations on labor issues such as occupational safety and child labor. Developing countries accept these labor standards in order to be allowed into regional trade agreements with developed countries. Policymakers in developing countries and many trade economists worry that these agreements might be *disguised protectionism,* inspired at least in part by a desire to increase the cost of production in low-wage countries.

The final type of international agreement discussed in the chapter is *multilateral environmental agreements,* which deal specifically with environmental policy. Many issues arise within the context of the WTO, which allows countries to maintain their own environmental regulations as long as these regulations are equally applied to foreign and domestic firms. A larger, perhaps more contentious, issue is whether international trade tends to harm the environment. This concern has theoretical justification, particularly in the case of *common property*. International trade can exacerbate the *tragedy of the commons,* leading to more rapid depletion of natural resources, and can give rise to a different form of the prisoner's dilemma. Once again, the existence of a prisoner's dilemma suggests the need for more extensive international agreements.

1 International Trade Agreements

ESSENTIAL CONCEPTS

Multilateral trade agreements and regional trade agreements are designed to reduce trade barriers between countries. Multilateral agreements involve a wide range of countries, whereas RTAs are often limited in scope to as few as two countries. With more than 150 member countries, the WTO is the crowning example of a multilateral trade agreement. The WTO owes its existence to the desire among its members to overcome a prisoner's dilemma. To illustrate the nature of the prisoner's dilemma, consider a world with two countries, Home and Foreign. Home exports good A and imports good B, and Foreign imports good A and exports good B. By imposing the optimal tariff on good B, Home can increase its welfare at Foreign's expense because its terms-of-trade gain exceeds its deadweight loss. Foreign's welfare falls by the sum of its terms-of-trade loss and its deadweight loss. Foreign can increase its welfare at Home's expense by applying a tariff on good A. When both countries apply a tariff, the terms-of-trade gains in their import goods are exactly canceled out by the terms-of-trade losses in the export goods, so all that is left is deadweight loss in both industries. The outcome is the Nash equilibrium to the prisoner's dilemma game. The WTO is designed to overcome the prisoner's dilemma by (1) imposing rules on the application of trade policies, (2) providing a forum for countries to negotiate lower tariffs on each other's goods, and (3) providing a dispute settlement mechanism.

An alternative to multilateral trade agreements is *regional trade agreements.* RTAs occur when several countries eliminate trade barriers between signatories to the agreement but maintain tariffs against countries outside the agreement. These agreements are inherently discriminatory because countries outside the agreement do not get the same treatment. This exception to the *most favored nation principle* is allowed in Article XIV of the GATT. Because these agreements are inherently discriminatory, their detractors often refer to them as *preferential trade agreements.*

RTAs come in two forms: *free-trade areas* and *customs unions.* Although both types of agreements involve free trade between members, customs unions require member countries to share a single tariff code on countries outside the agreement, whereas free-trade areas allow countries to have different tariff codes. Countries impose *rules of origin* to avoid the importation of goods into the lower-tariff country in a free-trade area followed by trans-shipment to the higher-tariff country.

Although RTAs lower trade barriers between countries, they may or may not increase welfare. RTAs have two types of effects on trading patterns. *Trade creation* occurs when a member country imports a product from another member country that it formerly produced for itself. *Trade diversion* occurs when a country switches its import supplier from a country outside the agreement to a country inside the agreement. Trade diversion can lead to a welfare loss for the importing country because it no longer collects tariff revenues. From a global point of view, trade diversion causes a less efficient use of the world's resources as production is reallocated away from a low-cost producer to a high-cost producer.

KEY TERMS

Use the space provided to record your notes on the following key terms.

Multilateral agreement _____

_____

_____

Terms-of-trade gain _____

_____

_____

Most favored nation principle _____

_____

_____

Prisoner's dilemma _____

_____

_____

Regional trade agreements _____

_____

_____

Preferential trade agreements _____

_____

_____

Free-trade area _____

_____

_____

Customs union _____

_____

_____

Rules of origin _____

_____

_____

Trade creation _____

_____

_____

Trade diversion _____

_____

_____

REVIEW QUESTIONS

Problem 1: The prisoner's dilemma set out in the textbook featured a world with two large countries. Would this logic hold if there were only one large country and many small countries? Explain. _____

_____

_____

Problem 2: Suppose that many small countries were to form a customs union. What impact might the customs union have on the prisoner's dilemma? _____

_____

_____

···

TIPS

The assumption that the two countries are identical in the formulation of the prisoner's dilemma is important. If one country gains more from following its optimal tariff than the other, it becomes less clear that country would benefit from international trade agreements.

···

Problem 3: Suppose that Home joins a free-trade area. Is it possible that Home simultaneously imports a homogeneous good from outside the free-trade area and exports the same good to a member of the free-trade area? Explain.

_____

_____

_____

Problem 4: Use the diagram for Home's market to show an example of trade creation in a RTA.

Home Market

Price

Quantity

Problem 5: Home's market could be served by its own producers, who have constant marginal cost of C_H; by Country B, whose producers have marginal cost C_B; or by Country A, whose producers have marginal cost C_A. Home has the largest marginal cost and Country A has the smallest marginal cost. Home initially applies the most favored nation tariff t to both A and B.

5a. If Home forms a regional trade agreement with Country A, could this agreement lead to trade diversion? If so, under what circumstances? _____

_____

_____

5b. If Home forms a regional trade agreement with country B, could this agreement lead to trade creation? If so, under what circumstances? _____

_____

_____

Now suppose that Home does not produce the good at all. The marginal costs for countries A and B and Home's demand are shown in Figure 9-1.

5c. Illustrate the case of trade diversion in Figure 9-1 by drawing the effect of the tariff on the cost of the country outside the regional free-trade arrangement.

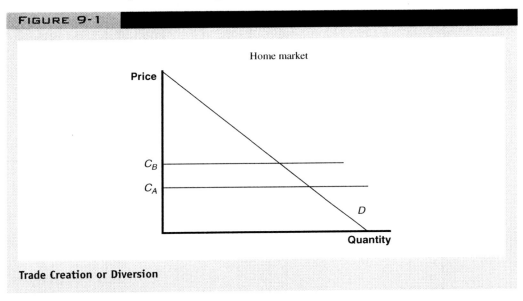

FIGURE 9-1

Home market

Trade Creation or Diversion

5d. In your diagram answer to question 5c, is there any welfare benefit from the RTA? Explain. _____

_____

_____

It is possible that even in a particular industry a regional trade diversion could improve a country's welfare if it leads to a substantial increase in imports. Experiment with different drawings of Figure 9-1 so that an RTA results in different magnitudes of changes in consumer surplus relative to loss tariff revenue. **TIPS**

2 International Agreements on Labor Issues

ESSENTIAL CONCEPTS

RTAs are often accompanied by *side agreements* that are not directly related to trade policies. When the levels of economic development differ substantially across countries within the RTA, these side agreements are often over *labor standards,* which cover areas such as occupational health and safety, child labor, and minimum wages. Consumers and policymakers favor labor standards out of concern for working conditions abroad. Labor unions often push for labor standards as part of trade agreements out of concern that poor labor standards abroad create more competition for U.S. workers.

Economists and policy makers in developing countries are skeptical about the motive for and benefits of attaching labor standards to trade agreements. Many see the emphasis on labor standards as a form of *disguised protectionism* because the regulations may result in much higher costs of production in the affected countries. Of particular concern is pressure to require developing country firms to pay a *living wage*. Although a living wage is not well defined, it can be construed to mean a wage that is higher than the norm in developing countries. Economic theory suggests that wages that are well above the market wage would either increase unemployment in developing countries or would force people into the unregulated informal sectors.

Finally, some evidence is presented that nongovernmental organizations (NGOs) have been effective at reducing some of the most egregious forms of abuse in developing countries by pressuring firms to improve their working conditions. Their successes suggest that bad publicity can be an effective tool for changing firms' behavior.

KEY TERMS

Use the space provided to record your notes on the following key terms.

Labor standards _____

_____

_____

Living wage _____

_____

_____

REVIEW QUESTIONS

Problem 6: According to a survey by the National Bureau of Economic Research, consumers were willing to pay a premium for items made under good working conditions. How could an NGO use this sentiment to improve working conditions in developing countries?

_____

_____

Problem 7: Explain why economists are wary of trade agreements with developing countries that include labor standards. _____

_____

_____

Problem 8: Suppose there are two sectors in an economy: the formal sector, which is subject to government regulations, and the informal sector, which is not subject to government regulations. Each sector has a specific factor associated with it, and labor is mobile between the two sectors. Prices of the goods produced by the two sectors are fixed on world markets. Suppose the government imposed a "living wage" on the formal sector that was above the market wage.

8a. What would happen to employment in the formal sector? Explain. _____

_____

_____

_____

8b. What would happen to the wage paid in the informal sector? Explain. _____

_____

_____

_____

3 International Agreements on the Environment

ESSENTIAL CONCEPTS

Many environmentalists are suspicious of international trade in general and the WTO in particular. Policies toward the environment can run afoul of WTO rules when they have consequences for international trade. For instance, the U.S. Marine Mammal Protection Act requires that tuna fishers use nets that do not inadvertently catch dolphins. When imports of tuna from Mexico were banned by the United States in 1991, the GATT (the WTO did not yet exist) ruled that the ban violated GATT rules on nondiscrimination. In looking at WTO rules, however, it is not obvious that they are stacked against the environment. *Article XX* of the GATT allows countries to adopt any environmental laws they please, provided that these laws are applied uniformly to domestic and foreign producers. The problem arises when a country regulates the *production process method* rather than the product itself. Past WTO rulings have not allowed countries to ban imports on the basis of their production process method, ruling that such a ban is essentially an effort to force one country's regulations onto another. The WTO has had no problem, however, with products being labeled in such a way to report the production process method so that concerned consumers can avoid products made in an environmentally unfriendly way.

Does international trade by its very nature accelerate the degradation of the environment? This is an open question, and plenty of examples can be found to support either side of the argument. For instance, in the United States the most fuel-efficient cars tend to be built by foreign manufacturers, so limiting these imports would worsen fuel efficiency in the United States. Those who are concerned that international trade has a negative impact on the environment can find plenty of theoretical support for their argument. This is particularly true in areas in which natural resources are *common property*. Common property tends to be overused, a phenomenon commonly referred to as the *tragedy of the commons*. International trade can exacerbate the tragedy of the commons by directing global demand toward the resource of a particular country or region, so that there is even more overuse of natural resources under free trade. Examples abound. For instance, the overharvesting of tropical wood is certainly encouraged by a large global market. Global pollutants, such as carbon dioxide emissions, present a problem similar to the tragedy of the commons: Weak regulation can give a country a production advantage while all countries suffer the consequences of the pollution. As another example of a prisoner's dilemma, this situation calls for multilateral agreements.

KEY TERMS

Use the space provided to record your notes on the following key terms.

Multilateral environmental agreements _____

_____

_____

Tragedy of the commons _____

_____

_____

Common property _____

_____

_____

Kyoto protocol _____

_____

_____

REVIEW QUESTIONS

Problem 9: Home requires the use of at least 40% recycled paper in cardboard boxes and bans imports of Foreign boxes because they use no recycled paper.

9a. If Foreign complains to the WTO, how is the WTO likely to rule? _____

_____

_____

9b. If Home were to require cardboard boxes manufacturers to label the recycled paper content of their boxes, would this violate WTO rules? _____

_____

_____

Problem 10: Suppose that rich countries have stronger feelings about protecting the environment than poor countries, that goods differ in the amount of pollution they create, and pollution regulations impose higher costs on "dirtier" industries. How might a reduction in tariffs brought about by the WTO affect pollution? _____

_____

_____

_____

Problem 11: The "sneed" industry produces a product that everyone needs as well as a great deal of pollution. Suppose that many identical countries have sneed firms. The pollution can be controlled using alternative production techniques, but this raises the marginal cost of production.

11a. If the pollution created by the sneed industry is primarily local, is an international agreement necessary? _____

_____

_____

Now suppose that the pollution created by the sneed industry is global.

11b. If all countries require the sneed industry to use the low pollution production technique, what happens to the price of sneeds on world markets? _____

_____

_____

11c. Suppose that your country is the only one not to sign on to an international agreement requiring the use of low pollution production techniques. What happens to producer surplus in your sneed industry once the agreement is put into place? _____

_____

_____

_____

11d. Given your answer to 11c, explain why might it be hard to get all countries to sign on to an international agreement on sneed production techniques. _____

_____

_____

••

Problem 10 gets at the "pollution haven hypothesis." The hypothesis is that tariff reduction is likely to lead to a migration of the production of dirty industries to poor countries with poor environmental regulations.

   Problem 11 makes the point that when there are many countries there is an incentive for individual countries to free ride on the beneficial actions of others.

TIPS

••

10

Introduction to Exchange Rates and the Foreign Exchange Market

Overview

The exchange rate is the price of one country's currency in terms of another country's currency. The exchange rate is one of the most important prices in the entire economy because movements in the exchange rate alter the competitiveness of a country's goods and change the rate of return on domestic assets relative to foreign assets. This chapter begins with a short description of the global market for foreign exchange covering (1) the types of foreign exchange contracts traded on this market, (2) the chief players in the market, and (3) the manner in which the market functions.

The chapter also introduces the important concept of arbitrage. By buying low and selling high, arbitrageurs alter supply and demand conditions so as to guarantee that all exchange rates are consistent across countries. In addition, it follows from the principle of arbitrage that if investors are not concerned about risk then the expected returns on all assets must be the same regardless of the currency in which they are denominated. This insight is used to derive the uncovered interest parity equation, which can be used to calculate the level of the exchange rate that equilibrates foreign exchange markets.

1 Exchange Rate Essentials

ESSENTIAL CONCEPTS

This section introduces some simple terms and conventions concerning the *exchange rate* that will be used throughout the remainder of the book. The exchange rate is the relative price of two currencies. A relative price and its reciprocal convey exactly the same information, but it is critical that the two are not confused because an increase in a relative price is associated with a decrease in its inverse. The important convention to remember is that the home country's exchange rate is the number of units of its own home currency that must be given up to buy one unit of the foreign country's currency. An increase in a country's exchange rate is called a *depreciation* because it takes more units of the domestic currency to buy foreign currency. A decrease in the exchange rate is called an *appreciation*. There are over a hundred currencies in the world, and it is possible that a country's exchange rate may be depreciating against one currency and appreciating against another. *Effective exchange rates* are used to measure the average change in the value of a country's currency. Changes in a country's effective exchange rate are equal to the weighted average of changes in its exchange rate across all of that country's trading partners. The weight Country A's currency receives in Country B's effective exchange rate is equal to Country A's share of Country B's total trade.

A key point made in this chapter is that if the prices of goods are fixed in a country's own currency then their foreign currency price moves proportionately with changes in the country's exchange rate. Hence, if the dollar appreciates against the yen, the dollar price of Japanese products becomes more attractive relative to American products. If the dollar depreciates against the yen, the dollar price of Japanese products becomes less attractive relative to American products.

KEY TERMS

Use the space below to record your notes on the following key terms.

Exchange rate _____

_____

_____

Appreciation _____

_____

_____

Depreciation _____

_____

_____

Effective exchange rate _____

_____

_____

REVIEW QUESTIONS

Problem 1: On day one the U.S. dollar bought one euro or 100 Japanese yen. On day two one euro cost 1.2 U.S. dollars, whereas one U.S. dollar bought 120 Japanese yen.

1a. Write the day two exchange rate between the dollar and the euro first in American terms and then in European terms. _____

_____

_____

1b. Between day one and day two, did the U.S. dollar appreciate or depreciate against the euro? By how much in percentage terms? _____

_____

_____

1c. Between day one and day two, did the euro appreciate or depreciate against the dollar? By how much in percentage terms? _____

_____

_____

1d. Write the day two exchange rate between the dollar and the yen first in American terms and then in Japanese terms. _____

_____

_____

1e. Between day one and day two did the dollar appreciate or depreciate against the yen? By how much in percentage terms? _____

_____

_____

1f. Suppose that the U.S. trade with Europe is worth $200 billion and its trade with Japan is worth $400 billion. Between day one and day two, did the effective exchange rate of the dollar appreciate or depreciate? (The basket of currency includes only the euro and the yen.) By how much? _____

_____

_____

TIPS

It is easy to mix up an appreciation with a depreciation and vice versa. Using the common convention, a country's currency is appreciating (often said to be rising or getting stronger in the media) when its exchange rate is going down. Think of an appreciation as allowing you to get more foreign currency for your dollar.

The big discrepancy between the amount that the dollar depreciated against the euro in problem 1b and the amount that the euro appreciated against the dollar in problem 1c is due to the very large size of the exchange rate movement. The bigger the movement in the exchange rate, the larger the discrepancy.

Notice that although the dollar depreciated against the euro by more than it appreciated against the yen, the effective exchange rate appreciated because (in this example anyway) the United States trades more with Japan than it does with Europe.

Problem 2: Volker, a disheveled businessman, travels frequently between Boston and his home town of Munich, Germany. The price of a glass of his favorite ale is $2 in Boston and €3 in Munich.

2a. At what U.S. exchange rate is the price of the ale the same in both countries when measured in a common currency? _____

_____

_____

2b. In which city is the ale cheaper if one dollar currently buys one euro? _____

_____

_____

··

TIPS When the prices of goods are sticky in their own currency, a depreciation of Home's currency makes all of its goods become more attractively priced relative to foreign goods.

··

2 Exchange Rates in Practice

ESSENTIAL CONCEPTS

An *exchange rate regime* describes the amount of effort that a government exerts to control the exchange rate. At one extreme, the government may not make any effort whatsoever to control the exchange rate, leaving the exchange rate to be freely determined on foreign exchange markets. This type of regime is known as a *floating* (or *flexible*) *exchange rate regime*. At the other extreme, the government may exert as much effort as is necessary to keep the exchange rate constant. This is what is known as a *fixed* (or *pegged*) *exchange rate regime*. When looking at exchange rate data, it is easy to distinguish a fixed exchange rate regime from a floating exchange rate regime because the fixed exchange rate is constant, whereas the floating varies (sometimes substantially) from day to day.

Most governments follow a policy toward their exchange rate that lies between the two extremes. For instance, a country might allow its exchange rate to float within a *band*, or range around some rate, but will take action if the exchange rate moves outside this band. Another problem that arises in classifying exchange rate regimes is a country might follow a fixed exchange rate system only to abandon it when the cost of maintaining that regime is high. In this case, the variability of the exchange rate can be very low at some times only to become very high at other times (exchange rate crises).

Countries that wish to maintain very stable exchange rates occasionally adopt a *currency board* system, under which governments tie their hands so as to make it harder to drop the fixed exchange rate. Still other countries dump their currency altogether in favor of adopting a relatively stable currency. Ecuador's adoption of the U.S. dollar as its currency in 2000 is an example of *dollarization*. Finally, some countries collectively share a single currency in a *currency union* so that there is no exchange rate variability across countries within the union. For instance, the euro is shared by an increasing number of European countries.

KEY TERMS

Use the space below to record your notes on the following key terms.

Exchange rate regime _____

_____

_____

Fixed (or pegged) exchange rate regime _____

_____

_____

Floating (or flexible) exchange rate regime _____

_____

_____

Band _____

_____

_____

Dollarization _____

_____

_____

Currency board _____

_____

_____

Currency (or monetary) union _____

_____

_____

Free float exchange rate regime _____

_____

_____

Managed float _____

_____

_____

Exchange rate crises _____

_____

_____

Crawl _____

_____

_____

REVIEW QUESTIONS

Problem 3: Suppose that a country called Home has many trading partners and each trading partner has its own currency.

3a. If each trading partner allows its currency to float, is it possible for Home to fix its exchange rate against all of its trading partners? Explain. _____

_____

3b. If Home wishes to reduce the variability of its effective exchange rate, what kind of exchange rate regime might it choose? Explain. _____

_____

_____

....

TIPS At this stage of the book, the study of exchange rate regimes is mostly memorization. The distinction between regimes becomes critical when we delve into a government's economic objectives and the policies that it can take to achieve these objectives.

....

3 The Market for Foreign Exchange

ESSENTIAL CONCEPTS

Exchange rates, or the price of one currency in terms of another, are determined in the *foreign exchange market*. This market, which is a collection of electronically linked corporations and institutions spread out over the globe, is the largest in the world, with over $3.2 trillion worth of transactions per day in April 2007. Foreign exchange transactions can take many forms, but most of these transactions (90%) are simple *spot contracts* for the immediate delivery of a foreign exchange. The rate at which currencies exchange is known as the *spot exchange rate.*

Newspapers typically report single exchange rates, but in fact different individuals pay different rates. Traders of foreign exchange advertise rates at which they sell a given currency and rates at which they buy the same currency. The difference between these rates is called a *spread*. These spreads, which reflect *market frictions* or *transaction costs,* differ between different clients and are lowest between the main players in the foreign exchange market, the commercial banks. Most foreign exchange transactions involve a transfer of deposits between commercial banks, known as *interbank trading.* In addition to other private players in the foreign exchange market, such as *nonbank financial institutions,* governments often intervene to affect exchange rates. Governments occasionally attempt to suppress foreign exchange trading by imposing *capital controls* or by *intervening* in the market by buying and selling foreign exchange rates.

Finally, there are many types of contracts in the foreign exchange market, including *forwards, swaps, futures,* and *options.* These contracts are termed *derivatives* because their prices are derived at least in part from the spot exchange rate. Because these contracts involve future trades in foreign exchange, they allow investors to hedge against risk or to take risk through speculation.

KEY TERMS

Use the space below to record your notes on the following key terms.

Foreign exchange (forex) market _____

_____

_____

Spot contract _____

_____

_____

Spot exchange rate _____

_____

_____

Spread _____

_____

_____

Market friction _____

_____

_____

Transaction cost _____

_____

_____

Derivatives _____

_____

_____

Forwards _____

_____

_____

Swaps _____

_____

_____

Futures _____

_____

_____

Options _____

_____

_____

Commercial banks _____

_____

_____

Corporations _____

_____

_____

Interbank trading _____

_____

_____

Nonbank financial institutions _____

_____

_____

Capital control _____

_____

_____

Official market _____

_____

_____

Black market _____

_____

_____

Intervention _____

_____

_____

REVIEW QUESTIONS

Problem 4: Why are the spreads facing individuals in their foreign exchange dealing larger than the spreads in transactions between large market players such as commercial banks?

_____

_____

_____

Problem 5: Suppose the dollar–euro spot rate is 1.20 and the current 30-day forward rate is 1.25.

5a. You have an obligation to pay a French supplier of wine 10 million euros in 30 days and have contracted with a U.S. distributor to sell the wine for $13 million. How many dollars can you make if you hedge your risk using the forward market? _____

_____

_____

5b. Is it possible that you could lose money if you do not hedge your risk? _____

_____

_____

5c. Suppose that you could get a call option that would allow you to buy euros in 30 days at 1.27. Describe the merits of buying this option relative to using the forward market as in problem 5a.

_____

_____

_____

5d. Now suppose you are a speculator facing the same spot and forward rates as above and you have $1 million. Suppose you bought euros forward. In 30 days, the spot rate for the dollar turns out to be 1.3. How many dollars did you make or lose from this transaction?

_____

_____

5e. Now suppose instead that the spot rate stayed the same over the next 30 days. If you bought euros forward, how many dollars did you make or lose from this transaction?

_____

_____

_____

As in your high school science classes, it is important to keep track of the units. If you are dividing where you should be multiplying or vice versa, then the units won't be correct, and you will spot your mistake.

TIPS

4 Arbitrage and Spot Exchange Rates

ESSENTIAL CONCEPTS

Although foreign exchange traders are spread out across the globe, fiber optic cables, computers, and the principle of *arbitrage* ensure that there is a single, unified foreign exchange market. For instance, suppose that a dollar will buy more euros in New York than in Paris. A quick investor will buy euros in New York, transfer them to Paris, and then sell them at the higher rate prevailing there. By buying low and selling high, the investor makes a profit, and her actions tend to raise the price of euros in New York and lower it in Paris until the prices are the same.

Arbitrage also ensures that all *cross rates* are the same in every market. Suppose a dollar investor wants to buy British pounds. The investor could buy pounds directly, or the investor could buy euros with the dollars and then use the euros to buy pounds. If the foreign exchange market is in equilibrium (and if transaction costs were very low), it should not matter which way the dollar investor obtains the pounds because the cross rates should be identical. That is, $E_{\$/£} = E_{\$/€}E_{€/£}$. If instead, $E_{\$/£} > E_{\$/€}E_{€/£}$, then the dollar investor could get more pounds by buying euros and then selling them for pounds than by buying them directly. Further, the investor could sell the pounds for dollars and actually make dollars in the transaction.

Whenever arbitrage opportunities arise, the market quickly adjusts to eliminate them. The foreign exchange market is in *equilibrium* when there are no opportunities for arbitrage (the so-called *no-arbitrage condition*). Finally, although there are over 160 different currencies in the world, almost all trading activity is limited to a handful of developed country currencies such as the U.S. dollar. This is because such *vehicle currencies* are sufficiently traded so that all traders are willing to buy or sell them, whereas the same cannot be said for rarely traded currencies.

KEY TERMS

Use the space below to record your notes on the following key terms.

Arbitrage _____

_____

_____

Equilibrium _____

_____

_____

No-arbitrage condition _____

_____

_____

Cross rate _____

_____

_____

Vehicle currency _____

_____

_____

REVIEW QUESTIONS

Problem 6: Suppose $E_{\$/€} = 3/2$ and $E_{\$/£} = 2$. What cross rate between the euro and the pound must prevail if there are no arbitrage opportunities?

    a. $E_{€/£} = \frac{3}{4}$

    b. $E_{€/£} = 3$

    c. $E_{£/€} = 3/4$

    d. $E_{£/€} = 1/3$

Problem 7: Suppose that $E_{¥/\$} = 100$, $E_{\$/€} = 2$, so

    a. $E_{€/¥} = 0.005$

    b. $E_{\$/¥} = 0.01$

    c. $E_{¥/€} = 200$

    d. All of the above

    e. None of the above

Problem 8: Suppose that you have $1 million. While staring at the computer screen, you notice that $E_{\$/£}=2$, $E_{¥/\$}=100$, and $E_{¥/£}=220$. If you have time for three quick trades, what dollar profit could you realize? Explain. _____

_____

_____

Problem 9: Could capital controls cause an exchange rate to be different in two cities? Explain.

_____

_____

TIPS Problem 8 demonstrates how arbitrage opportunities can arise when the cross rates are inconsistent. Don't expect to make money this way, however, unless you have a supercomputer and lightning-speed communications!

5 Arbitrage and Interest Rates

ESSENTIAL CONCEPTS

When arbitrage is possible, then two equivalent items must have the same price. In financial markets this means that two assets, even if they have different names, must have the same price as long as the characteristics for which investors care are the same. In general, there are three characteristics of an asset that are important to investors: (1) its *rate of return,* (2) its *liquidity,* and (3) its *risk.* If two assets are identical in terms of their liquidity and risk, then they should have the same rate of return if investors are free to choose assets. For the bulk of this book, it is assumed that assets are identical in terms of their risk and liquidity so that we may apply simple, no–arbitrage conditions.

In comparing the rates of return for assets whose price, and whose return, is valued in different currencies, we must distinguish between the asset's local currency return and its return in foreign currencies. For instance, the dollar return on a foreign deposit is equal to the interest rate on the foreign deposit (local return) plus the percent change in the dollar exchange rate between the time when the foreign deposit was purchased and the time when the deposit was sold (rate of depreciation or appreciation). A dollar-based investor must decide how to convert foreign currency earnings back into dollars. On the one hand, they might use the forward market to "lock in" the percent change in the exchange rate. On the other hand, they may calculate the expected return on the foreign asset (rather than its "for sure" return), using the expected rate of dollar depreciation over the period that they own the foreign deposit. The first method avoids risk, but if investors care only about expected returns, then the two methods should be equivalent in the eyes of an investor choosing between them.

The *uncovered interest parity* (*UIP*) condition holds when arbitrage equalizes the expected common currency return on domestic and foreign deposits. For instance, if the interest rate on U.S. deposits is $i_\$$ and the interest rate on British deposits is i, then the (approximated) uncovered interest parity condition is

$$i_\$ = i_\pounds + \Delta E^e_{\$/\pounds} / E_{\$/\pounds},$$

where the right-hand side of this equation is the expected dollar rate of return on British deposits (the local currency return i and the *expected rate of depreciation* of the dollar $\Delta E^e_{\$/\pounds} / E_{\$/\pounds}$) and the left-hand side of this equation is the dollar return on U.S. deposits. It is very important to understand that the home country return on assets denominated in a foreign currency has two components, whereas the return on home assets only has one. This means that if the interest rate in the United States exceeds the interest rate in the U.K. then the dollar must be expected to depreciate relative to the pound. If in addition one knew the expected future spot rate, then one could compute the spot rate that must prevail on foreign exchange markets.

KEY TERMS

Use the space below to record your notes on the following key terms.

Forward exchange rate _____
_____
_____

Covered interest parity _____

_____

_____

Expected exchange rate _____

_____

_____

Uncovered interest parity _____

_____

_____

Rate of return _____

_____

_____

Risk _____

_____

_____

Liquidity _____

_____

_____

Expected rate of return _____

_____

_____

Expected rate of depreciation _____

_____

_____

Forward premium _____

_____

_____

REVIEW QUESTIONS

Problem 10: Suppose that the U.S. nominal interest rate is 5% and the European nominal interest rate is 3%. The dollar is expected to

    a.   appreciate by 8%

    b.   depreciate by 8%

    c.   appreciate by 2%

    d.   depreciate by 2%

    e.   depreciate by 15%

Problem 11: Suppose the interest rate in U.S. deposits is 5% per year and the interest rate in Germany is 3% a year. The spot rate for the dollar is $E_{\$/€} = 1.25$. You are an investor with $1 million.

11a. Suppose you used all of your dollars to buy euro deposits. What would the value of these deposits (in euros be)? _____

_____

11b. At the end of one year, how many euros would you have? _____

_____

11c. If instead you used your $1 million to buy U.S. deposits, how many dollars will you have at the end of the year? _____

11d. What would the one-year forward exchange rate have to be for you to be indifferent between these two investments? Assume that international transactions are costless. Explain.

_____

_____

11e. Why would the forward rate that is your answer to 11d be a coherent predictor of the spot rate one year in the future? _____

_____

_____

11f. Given your answer to 11e, what is the expected rate of depreciation of the dollar?

_____

_____

11g. If dollar deposits were perceived to be more liquid and less risky than German deposits, then how might you adjust your answer to 11e? _____

_____

_____

Problem 12: Assume that uncovered interest parity holds. In the following questions, assume that all other exogenous variables (everything but the exchange rate) stay the same.

12a. What would happen to the spot rate $E_{\$/£}$ if British interest rates rose? _____

_____

_____

12b. If U.S. interest rates rise, what must happen to the expected dollar return on British deposits? _____

_____

_____

12c. What could explain a sudden depreciation in the dollar if U.S. and British rates do not change? Explain. _____

_____

_____

The uncovered interest parity condition is perhaps the most important equation in the international macroeconomics portion of the book. The sooner you understand its implications, the better off you will be.

The uncovered interest parity condition is used to predict the spot rate given the expected future spot rate. That is, the current price in the market must reflect what people expect the spot rate to be in the future. This is the source of frequent confusion.

Expectations about the future can change instantaneously and without warning, and when they do, they affect the economy immediately. The study of how expectations are formed is central to macroeconomics.

Note that the approximation used in the book is fine for small interest rates. As interest rates get higher, the approximation can become quite poor.

11

Exchange Rates I: The Monetary Approach in the Long Run

Overview

In the long run, countries experiencing rapid money supply growth also tend to experience high inflation and a depreciating currency. This chapter presents a model that relates the price level and exchange rate in the long run to monetary conditions and so is called the *monetary approach to the exchange rate*. The monetary approach is built on three assumptions: (1) Goods are freely traded, (2) assets are freely traded, and (3) prices are perfectly flexible. This last assumption in particular gives the model a distinctly long-run flavor.

Because goods can be freely traded in international markets, goods' prices must be the same in all countries when measured in the same currency, a situation known as purchasing power parity (PPP). Given price levels in each country, the long-run exchange rate, therefore, must adjust to ensure PPP. Because assets are freely traded, uncovered interest parity holds. When uncovered interest parity and PPP hold simultaneously, a country's interest rate must be equal to the world *real interest rate* plus the expected rate of inflation in that country. Standard monetary theory and the assumption of perfectly flexible prices complete the model. Prices and the rate of inflation depend on the level and rate of change of nominal money supply and of real money demand.

Because the model relies on perfectly flexible prices, it is not an appropriate model of the exchange rate in the short run. However, because short-run models of the exchange rate rely on expectations of the long-run level of the exchange rate, the long-run model is a crucial input into short-run models of the exchange rate.

1 Exchange Rates and Prices in the Long Run: Purchasing Power Parity and Goods Market Equilibrium

ESSENTIAL CONCEPTS

Suppose that we lived in a world in which goods and services cross borders without cost and prices are perfectly flexible. In such a world, the prices of all goods and services would have to be the same in every country when measured in the same currency, for if they were not, arbitrageurs would buy goods in low-cost locations and sell them in high-cost locations. The *law of one price* (*LOOP*) states exactly this. Further, the prices of any given basket of goods when measured in a common currency would have to be the same in every country. This is the idea of *absolute purchasing power parity* (*APPP*).

It is useful to define the relative price of a basket of goods and services in two different countries as

$$q_{US/Japan} = (E_{\$/\yen} \times P_{Japan}) / P_{US}$$

where P_{US} is the price in dollars of the basket in the United States, P_{Japan} is the price in dollars of the basket in Japan, and $E_{\$/\yen}$ is the dollar–yen exchange rate. This relative price is called the real exchange rate because it describes the rate at which real (rather than nominal) things are traded. When $q_{US/Japan}$ is less than one, the U.S. dollar is said to be *overvalued* because it takes less than one American basket to buy the exact same basket in Japan; the basket is less expensive in Japan, and therefore the yen is undervalued (in other words, that the dollar is undervalued). The dollar is said to be *undervalued* when the real exchange rate is above one; the basket is less expensive in Japan, and therefore the yen is overvalued (the dollar is overvalued). APPP holds only when the real exchange rate is equal to one.

A similar concept that can hold even when the real exchange rate is not equal to one is *relative purchasing power parity* (*RPPP*), which relates rates of change in exchange rates to the difference of rates of change in prices (inflation rates) across countries. When the real exchange rate is constant, changes in prices in Japan or in the United States must be offset by changes in the nominal exchange rate to keep the relative price of Japanese and U.S. goods constant. Hence, if inflation is higher in Japan than in the United States, P_{Japan} / P_{US} is increasing, so $E_{\$/\yen}$ must be falling (the U.S. dollar must be appreciating) at the same rate.

Concepts of PPP are important because they provide a method of predicting the exchange rate. Suppose that APPP were to hold. Then, given price levels P_{Japan} and P_{US}, the exchange rate that makes PPP hold is

$$E_{\$/\yen} = P_{US} / P_{Japan}.$$

In such a world, all we would need to do to forecast exchange rates would be to forecast price levels. In the real world, APPP is a reasonable approximation over a horizon of many years or decades, but it has little to say about short-run movements in exchange rates. This is because the real world involves many frictions in the international exchange of goods, including (1) transaction costs (such as trade barriers such as tariffs and quotas and shipping costs), (2) the existence of non-traded goods, (3) imperfect competition that gives firms pricing power in different markets, and (4) stickiness in domestic price levels. Despite its drawbacks as a predictor of exchange rates in the short run, APPP is useful because it provides a guide to the exchange rate in the long run, where long run is defined as the time necessary for prices to be flexible and for firms to overcome trade barriers.

KEY TERMS

Use the space below to record your notes on the following key terms.

Monetary approach to exchange rates _____

_____

_____

Law of one price (LOOP) _____

_____

_____

Purchasing power parity (PPP) _____

_____

_____

Real exchange rate _____

_____

_____

Real appreciation _____

_____

_____

Real depreciation _____

_____

_____

Overvalued _____

_____

_____

Undervalued _____

_____

_____

Absolute PPP _____

_____

_____

Inflation _____

_____

_____

Relative PPP _____

_____

_____

REVIEW QUESTIONS

Problem 1: The price of an apple in the United States is \$1, and the exchange rate is $E_{\$/\euro}$ = 1.25. If international trade in apples is frictionless, then what must the price of an apple be in Germany?

_____

_____

Problem 2: Suppose that in the United States, the price of guns is $200 and the price of doctor's visits is $150. Suppose that in France, the price of guns is €300 and the price of doctor's visits is €50. Guns and doctor's visits receive an equal weight in a basket of goods.

2a. Is there any exchange rate that would make the law of one price hold for both goods?

_____

_____

2b. What is the dollar price of a U.S. basket? _____

_____

_____

2c. What is the euro price of a French basket? _____

_____

_____

2d. If $E_{\$/\epsilon} = 1$, does APPP hold? _____

_____

_____

2e. Suppose that $E_{\$/\epsilon}$ were to increase. Would this result in a real appreciation or a real depreciation of the dollar? _____

_____

_____

2f. Provide any value of $E_{\$/\epsilon}$ such that the dollar is overvalued. Explain. _____

_____

_____

2g. If, instead, guns received a weight of 3/5 in an American basket and only 2/5 in a French basket, would APPP hold when $E_{\$/\epsilon} = 1$? _____

_____

_____

TIPS Problem 2 provides an example in which the law of one price may not hold for any good but APPP holds. Problem 2g gets at a practical problem in comparing price levels across countries: if different countries use different baskets, then different exchange rates are implied for PPP than if all countries used the same baskets.

Problem 3: Home's currency (the dollar) is depreciating relative to Foreign's currency (the blot) at a rate of 5%. Home's inflation rate is 8%. Foreign's inflation rate is 2%. Is Home's real exchange rate appreciating or depreciating and by how much?

_____

_____

Problem 4: (Multiple Choice) Suppose that inflation in Home is 6%, and inflation is 1% in Foreign. Then,

    a.   Home's real exchange rate is appreciating.

    b.   RPPP would predict that Home's currency will buy fewer of Foreign's currency next year.

    c.   The price level is higher in Home than in Foreign.

    d.   none of the above

Problem 5: (True or False. Please explain your answers.) Assess the following statement, "relative PPP is a better approximation of reality when one of the two countries is suffering high inflation and the other is not."

_____

_____

Problem 6: (Multiple Choice) If the law of one price holds for all goods and services, then

    a.   the real exchange rate must equal one.

    b.   APPP holds.

    c.   RPPP holds.

    d.   all of the above

    e.   none of the above

Problem 7: (Multiple Choice) Which of the following might explain why PPP doesn't hold in the short run?

    a.   Prices are sticky.

    b.   Governments impose tariffs on goods.

    c.   Firms engage in imperfect competition.

    d.   all of the above

    e.   none of the above

2 Money, Prices, and Exchange Rates in the Long Run: Money Market Equilibrium in a Simple Model

ESSENTIAL CONCEPTS

Given information on future price levels in the long run, PPP can be used to make predictions on future exchange rates. Developing a model of future price levels is therefore the focus of this section. In the long run, price levels are determined by equilibrium in the market for *money*. To keep the analysis simple, we assume that the *central bank* directly determines the *money supply, M. Money demand, M^d,* is generated by its three key uses: as a store of value, as a unit of account, and as a medium of exchange. Specifically, we rely on the *quantity theory of money* to provide a demand equation: the demand for money is equal to the price level (P) multiplied by real output (Y) multiplied by a constant ($\overline{L}$) or

$$M^d = P \times Y \times \overline{L}.$$

The idea is that people require a certain amount of money to carry out their transactions, and the volume of transactions is equal to the size of the economy, $P \times Y$. In equilibrium, the price must adjust so that the demand for money is equal to the supply of money made available by the central bank. Hence, for the United States, the price level should be

$$P_{US} = \frac{M_{US}}{\overline{L}Y_{US}}.$$

A similar equation would have to hold for each other country.

By combining the APPP equation with one price equation for each country, we have the *fundamental equation of the monetary approach to exchange rates*:

$$E_{\$/Y} = \left(\frac{M_{US}}{M_{Japan}} \right) \left(\frac{\overline{L}_{Japan} Y_{Japan}}{\overline{L}_{US} Y_{US}} \right)$$

This equation tells us what matters for the exchange rate in the long run. For instance, holding everything else equal, an increase in real output in the United States will tend to raise money demand and so will lower prices in the United States. Lower prices in the United States will make the dollar appreciate. Other variables that matter are the relative supplies of monies in the two countries and the proportion of real income that people want to hold in real balances. The fundamental equation can also be expressed in terms of changes over time. For instance, holding fixed all other variables, if the U.S. money supply grows faster than real output, then it must be that the dollar depreciates at the rate at which M_{US} / Y_{US} is increasing.

KEY TERMS

Use the space below to record your notes on the following key terms.

Money _____

_____

_____

Central bank _____

_____

_____

Money supply _____

_____

_____

Money demand _____

_____

_____

Quantity theory of money _____

_____

_____

Fundamental equation of the monetary model of the price level _____

_____

_____

Fundamental equation of the monetary approach to exchange rates _____

_____

_____

REVIEW QUESTIONS

Problem 8: Home's money supply grows at 3% and Foreign's grows at 5%. Home's currency should

    a.   appreciate at a rate of 2%.

    b.   appreciate at a rate of 3/5%.

    c.   depreciate at a rate of 5/3%.

    d.   depreciate at a rate of 2%.

    e.   none of the above

Problem 9: In the United States, the level of real output is 100 units, and money demand is equal to half of nominal output. In Japan, the level of real output is 80 units, and money demand is equal to three quarters of nominal output. The money supply in the United States is $25. Assume that the monetary approach to the exchange rate holds.

9a. What is the price level in the United States? _____

_____

_____

9b. If $E_{\$/¥}$ is 0.1, then what is the price level in Japan? _____

_____

_____

9c. Given your answer to 9b, what is the supply of money in Japan? _____

_____

_____

Problem 10: Suppose that U.S. money growth is 5% per year and U.S. economic growth is 3% a year. Suppose that money growth in Canada is 7% a year and the economy is shrinking at 2% a year.

10a. What is the inflation rate in the United States? _____

_____

_____

10b. What is the inflation rate in Canada? _____

_____

_____

10c. What does the monetary approach to the exchange rate predict about the movement of the Canadian dollar? _____

_____

_____

···

The monetary approach to the exchange rate is really pretty simple. In the long run, PPP (one equation) and the quantity theory of money (two equations) hold. End of story.

TIPS

···

3 The Monetary Approach: Implications and Evidence

ESSENTIAL CONCEPTS

This short section presents evidence on the link between money growth rates and exchange rates movements. As predicted by the monetary approach, there is a tight positive relationship between monetary growth rates and exchange rate movements over the long run. In addition, the evidence presented in this section suggests an improvement that can be made over the approach presented in the previous section. In the previous section, we assumed that money demand was a fixed proportion of nominal output. The evidence suggests that real money demand (M / P) falls dramatically as inflation rates become very high. The empirical evidence motivates a need to generalize our model of money demand, which is done in the next section.

KEY TERMS

Use the space below to record your notes on the following key term.

Hyperinflation _____

_____

_____

REVIEW QUESTIONS

Problem 11: Provide an intuitive explanation for why demand for real money balances collapses during periods of very rapid money growth (hyperinflations).

_____

_____

Problem 12: There are two countries, Home and Foreign. Assume that the monetary approach to the exchange rate accurately predicts the exchange rate. What is the effect on Home's exchange rate if Home's demand for liquidity constant, $\overline{L}$, were to decrease?

_____

_____

4 Money, Interest, and Prices in the Long Run: A General Model

ESSENTIAL CONCEPTS

In this section the monetary approach to the exchange rate is improved by using a more standard, and realistic, model of money demand. Rather than assume that money demand is a fixed, constant proportion of nominal output, it is assumed that the demand for liquidity (the liquidity ratio) is a decreasing function of the interest rate i. In this case the demand for real balances can be written

$$\frac{M^d}{P} = L(i) \times Y,$$

where $L(i)$ is the liquidity ratio (decreasing in i) and Y is real output. The assumption that demand for real balances falls with the interest rate is motivated by the following logic: Because money does not pay interest, an increase in the interest rate on deposits increases the opportunity cost of holding money and so reduces demand for money. Put another way, individuals are more willing to put up with the inconvenience of having their wealth tied up in less liquid assets if the return to those assets is higher.

Now that we have the interest rate in the money demand equation, we need to have a model of what determines interest rates when prices are perfectly flexible. The first step is to notice that the uncovered interest parity condition links interest rate differentials to expected changes in the exchange rate which relative PPP links in turn to differences in inflation rates across countries. For two countries, Home and Foreign, this means

$$i_H - i_F = \pi_H^e - \pi_F^e.$$

If the interest rate is higher in Home than in Foreign in the long run, then it must be because Home's expected rate of inflation (π_H^e) is higher than the expected rate of inflation in Foreign (π_F^e). This is known as the *Fisher effect*.

Up until now, we have spoken exclusively about nominal interest rates, which tell us the return of a deposit in terms of money. The *real interest rate* is the return of an investment in terms of how much goods and services we can buy, or the nominal interest rate minus the rate at which money is expected to lose value relative to goods and services: $r = i - \pi^e$. By rearranging the Fisher effect equation, we find that as long as uncovered interest parity and RPPP hold, then real interest rates must be the same in both countries and equal to the *world real interest rate*. Arbitrage in financial and goods markets causes *real interest parity*. For a country taking real interest rates as given (determined on world markets), the nominal rate of interest must be equal to the sum of the fixed world interest rate r and the expected local rate of inflation π^e. In the long run the rate of inflation is equal to the rate of money growth less the rate of output growth. This observation completes the model. Monetary policy simultaneously determines (1) price levels and the inflation rate, (2) interest rates, and (3) exchange rates and depreciation rates.

Relative to the monetary approach described earlier in the chapter, the more general approach differs in two important respects: (1) Changes in monetary policy alter the nominal interest rate, and (2) changes in this interest rate have direct effects on price levels and exchange rates. Hence, a sudden change in money growth rates leads to a leap in prices and exchange rates that work through changes in money demand that in turn are induced by changes in interest rates.

KEY TERMS

Use the space below to record your notes on the following key terms.

Real money demand function _____

_____

_____

Fisher effect _____

_____

_____

Real interest rate _____

_____

_____

Real interest parity _____

_____

_____

World real interest rate _____

_____

_____

REVIEW QUESTIONS

Problem 13: In a long-run equilibrium, Country A has an interest rate of 10%, whereas Country B has an interest rate of 7%. Real output in each country is growing at 2% per year. The money growth rate in Country B is 6%.

13a. Which country has a higher inflation rate? _____

_____

13b. Which country has a higher real interest rate? _____

_____

13c. What is the inflation rate in Country B? _____

_____

13d. What is the inflation rate and money growth rate in Country A? _____

_____

Suppose that the central bank of Country B announces at time T that the country will henceforth have a money growth rate that will be 2% per year.

13e. What is the effect of the decrease in money growth on nominal interest rates in Country B at time T? _____

_____

_____

13f. What is the effect of the decrease in money growth rate on the liquidity ratio $L(i)$?

_____

_____

13g. What is the effect of the decrease in the money growth rate on the price level in Country B?

_____

_____

_____

13h. What is the effect of the decrease in the money growth rate on Country B's exchange rate at time T? _____

_____

_____

13i. How does Country B's exchange rate change after time T? _____

_____

_____

Problem 14: (Multiple Choice) Which of the following could explain a sudden depreciation in a country's exchange rate?

    a.   a decrease in the expected rate of inflation

    b.   an increase in the real level of output

    c.   a decrease in the money supply

    d.   all of the above

    e.   none of the above

Problem 15: (Multiple Choice) Suppose that prices are perfectly flexible. Home is growing at a faster rate than Foreign. Money supplies in each country are fixed. Which of the following is predicted by the monetary approach?

    a.   Home's currency is depreciating relative to Foreign's currency.

    b.   The exchange rate is constant between the two countries.

    c.   Interest rates are lower in Home than in Foreign.

    d.   none of the above

Problem 16: Imagine a world with two countries, Home and Foreign. Home's currency is the dollar and Foreign's currency is known as the blot. Trade in goods and in assets is completely free. In a long-run equilibrium Home's money supply grows at 10%, and Foreign's money supply grows at 5%. Assume that *prices are perfectly flexible.*

16a. At what rate does Home's currency appreciate or depreciate? _____

_____

_____

16b. Is Home's interest rate higher or lower than Foreign's interest rate and by how much?

_____

_____

Suppose that at time *t,* Home's central bank announces that henceforth the money growth rate will be 5% instead of 10%.

16c. What happens to Home's interest rate at time *t?* _____

_____

_____

16d. What happens to Home's exchange rate at time *t?* _____

_____

_____

16e. After time *t,* what happens to the value of the dollar relative to the blot?

_____

_____

In the long-run model presented in this section, a country with higher inflation also has a higher interest rate. This positive relationship between interest rates and inflation rates may seem backwards to students raised in low-inflation countries. The important thing to remember is that this is a *long-run model.*

    The more complicated money demand equation affects only some of the model's predictions. An increase in money growth rate will alter the rates of changes of prices and exchange rates in the same way, but the "jump" at time *T* happens only because of the adjustment in the interest rate.

5 Monetary Regimes and Exchange Rate Regimes

ESSENTIAL CONCEPTS

High and/or volatile inflation rates tend to destabilize an economy and retard its long-run growth. For this reason, countries frequently set an *inflation target* and structure their monetary policies to achieve this target. To meet long-run targets, governments often choose a *monetary regime* featuring a *nominal anchor*. The government chooses a nominal variable to target the rate of inflation in prices, another nominal variable.

Three potential nominal anchors are considered. The first nominal anchor is motivated by RPPP. Rearranging the basic RPPP equation yields

$$\pi_H = \frac{\Delta E_{H/F}}{E_{H/F}} + \pi_F.$$

While Home's government has no control over Foreign's inflation rate, it can target the rate at which its currency appreciates or depreciates relative to Foreign's currency. In this case, the government imposes an *exchange rate target*. For instance, a government could fix its exchange rate vis-à-vis a low-inflation country so that Home's inflation becomes equal to Foreign's inflation rate. The second nominal anchor is the growth rate of the nominal money supply. The fundamental equation for the price level implies that the rate of inflation is

$$\pi_H = \mu_H - g_H,$$

where g_H is the rate of growth of real output and μ_H is the nominal anchor, the growth rate of the money supply. In this case the government announces a *money supply target*. Finally, the Fisher effect implies another nominal anchor, the nominal interest rate. Because the nominal interest rate is equal to the real interest rate plus inflation, and because the real interest rate is fixed from the perspective of the government, a government that controls nominal interest rates *(inflation plus interest rate target)* also controls inflation rates.

The key problem facing a government pursuing a monetary regime with a nominal anchor is that the government must be committed to its target. This means that a country with a nominal anchor sacrifices monetary policy autonomy in the long run. To be able to pursue such a policy (which often has negative, short-run political consequences), it is often necessary for *central bank independence* so that government officials cannot order the bank to change its policies.

KEY TERMS

Use the space below to record your notes on the following key terms.

Nominal anchors _____

_____

_____

Monetary regime _____

_____

_____

Exchange rate target _____

_____

_____

Money supply target _____

_____

_____

Inflation target plus interest rate policy _____

_____

_____

Central bank independence _____

_____

_____

REVIEW QUESTIONS

Problem 17: Suppose the economy of Home grows at a rate of 3% and inflation in Foreign runs at a rate of 5%. Home's inflation target is 2%.

17a. What exchange rate target would allow Home to meet its inflation target?

_____

_____

17b. What money supply target would allow Home to meet its inflation target?

_____

_____

17c. If foreign interest rates are 8%, what interest rate should the government target to meet its inflation target? _____

_____

_____

17d. If the growth rate of real output were to fall to 1%, how would the government have to adjust its nominal anchor policies? Consider all three nominal anchors. _____

_____

_____

_____

12

Exchange Rates II: The Asset Approach in the Short Run

Overview

The theory of exchange rates is built on two arbitrage arguments. First, if assets can be traded internationally, then the expected return of deposits in each country should be the same when measured in the same currency. Second, if goods and services can be procured from different countries, then the exchange rate should adjust so that a given basket of goods and services has the same price in each country when measured in the same currency. The first arbitrage condition, uncovered interest parity (UIP), applies at all times. Given interest rates on deposits in different countries, UIP tells us how much a currency is expected to change in value over a given time horizon, but it does not tell us the expected level of the exchange rate. The second arbitrage condition, purchasing power parity (PPP), is assumed to apply only after some time has passed. Given expected levels of prices in the long run, PPP tells us the level of the exchange rate to expect in the long run. Only by using the two arbitrage conditions together can we predict the effect of various economic shocks on the level of spot exchange rate.

In order to make use of either arbitrage condition, we need to be able to predict monetary phenomena. To use PPP to forecast expected exchange rates, we need to be able to forecast expected price levels. To use the UIP condition (in conjunction with PPP) to forecast spot rates, we need to be able to predict interest rates in the short run. By assuming that price levels are sticky in the short run but perfectly flexible in the long run, we are able to use the same equation for equilibrium in the money market to predict the effect of economic changes on both the short-run interest rate and the long-run price level.

Once formulated, our complete theory of exchange rate determination shows that permanent monetary and economic shocks have much larger impacts on the exchange rate than do temporary monetary and economic shocks. That is, permanent shocks result in exaggerated exchange rate movements in the foreign exchange (forex) market that cause the exchange rate to overshoot its new long-run level. Finally, our theory can be used to demonstrate some fundamental results in international economics: Countries that allow free trade in financial assets cannot independently target both the exchange rate and the money supply simultaneously.

1 Exchange Rates and Interest Rates in the Short Run: UIP and FX Market Equilibrium

ESSENTIAL CONCEPTS

The asset approach to exchange rates is built upon the idea of arbitrage in the international market for financial assets. According to UIP, free international trade in financial assets causes the common currency return on deposits denominated in different currencies to be equal. For the case of the United States and Europe, the UIP condition is

$$i_\$ = i_€ + (E^e_{\$/€} - E_{\$/€}) / E_{\$/€}$$

which states that the expected return on European deposits measured in dollars (the right-hand side) is the same as the return on deposits in the United States (the left-hand side). This equation can be rewritten

$$E_{\$/€} = E^e_{\$/€} / (1 + i_\$ - i_€).$$

The UIP equation is the *fundamental equation of the asset approach to exchange rates* because it predicts the current spot rate $E_{\$/€}$ as a function of three different monetary variables: (1) interest rates in a "home" country, $i_\$$; (2) interest rates in a "foreign" country, $i_€$; and (3) expected future spot exchange rates, $E^e_{\$/€}$, between home and foreign currencies. If an investor can predict these three monetary variables, then the investor can predict the exchange rates. The *FX market diagram* expresses this information in graph form: Given interest rates and expected future exchange rates, there is only one exchange rate that equalizes home and foreign returns.

KEY TERMS

Use the space below to record your notes on the following key terms.

Asset approach to exchange rates _____

_____

_____

Fundamental equation of the asset approach to exchange rates _____

_____

_____

FX market diagram _____

_____

_____

REVIEW QUESTIONS

Problem 1: Suppose that the U.S. nominal interest rate is 5% and the European nominal interest rate is 3%. The dollar is expected to

   a. appreciate by 8%.

   b. depreciate by 8%.

   c. appreciate by 2%.

   d. depreciate by 2%.

   e. none of the above

Problem 2: Suppose that the interest rate on one-year deposits is 4% in the United States and 2% in the European Union. UIP is assumed to hold.

2a. How much is the U.S. dollar expected to depreciate against the euro over the next year?

_____

_____

2b. If the current U.S. dollar–euro exchange rate were one, then what does the foreign exchange market expect the spot rate to be next year? _____

_____

_____

2c. Suppose that the American interest rates increased to 5% at time T. Has the expected rate of dollar depreciation over the next year increased or decreased? Explain. _____

_____

_____

2d. If the future expected spot rate remained unchanged after the increase in interest rates at time T, what happens to the spot rate at time T? _____

_____

_____

2e. In the diagram below, draw the expected dollar return on American and European assets as a function of the American exchange rate before and after the change in American interest rates.

**Expected
return, percent
per annum**

$E_{\$/€}$

Suppose that U.S. interest rates are 4% per year and E.U. interest rates are initially at 2% per year. At time T, E.U. interest rates rise to 3% per year.

2f. At time T, does the rate of expected depreciation of the dollar increase or decrease? Explain. _____

_____

_____

2g. If at time T the expected future spot rate were to remain unchanged, what would happen to the current spot rate? Explain. _____

_____

_____

2h. In the diagram below, draw the expected dollar return on U.S. and European assets as a function of the U.S. exchange rate before and after the change in European interest rates.

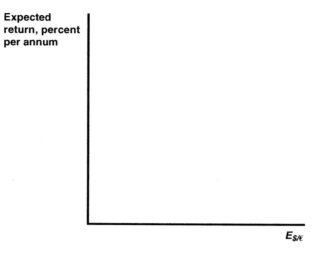

....

Problem 2 highlights an important feature of equilibrium in the foreign exchange market. The increase in the U.S. interest rate caused the dollar to appreciate when it occurred, but it also led to a greater rate of expected depreciation of the dollar over the next year.

The diagrams above may look like supply and demand diagrams, but they are not. If the return on one kind of asset is greater than the return of an equivalent asset, then *everybody* prefers the asset with the higher return, and markets must adjust.

Notice that the textbook takes the trouble to review the concept of UIP in great detail. This demonstrates the importance of this material!

....

2 Interest Rates in the Short Run: Money Market Equilibrium

ESSENTIAL CONCEPTS

Economists have long observed that an increase in the money supply will eventually lead to an increase in prices if everything else is held equal. They have also observed that the process of price adjustment can be quite slow and that prices may reasonably be treated as fixed in the short run. In this section, we explore the implications of this short-run *nominal rigidity* for our model of exchange rates.

Equilibrium in the money market requires (in both the short and long run) that the supply of real balances be equal to the demand for real balances:

$$\frac{M}{P} = L(i)Y$$

If the price level P and real output Y are fixed in the short run, then equilibrium in the money market requires that interest rate (i) adjust so that people are willing to hold the quantity of money supplied by the central bank (M). A temporary increase in M has no long-run effect on the price level P, but it must lower the interest rate. A permanent increase in the money supply must also reduce the interest rate in the short run because prices are fixed in the short run, even if it will increase prices (i.e., cause inflation) in the long run. Note that temporary or permanent changes in Y have the opposite effects of temporary or permanent changes in M.

KEY TERMS

Use the space below to record your notes on the following key term.

Nominal rigidity _____

_____

_____

REVIEW QUESTIONS

Problem 3: Consider a country that has seen its money supply (M) and real gross domestic product (GDP) (Y) fixed for a long time. At time T, M unexpectedly increases by 10% and stays constant at that level forever. Assume that prices are sticky in the short run.

3a. What is the effect of the increase in M on prices at time T? _____

_____

_____

3b. What is the effect of the increase in M on the interest rate at time T? Use the following diagram to answer the question. _____

_____

_____

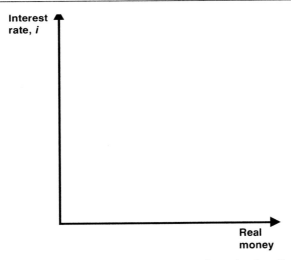

3c. What is the long-run effect of the increase in M on the price level?

_____

_____

3d. What is the long-run effect of the increase in M on the interest rate?

_____

_____

Problem 4: Consider a country that has seen its money supply (M) and real GDP (Y) fixed for a long time. At time T, Y unexpectedly increases by 10% and stays constant at that level forever. Assume that prices are sticky in the short run.

4a. What is the effect of the increase in Y on prices at time T?

_____

_____

4b. What is the effect of the increase in Y on the interest rate at time T? Use the following diagram to answer the question.

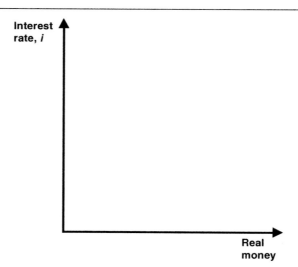

4c. What is the long-run effect of the increase in Y on the price level?

4d. What is the long-run effect of the increase in Y on the interest rate?

....

TIPS   How long is the short run? How short is the long run? These are quite reasonable questions that students frequently ask. There is no easy answer to these questions because the degree to which prices are sticky is not well understood.

Problems 3 and 4 emphasize the difference between the long run and the short run. Note that there is no long-run effect on the interest rate because in the long run, money supply growth is expected to be zero, so there is NO long-run inflation.

Note that in problems 3 and 4, real and nominal interest rates move in the same direction in the short run because the Fisher effect only applies to the long run.

....

3 The Asset Approach: Applications and Evidence

ESSENTIAL CONCEPTS

In this section, the UIP condition (or fundamental equation to the asset approach to exchange rates) is combined with the money market equilibrium condition in order to consider the effect of temporary changes in the money supply on the exchange rate. Because the changes in money supply are temporary, they have no effect in the long run and so do not have an effect on the expected future spot rate. However, because price levels are fixed in the short run, changes in the money supply or in real output in either of the two countries cause interest rate differentials to change and so affect the current spot rate through the UIP condition.

REVIEW QUESTIONS

Problem 5: Use the diagrams below to show the effect of a temporary increase in Home's money supply on its interest rate and on its exchange rate. (All nominal variables are in terms of Home dollars.) Explain your diagram.

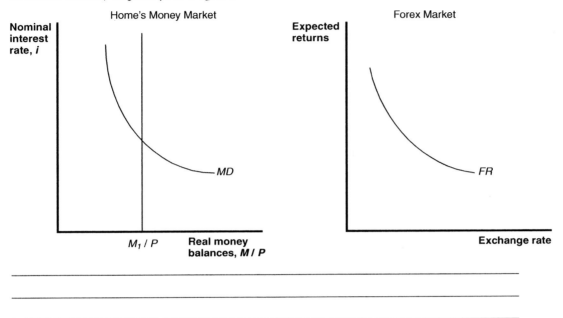

_____

_____

_____

Problem 6: Use the diagrams below to show the effect of a temporary increase in Home's GDP (Y) on its interest rate and on its exchange rate. Explain your diagram.

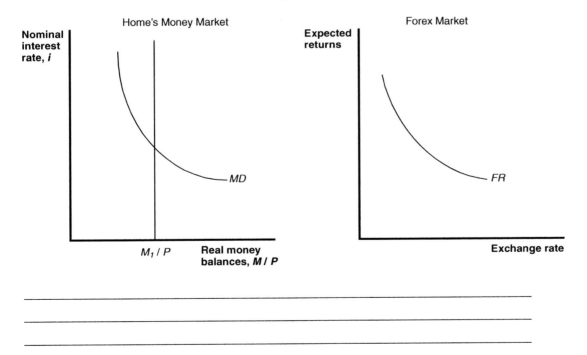

_____

_____

_____

Problem 7: Use the diagrams below to show the effect of a temporary increase in Foreign's GDP (Y) on Home's interest rate and on the exchange rate (Home dollars in terms of Foreign). Explain your diagram. _____

_____

_____

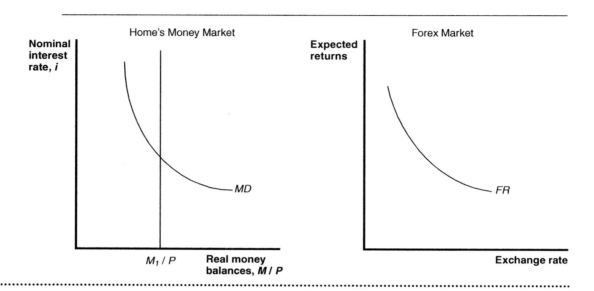

TIPS

Because capital controls prevent arbitrage in expected returns, they break the link between interest rates and exchange rates.

It is crucial that the word "temporary" appeared in each question. Permanent changes would alter future expectation and would have an additional impact on the exchange rate as we will learn in the next section.

The problems also highlight the fact that temporary shocks to the supply of real balances (M / P) can have similar effects to temporary shocks to the demand for real balances caused by changes in Y.

Sometimes it is asserted in the media that "strong economies have strong currencies." The problems above rationalize this type of statement. An increase in real output raises money demand and so leads to an appreciation of the currency.

··

4　A Complete Theory: Unifying the Monetary and Asset Approaches

ESSENTIAL CONCEPTS

The complete theory uses the equilibrium in the home and foreign money markets to solve for all three variables in the fundamental equation of the asset approach to the exchange rate. In the short run, monetary equilibrium plus sticky prices determines the interest rate in each country. In the long run, monetary equilibrium plus the Fisher effect determines expected price levels in each country, and PPP translates expected price levels into an expected future spot rate.

The benefit of the complete model is that it allows us to analyze the effect of *permanent* shocks to the money supply or to real output. Permanent shocks have the same short-run effects on interest rates as temporary shocks. For instance, a permanent increase in Home's money supply lowers the interest rate on Home's deposits in the short run. A permanent increase in the money supply (or decrease in real output) must also increase the long-run price level and so must lead to a higher (depreciated) exchange rate in the long run. Because the shock is permanent, foreign exchange arbitrageurs immediately anticipate the long-run change in the exchange rate: The expected future spot rate shifts up at the **same** time that interest rates fall. Thus, the short-run and long-run effects reinforce one another in an immediate response of the exchange rate to the permanent increase in the money supply, leading to a sharp jump in the exchange rate. The sharp depreciation is followed by a slow appreciation of the exchange rate toward its new long-run level as the short-run effect dissipates. Thus, the complete model predicts that permanent shocks to the money supply cause the exchange rate to *overshoot* its new long-run level. An immediate implication of the model is that countries that do not have compelling nominal anchors are likely to experience very high levels of exchange rate volatility.

KEY TERMS

Use the space below to record your notes on the following key term.

Overshooting _____

_____

_____

REVIEW QUESTIONS

Problem 8: True, False, or Uncertain. Please explain your answers.

8a. If prices were perfectly flexible, then exchange rates would never overshoot. _____

_____

_____

8b. Suppose the dollar were to depreciate sharply. Does this necessarily imply an increase in the expected rate of inflation in the United States? _____

_____

_____

8c. Does an increase in interest rates predict an exchange rate appreciation? _____

_____

_____

Problem 9: Consider the exchange rate of the dollar for the euro. Suppose that the liquidity function $L(i)$ is the same in both the United States and in Europe. The United States and Europe are initially in long-run equilibrium. The money supply in the United States is $1,000, and its real GDP is 10,000 units. The price level in the United States in this long-run equilibrium is $1 per unit of output. The money supply in Europe is €500, and its real GDP is 5,000 units. At time T, the United States permanently (and unexpectedly) increases its money supply to $1,500. At time T, interest rates in the United States fall from 5% to 2%.

9a. What is the exchange rate prior to time T? _____

_____

_____

9b. What is the expected future spot rate at time T (after the permanent increase in the money supply)? _____

_____

_____

9c. What are interest rates in Europe before and after time T? _____

_____

_____

9d. What is the expected rate of depreciation/appreciation of the dollar immediately following time T? _____

_____

_____

9e. What is the exchange rate immediately after the permanent increase in the money supply in the United States at time T? _____

_____

_____

Problem 10: Suppose the spot exchange rate between the U.S. dollar and the euro is well described by the "overshooting" model. The countries are in a long-term equilibrium when U.S. GDP increases permanently. No other exogenous variables change.

10a. What is the immediate impact of this "shock" on the U.S. interest rate and on the current spot exchange rate? Use the following diagrams to answer the following questions.

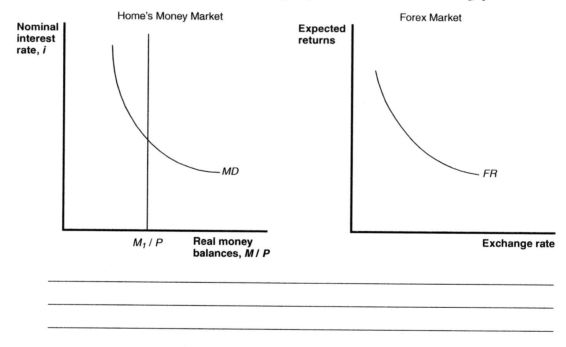

_____

_____

_____

10b. What is the impact of this "shock" on the U.S. interest rate, the U.S. price level, and the spot exchange rate in the long run?

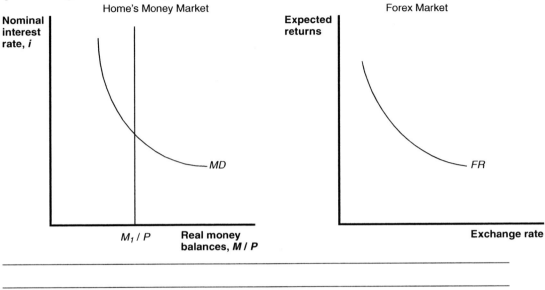

....

Note that the problems in this chapter do not consider cases of long-run inflation as in Chapter 11. This simplifies matters considerably because the long-run interest rate is unchanged. Problem 9 illustrates using numbers to "overshoot" of the exchange rate. Problems 9 and 10 are quite involved, but they do make use of most of the concepts discussed in this chapter. If you can understand each step, you are in good shape.

....

5 Fixed Exchange Rates and the Trilemma

ESSENTIAL CONCEPTS

As noted in Chapter 10, countries often choose to fix their exchange rate. What does the complete theory tell us about fixed exchange rate systems? A key result in all of international economics is that a country that fixes its exchange rate and does not impose capital controls loses its control over its monetary policy. To see this, note that under a fixed exchange rate system, the expected depreciation of the exchange rate becomes zero. This means that the interest rate in the country fixing its exchange rate must be exactly equal to the interest rate abroad. The textbook shows that this happens in practice: When Denmark fixes its currency relative to the euro, Danish interest rates converge to Eurozone levels. Using the money demand equation, it is then clear that a country with a fixed exchange rate does not have control over its money supply in the short run because there is only one level of the money supply that keeps interest rates equal to foreign levels. In summary, a country that maintains free mobility of capital faces a dilemma: it can either choose its exchange rate or its money supply, but it cannot do both.

When a country imposes capital controls, it becomes much harder for investors to arbitrage differences in interest rates across countries, and the UIP condition no longer holds. Hence, a country that imposes capital controls regains control over both its exchange rate and its money supply at least in the short run. Why don't countries impose capital controls? Countries benefit from being able to engage in international borrowing and lending with the rest of the world. Therefore there exists a *trilemma*. It is impossible to choose both the exchange rate and the money supply and to allow for capital mobility simultaneously.

KEY TERMS

Use the space below to record your notes on the following key term.

Trilemma _____

_____

_____

REVIEW QUESTIONS

Problem 11: Suppose PPP holds in the long run. In the *long run,* does a country imposing capital controls have control over both the exchange rate and the money supply? Explain.

_____

_____

Problem 12: Suppose that Home has pegged its currency to Foreign's currency. Home and Foreign allow free movement of capital.

12a. If Foreign's interest rate increases, what happens to the interest rate in Home?

_____

_____

12b. Suppose that Home's national output (*Y*) increases. What must happen to the money supply in Home?

_____

_____

TIPS

Problem 11 makes the point that control over the money supply and exchange rate separately is only relevant in the short run. In the long run, PPP ties down the exchange rate as a function of the money supply via the price level.

13

National and International Accounts: Income, Wealth, and the Balance of Payments

Overview

Sound economic policy relies on careful measurement of economic phenomenon. The national income and product accounts and the balance of payments are the two intricate accounting systems used to keep track of the circular flow of payments within and between economies. This chapter explains these important accounting concepts and uses them to analyze features of the international economic system. The chapter begins by deriving a series of "identities" that relate national income to national expenditure and to transactions with foreigners. The national income identity will play a crucial role in our macroeconomic analysis later in the book.

The balance of payments accounts summarize a nation's transactions with the rest of the world. The balance of payments accounts balance because every transaction involves an exchange of two items of equal value so that each credit is offset by a debit. The balance of payments can be used to analyze how a nation finances the gap between the value of its expenditures and its output. The financial flows that are documented in the balance of payments are one component of the evolution of countries' external wealth. A country that consistently spends less than it produces will tend to see its wealth increase. A country that persistently spends more than it produces will tend to see its wealth decline. Finally, the importance of capital gains and losses on countries' external wealth is analyzed.

The chapter is very vocabulary-intensive and requires a substantial amount of memorization. The subject matter is important to master because economic analysis of real-world phenomena requires sensible measurement, as the chapter illustrates through a series of case studies.

1 Measuring Macroeconomic Activity: An Overview

ESSENTIAL CONCEPTS

This section presents an overview of the accounting systems used by macroeconomists to trace economic activity. To introduce the accounting concepts, the chapter begins with the simple case of the closed economy (i.e., an economy that is not linked to the outside world). In a closed economy, one can easily perceive a "circular flow of payments." In the national product and income accounts of a closed economy, the amount that the consumers of final goods and service spend, or *gross national expenditure* (*GNE*), is equal to the value of goods and services created, or *gross domestic product* (*GDP*). GDP, which only counts *value added* at each stage of production by the economy's productive resources (factors), generates income, or *gross national income* (*GNI*), which is paid out to domestic citizens. Completing the circle of payments, GNE is financed out of GNI.

In an open economy, the links with the rest of the world occur at each stage along the circular flow of payments. Not all expenditures on goods and services are spent on domestically produced goods and services. For instance, some expenditure falls on imports, whereas some of the value of final output is sent abroad as exports. The difference between GNE and GDP is equal to the difference between exports and imports, which is called the *trade balance*. GDP and GNI tend to differ in an open economy because some of the value of domestic output accrues to foreign factors, such as the domestic affiliates of multinational firms or foreign workers working in the country (an example of factor service imports), and some of the value of national income is generated by the country's factors working abroad, such as interest payments on outstanding loans to foreigners (an example of factor service exports). Hence, GNI is equal to GDP plus *net factor income from abroad* (*NFIA*). Finally, the amount of disposable income has to be adjusted because some of the income may either be given away to residents of foreign countries or residents of foreign countries may transfer income to domestic residents (*net unilateral transfers* [*NUT*]). A key feature of an open economy is that international trade in assets allows a country's GNE to exceed its *gross national disposable income* (*GNDI*) (net borrowing) or vice versa (net lending).

The various international transactions that account for the difference between GNE and GNDI sum to the *current account* balance. How does a country that spends more than its income finance that expenditure? The answer is that this additional expenditure is financed via the sale of assets to foreign residents. The difference between GNDI and GNE is equal to the sum of the *financial account* and the *capital account*. The flows in the domestic circle of payments (*national income and product accounts*) require that the current account is equal to the sum of the financial account and the capital account (*balance of payments accounts*).

KEY TERMS

Use the space below to record your notes on the following key terms.

National income and product accounts _____

_____

_____

Balance of payments accounts _____

_____

_____

Gross national expenditure (GNE) _____

_____

_____

Gross domestic product (GDP) _____

_____

_____

Gross national income (GNI) _____

_____

_____

Trade balance (TB) _____

_____

_____

Net factor income from abroad (NFIA) _____

_____

_____

Net unilateral transfers (NUT) _____

_____

_____

Gross national disposable income (GNDI) _____

_____

_____

Current account (CA) _____

_____

_____

Financial account (FA) _____

_____

_____

Capital account (KA) _____

_____

_____

REVIEW QUESTIONS

Problem 1: True or false. Please explain your answers.

1a. A country whose GNE exceeds its GDP must be a net exporter of assets. _____

_____

_____

1b. A country's GNE must equal its GDP if it does not engage in trade with the rest of the world. _____

_____

_____

1c. A country's GDP is equal to the total value of the sales of all its firms.

_____

_____

_____

1d. The current account balance is equal to the difference between GNDI and GNE.

_____

_____

TIPS   Figure 13-2 in the textbook is an excellent resource for understanding the structure of the national income and products account and the balance of payments accounts. If you understand and memorize this figure, you are well on your way to doing well in this chapter.
In the "good old days," the financial and capital accounts were collectively called the capital account. Many instructors will have "grown up" using the older nomenclature, and it may slip into their lectures.

2 Income, Product, and Expenditure

ESSENTIAL CONCEPTS

This section carefully describes how the various aggregate measures of economic activity called the national accounts are constructed and provides a flavor of how these measures are used. In a closed economy, aggregate economic activity can be measured by three equivalent measures. The expenditure approach counts total spending on final goods and services in the economy (GNE), the product approach measures the total value of final goods produced by domestic firms (GDP), and the income approach measures the total income of payments to productive factors in the economy (GNDI). In an open economy GNE, GDP, and GNDI differ from each other because of flows between the domestic economy and the rest of the world. These measures are defined in the textbook as a series of identities. For instance, the GDP identity is GDP = GNE + *TB*, where *TB* is the trade balance; and the *national income identity* is GNDI = $Y = C + I + G + CA$ = GNE + *CA,* where *CA* is the current account balance. The national income identity is the most meaningful of the various measures of national well-being because it most closely corresponds to the resources available to a nation's households.

These identities demonstrate that governments must carefully measure a country's transactions with foreigners (the trade balance, net factor income accounts, and unilateral transfers) to measure changes in national welfare. A key example given in the textbook of how the distinction between GDP and GNDI matters is the experience of Ireland. Because of the large portion of Irish manufacturing that is undertaken by foreign multinationals, Irish GDP is much larger, and traditionally faster growing, than Irish GNDI.

Another important identity that can be derived from the national income identity is the *current account identity*,

$$S = I + CA$$

which states that a country's *national savings* $(S = Y - C - G)$ must be equal to the sum of investment (I) and the current account balance. A country that wishes to reduce its current account deficit must either increase its savings or reduce its investment. Savings can be broken down further into *private savings* $(Y - C - T)$ and *government savings* $(G - T)$. In the case of the United States, the rapid increase in the size of its current account deficit is driven by a decline in both private savings and government savings, whereas investment has remained roughly unchanged.

KEY TERMS

Use the space below to record your notes on the following key terms.

National income identity _____

_____

_____

National savings _____

_____

_____

Current account identity _____

_____

_____

Private savings _____

_____

_____

Government savings _____

_____

_____

REVIEW QUESTIONS

Problem 2: Would you expect GNDI to be greater than or less than GDP in a country in which many of the country's citizens work abroad? Explain. _____

_____

_____

Problem 3: Holding fixed other components of aggregate demand, what impact does an increase in investment have for the current account balance? _____

_____

_____

Problem 4: Is it possible for a country's GDP to exceed both its GNE and its GNI?

_____

_____

Problem 5: Consider the following aggregates for a fictional country for the year 2006: $I = 10$, $C = 80$, $G = 10$, and its GNDI is 95.

5a. What is the country's GNE? _____

5b. What is the country's national savings? _____

5c. What is the country's current account balance? _____

5d. Was the country a net exporter or importer of assets? _____

Problem 6: How might a country's birth rate affect its current account? _____

_____

_____

Problem 7: Imagine a world in which all countries are identical except that one country has an unusually good investment climate. Would you expect this country to run a current account surplus or deficit? _____

_____

_____

Problem 8: True, False, or Uncertain. Please explain your answers.

8a. Holding everything else in the economy constant, a decrease in government spending lowers the current account deficit (or raises the surplus). _____

_____

_____

8b. After everything in the economy is allowed to adjust, a decrease in government spending lowers the current account deficit (or raises the surplus). _____

_____

_____

Problem 9: (Multiple choice) Home's GDP rises by more than its GNDI. Which of the following are possible explanations?

    a.   Home has received government aid from a foreign country.

    b.   A foreign multinational affiliate has just begun production in Home.

    c.   Many of Home's workers work overseas.

    d.   all of the above

    e.   none of the above

3 The Balance of Payments

ESSENTIAL CONCEPTS

The national income accounts include all international transactions involving goods, services, factor services, and nonmarket transactions. The full set of all international transactions, including trade in financial assets and capital transfers, is documented in a country's balance of payments (BOP) accounts. Because the current account was already covered in detail in the last section, the focus of this section is primarily international trade in assets. There are two types of asset exports. First, domestic residents can sell claims on their home country to foreigners (thereby increasing the country's *external liabilities*). Second, domestic residents can sell claims on foreigners to foreigners (thereby decreasing the country's *external assets*). Similarly, domestic residents can import assets by buying back claims on themselves or by buying claims on foreigners. The actual "movement" that occurs in the asset trade is movement from one country's ownership of an asset to another country's ownership of it. The capital account works similarly but involves capital transfers rather than market transactions.

Now consider the links between the flows of goods, services, income, and assets. By the construction of the national accounts, GNE is equal to the sum of GNDI, the financial account balance (*FA*), and the capital account balance (*KA*):

$$GNE = GNDI + FA + KA$$

which states that expenditure is financed out of earnings or asset sales. GNDI is in turn equal to GNE plus the current account:

$$GNDI = GNE + CA$$

Combining the two expressions yields the *BOP identity*,

$$CA + FA + KA = 0$$

which states that all international transactions either expand or contract the resources available for expenditure in the home country so that a deficit (surplus) in one type of transactions must be balanced by a surplus (deficit) in a different type of transaction. If every international transaction were accurately recorded, the balance of payments would sum to zero by construction because each market transaction involves the exchange of two items of equal value. Every time a domestic resident conducts a transaction with a foreign resident, there must be a *BOP credit* that is exactly offset by a *BOP debit* recorded by balance of payments statisticians. For instance, suppose a Home firm imports a tractor from a Foreign firm and pays by running down its account at a foreign bank. The import is recorded as a debit in the current account balance, and the reduction in the claims on a foreign bank is treated as an asset export in the financial account.

In the aggregate, a country that runs a current account surplus is either running up its stock of claims of foreigners or it is disposing of its liabilities held by foreigners. By convention such a country is called a *(net) lender* because it is in essence providing purchasing power to foreigners. Because the country is buying more assets abroad than foreigners are buying in that country, this is also referred to as a financial outflow. A country that runs a current account deficit is called a *(net) borrower* because its GNE is greater than its GNDI. The gap between expenditure and income is filled by a financial inflow from abroad.

KEY TERMS

Use the space below to record your notes on the following key terms.

External asset _____

_____

_____

External liability _____

_____

_____

BOP identity _____

_____

_____

BOP credit _____

_____

_____

BOP debit _____

_____

_____

(Net) lender _____

_____

_____

(Net) borrower _____

_____

_____

REVIEW QUESTIONS

Problem 10: (Multiple Choice) Home has a current account deficit of $8 billion, and the capital account balance is zero. Which of the following must be true?

   a.   Home must have a financial account surplus.

   b.   Home must be exporting assets to the rest of the world.

   c.   GNDI must be less than GNE.

   d.   all of the above

   e.   none of the above

Problem 11: True, False, or Uncertain. Please explain your answers. A country that runs a current account surplus must be running up its stock of claims on foreigners. _____

_____

_____

Problem 12: How are the balance of payments accounts of a country with a fixed exchange rate system likely to differ from the accounts of a country with a floating exchange rate system?

_____

_____

_____

Problem 13: Classify the following transactions on the U.S. balance of payments. Make sure to record both the debit and credit and the appropriate categories (export of good, import of asset on financial account, etc.). Do not concern yourself with the magnitudes involved.

13a. A U.S. manufacturer sells a tractor to a Russian company and the Russian company pays by drawing a check on a Russian bank. _____

_____

13b. A U.S. bank makes a loan to an Argentine firm and creates a deposit in the name of the Argentine firm. _____

_____

13c. The U.S. government gives food to Zimbabwe. _____

_____

13d. A U.S. consultant is paid by a British firm. The British firm draws the funds from its account at an American bank. _____

_____

13e. A middle-aged British rock star plays a free concert for an American audience.

_____

13f. A Chinese student enrolls in an American university and pays by drawing on an account at an American bank. _____

_____

13g. An Argentine bank makes an interest payment on its debt to an American bank. It pays by drawing on its deposit at the American bank. _____

_____

13h. An interest payment comes due on an Argentine bank's debt to an American bank. The Argentine bank fails to make the payment. _____

_____

....

Balance of payments accounting questions are tedious, but it is important to understand the structure of these accounts.
Problem 13h can be confusing because it doesn't seem to involve two items of equal value. There are always two items; you must persevere to identify both parts.

TIPS

....

4 External Wealth

ESSENTIAL CONCEPTS

A country's *external wealth* is the difference between the value of its total claims on foreigners and the value of foreigners' total claims on it. If this number is positive, we say that the country is a *net creditor*. If this number is negative, as is the case for the United States, we say that this country is a *net debtor*. There are three ways that a country's net wealth can change. First, the financial account of a country records net changes in assets. As is the case for an individual, a country whose income exceeds its expenditure will accumulate external wealth. Second, as wealth is stored in financial assets and the prices of assets vary from day to day, a country's external wealth changes due to valuation effects. For instance, a country that invests in low-risk but low-return assets will tend to see few surprise changes in its external wealth, experiencing little in the way of capital gains or losses. A country that invests in higher-risk but higher-yielding foreign assets could see large swings in its external wealth, but on average it will see a positive valuation effect. Finally, a country's external wealth can change if it receives gifts of assets or if it gives assets to others. A prime example of this sort is debt forgiveness of developing country debt by developed countries.

In practice the size of the valuation effects can be very large relative to the size of financial flows. As pointed out in the textbook, the United States has done well in terms of valuation effects: In 2006 the United States experienced a net financial inflow of $804 billion but saw its external wealth fall by only $302 billion as it enjoyed a half trillion dollar capital gain! These gains were driven in part by the fact that many of the financial claims on the United States are denominated in dollars, whereas most of the financial claims of the United States on foreigners are denominated in other currencies. As the dollar has fallen, the value of its assets has risen relative to the value of its liabilities.

KEY TERMS

Use the space below to record your notes on the following key terms.

External wealth _____

_____

_____

Net creditor _____

_____

_____

Net debtor _____

_____

_____

REVIEW QUESTIONS

Problem 14: Home's current account balances and external wealth (in $ billions) for the years 1990–2000 are shown in the table below. Home's external wealth at the end of 1989 was zero. All external wealth figures are measured at the end of the year (so they include the effects of any borrowing during the year). Assume that KA = 0.

Year	Current Account Balance ($ Billions)	External Wealth at Year-End ($ Billions)
1990	10	6
1991	3	10
1992	1	12
1993	−4	8
1994	−7	4
1995	−2	5
1996	3	6
1997	8	15
1998	12	22
1999	10	29
2000	16	43

14a. If there had been no valuation effects over the period, what would Home's external wealth be by the end of the year 2000? _____

_____

_____

14b. What was the total size of valuation effects over the period? _____

_____

_____

14c. In which years (if any) were valuation effects positive? _____

_____

_____

Problem 15: At the end of 2001, Home residents owned €10 million worth of Foreign bonds and $10 million worth of foreign deposits. In turn, foreigners owned $25 million worth of Home bonds. The exchange rate of the dollar in terms of euros was 1. Over the course of 2002, the dollar depreciated against the euro to the rate of 1.5, and Home ran a current account deficit of $5 million. What was Home's external wealth at the end of 2002?

_____

_____

Problem 16: The external assets of the United States are greatly exceeded by its external liabilities. The NFIA for the United States is positive. Why do economists have difficulty reconciling these two facts? _____

_____

_____

14

Output, Exchange Rates, and Macroeconomic Policies in the Short Run

Overview

Temporary "macroeconomic shocks" can destabilize a country's economy. Some of these shocks have a domestic origin, such as a drop in consumer spending, and some of these shocks originate abroad, such as an increase in international interest rates. This chapter introduces a Keynesian-type model of the macroeconomy to analyze the effect of domestic and international shocks on key macroeconomic aggregates and to analyze the ability of the government to offset these shocks through changes in its policy. The model highlights the role of international markets for goods and assets in determining domestic outcomes. Critically, government policies that affect the return on domestic deposits alter the exchange rate, which in turn alters the trade balance through a phenomenon known as expenditure switching.

A country's choice of exchange rate regime is shown to be paramount in determining the effect of shocks on the economy and in the efficacy of monetary policy for stabilizing the economy. In a country with a fixed exchange rate system, the interest rate must be equal to the world interest rate, which has the implication that the government can only use fiscal policy to combat adverse economic shocks. In a country with a flexible exchange rate system, there is no such constraint on the use of monetary policy because both the exchange rate and the interest rate are free to vary. Finally, real world difficulties in the implementation of policies to stabilize the economy are discussed.

1 Demand in the Open Economy

ESSENTIAL CONCEPTS

The Keynesian model introduced in this chapter attributes fluctuations in national output to shocks to demand for national output. As discussed in Chapter 13, demand for national output is equal to gross national expenditure (GNE) plus the trade balance and so is given by

$$D = C + I + G + TB$$

where C stands for *consumption,* I stands for *investment,* G stands for *government consumption,* and TB stands for the trade balance, or the difference between a country's exports and its imports. This section discusses the model's assumptions over the way in which these four components of aggregate demand behave. Much of the behavior of these components of demand can be attributed to the model's assumption that prices are "sticky," or fixed in the short run.

Demand by consumers is described by the consumption function, $C = C(Y - T)$. This posits that the level of consumption is increasing in *disposable income,* which is the difference between national income, Y, and taxes, T. The rate at which consumption rises with disposable income is known as the *marginal propensity to consume.* Consumption can also shift as consumer sentiment changes. This is an example of a demand shock.

Demand by investors is assumed to be determined by investor sentiments and by the *expected real interest rate.* The higher is the interest rate, the higher the return that any given investment project would have to generate in order to be profitable. An increase in the interest rate thus reduces aggregate investment as fewer investment projects are undertaken. In summary, the investment function is given by $I = I(i)$, where I is decreasing in i (note that inflation expectations are assumed to be zero so that the nominal interest rate is equal to the real interest rate).

Government consumption, G, and the taxes levied by the government, T, are assumed to be determined only by the government via its fiscal policy. Note that not all government spending counts as government consumption, as some spending takes the form of *transfers programs,* such as social security, which do not generate demand for goods and services directly.

The final component of aggregate demand is the trade balance, which is equal to the difference between the value of exports and the value of imports. Demand for a country's exports is assumed to depend on the *real effective exchange rate,* on the level of disposable demand in other countries $(Y^* - T^*)$, and on consumer preferences abroad. A country's import demand is also assumed to depend on the real effective exchange rate, on the level of disposable income in the home country $(Y - T)$, and on domestic consumer preferences. As a country's real exchange rate depreciates, its goods and services become cheaper relative to foreign goods and services, inducing consumers at home and abroad to engage in *expenditure switching:* Exports are increasing and imports are decreasing in the *real effective exchange rate.* This assumption is generally consistent with the data in the long run but may not hold in the short run, a phenomenon known as the *J curve.* In summary, the trade balance can be written as a function of its determinants: $TB(EP^*/P, Y - T, Y^* - T^*)$.

KEY TERMS

Use the space below to record your notes on the following key terms.

Consumption _____

_____

_____

Disposable income _____

_____

_____

Marginal propensity to consume (MPC) _____

_____

_____

Expected real interest rate _____

_____

_____

Government consumption _____

_____

_____

Taxes _____

_____

_____

Transfer programs _____

_____

_____

Expenditure switching _____

_____

_____

Real effective exchange rate _____

_____

_____

Pass-through _____

_____

_____

J curve _____

_____

_____

REVIEW QUESTIONS

Problem 1: Consider the following consumption function, $C = 5 + 0.75 \cdot (Y - T)$. Y is national income and T is government taxes.

1a. What is the marginal propensity to consume? _____

_____

1b. If disposable income is 100, what are consumers' savings? _____

_____

1c. What form might a "consumption shock" take given the structure of this consumption function? _____

_____

1d. If each individual consumer had the same consumption function, would a government transfer program, such as social security, affect aggregate consumption? _____

_____

_____

1e. True or False. Please explain your answer. If the government were to cut taxes T by 15 units and Y were to stay the same, aggregate demand would increase by 11.25. (Hint: Take into account demand for foreign goods and services.) _____

_____

_____

....

TIPS

Savings and consumption are assumed to not rely directly on the interest rate. This assumption may be different than in other textbooks.

Transfer programs can affect aggregate consumption spending if the marginal propensity to consume differs across consumers with different income levels.

....

Problem 2: There are seven potential investments available in Home. Each investment requires 1 unit of input. The rate of return on each investment is shown in the following table.

Project	Rate of Return
1	10
2	9
3	6
4	5
5	3
6	2
7	1

2a. If the real interest rate were 4%, how many units of output are demanded for investment?

_____

_____

2b. If the interest rate were to rise to 7%, how many units of output would be demanded for investment? _____

_____

2c. Suppose that there was a productivity boom so that the rate of return on each investment doubled. If the interest rate continued to be 7%, how many investments would be undertaken? _____

_____

Problem 3: Home's exchange rate is fixed for many years. At time t, the currency appreciates. Use the following graphs to plot the response of Home's exports, imports, and trade balance over time. (Hint: Think about the J curve.)

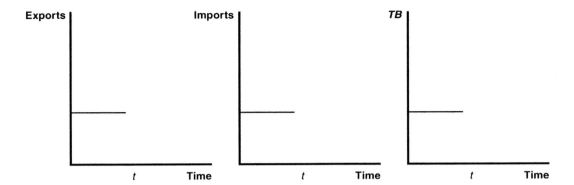

Problem 4: (Multiple Choice) A 10% depreciation is observed to lead to a 4% increase in import prices. Which of the following phenomena could explain the incomplete pass-through?

    a.   dollar invoicing

    b.   distribution costs

    c.   J curve effects

    d.   a & b

    e.   all of the above

Problem 5: (Multiple Choice) Home's trade balance surplus might increase as a result of

    a.   a real effective exchange rate depreciation.

    b.   a decrease in Home's disposable income.

    c.   an increase in the rest of the world's disposable income.

    d.   all of the above

    e.   none of the above

2 Goods Market Equilibrium: The Keynesian Cross

ESSENTIAL CONCEPTS

In a Keynesian model all changes in short-run aggregate supply are induced by a shock (change) in one or more components of aggregate demand D. Because aggregate demand is a function of the same variables on which its components depend, it can be written

$$D(Y - T, I, G, EP^*/P, Y^* - T^*) = C(Y - T) + I(i) + G + TB(EP^*/P, Y - T, Y^* - T^*)$$

Holding fixed national income Y, an increase in G, E, i, P^*, or Y^* or a reduction in P^*, T or T^* will raise some component of aggregate demand, so aggregate demand will increase as well. The short-run equilibrium in the goods market requires that aggregate supply Y equals aggregate demand D or

$$D(Y - T, I, G, EP^*/P, Y^* - T^*) = Y$$

The level of output that satisfies this *goods market equilibrium condition* is generally analyzed using the *Keynesian cross* diagram shown in Figure 14-1.

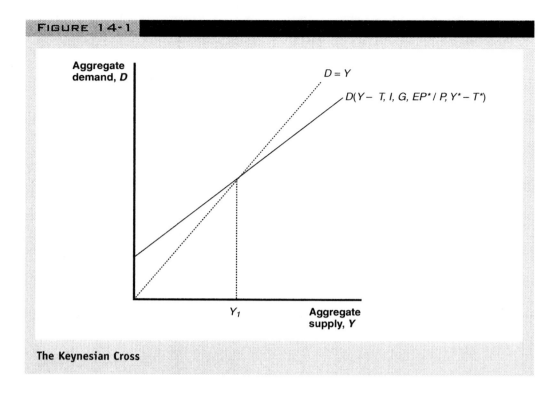

FIGURE 14-1

The Keynesian Cross

   The solid upward sloping line D is the aggregate demand curve. Aggregate demand is increasing in national output because consumption expenditure rises in national income. The slope of D is less than 1 because the marginal propensity to consume is less than 1 and because some of consumption falls on foreign rather than domestic goods. The equilibrium level of output Y_1 induces a level of aggregate demand that is exactly equal to that level of output. From Figure 14-1 it is clear that any shock that increases aggregate demand for any level of national output causes the aggregate demand curve to shift up, causing the short-run equilibrium level of output to rise.

KEY TERMS

Use the space below to record your notes on the following key terms.

Goods market equilibrium condition _____

_____

_____

Keynesian cross _____

_____

_____

REVIEW QUESTIONS

Problem 6: What is the effect of the following shocks on the short-run level of national output?

6a. A fall in interest rates? _____

_____

6b. An appreciation of the Home currency? _____

_____

6c. A tax cut? _____

6d. A tax cut in Foreign? _____

_____

6e. A drop in consumer confidence (consumers want to spend less)? _____

_____

6f. News that imported products make you sick? _____

_____

With prices sticky in the short run, we assume that any change in demand is immediately translated into a change in supply. Put another way, firms and workers have committed themselves to supply whatever is demanded no matter how big or small.

"Shocks" to aggregate demand shift the D curve up and down. Clearly, any shock to demand can be directly offset by a change in G and indirectly through a change in T, i, or E. Later in the chapter, we will see this observation motivate an activist government policy.

TIPS

---

3 Goods and Forex Market Equilibria: Deriving the IS Curve

ESSENTIAL CONCEPTS

The *IS curve* shows the combinations of the nominal interest rate and national output (i, Y) that are consistent with goods market equilibrium when all other determinants of aggregate demand are held fixed. There are two channels that connect interest rates to national output. First, a change in interest rates directly lowers investment spending $I(i)$. Higher interest rates make investment less attractive. Second, changes in interest rates also spark changes in exchange rates. In the short run, prices are sticky so that all changes in nominal exchange rates are also changes in real exchange rates. A reduction in interest rates leads to a real depreciation, which induces expenditure switching and a higher trade balance. Because these two effects reinforce each other, an increased interest rate lowers aggregate demand and so lowers national output: The IS curve is downward sloping.

A change in *any* other variable that affects aggregate demand D other than the interest rate will induce a *shift* in the IS curve. For instance, an increase in government spending directly increases aggregate demand and so increases the volume of output in the short run for any initial level of interest rates. As a result, the new relationship between interest rates and national output features a higher level of national output for each level of interest rates.

KEY TERMS

Use the space below to record your notes on the following key term.

IS curve _____

_____

_____

REVIEW QUESTIONS

Problem 7: How do the following shocks shift the IS curve? Explain.

7a. A fall in interest rates? _____

_____

7b. An increase in the expected future exchange rate? _____

_____

7c. A tax cut? _____

_____

7d. A tax cut in Foreign? _____

_____

7e. A drop in consumer confidence (consumers want to spend less)? _____

_____

_____

7f. News that imported products make you sick? _____

_____

_____

TIPS

Any change in a component of aggregate demand that changes the level of output for a given level of the interest rate (see Problem 6) will *shift* the IS curve. Changes in components of aggregate demand that are due to a change in the interest rate are associated with a movement *along* the existing IS curve.

4 Money Market Equilibrium: Deriving the LM Curve

ESSENTIAL CONCEPTS

The *LM curve* is used to summarize the combinations of the nominal interest rate and national output that are consistent with equilibrium in the money market while holding fixed the real money supply and any other determinants of money demand. The key equation is

$$M/P = L(i)Y$$

An increase in the interest rate i lowers money demand, whereas an increase in real output Y increases money demand. Hence, an increase in real output is associated with an increase in interest rates. This means that the LM curve is upward sloping.

There are only two shocks that can shift the LM curve. First, a change in the nominal money supply M or a change in the price level P both alter the real money supply. An increase in the real money supply is associated with a downward shift in the LM curve. Second, the function L can shift. For example, if people become concerned about the health of the financial system and want to hold more cash, the function L would shift up (a rush to liquidity). An increase in money demand holding fixed i must shift the LM curve up.

KEY TERMS

Use the space below to record your notes on the following key term.

LM curve _____

_____

_____

REVIEW QUESTIONS

Problem 8: (Multiple Choice) Which of the following could result in a shift of the LM curve?

    a.   a depreciation of the exchange rate

    b.   a rise in consumer spending

    c.   an increase in investment

    d.   a fall in the price level

    e.   all of the above

Problem 9: True or False. Please explain your answer. The LM curve is upward sloping because prices are assumed to be sticky. _____

_____

_____

5 The Short-Run IS-LM-FX Model of an Open Economy

ESSENTIAL CONCEPTS

In a short-run equilibrium, the nominal interest rate and level of real output make aggregate demand equal to aggregate supply in the goods market and ensure that the demand for real balances is equal to the real money supply. In other words, the interest rate and level of real output are determined by the intersection of the IS curve and the LM curve. In the background (and on a separate diagram typically drawn to the right of the IS-LM diagram), the interest rate and exchange rate lead to equilibrium in the foreign exchange market.

In this section, we use the complete model to analyze the effect of temporary shocks to the economy on the endogenous variables, such as national output, exchange rates, and trade balances. It is important to understand that a temporary shock is one that has no impact in the long run and so has no impact on people's expectations concerning future variables. For instance, a temporary investment boom results in an increase in one component of aggregate demand and so shifts the IS curve at the moment, but everyone in the economy understands that investment will soon fall and the IS curve will shift back to its initial location. The textbook's focus is on shocks that are created by changes in a government's *fiscal policy* (government consumption and taxation) and in its *monetary policy* (the money supply).

The effects of changes in fiscal and monetary policy on the economy depend on the country's exchange rate regime. The government of a country that has a flexible exchange rate system is in principle free to shift its IS curve (through fiscal policy) or its LM curve (through monetary policy). Mixtures of monetary and fiscal policy can be used to target particular interest rates and levels of national output. As noted in Chapter 12, a country that chooses to have a fixed exchange rate system and allows capital movements between countries loses control of its interest rate. To maintain the fixed exchange rate system, the government must adjust the country's money supply (and hence its LM curve) to keep the interest rate fixed. A change in fiscal policy that would tend to change the interest rate can only be achieved if the central bank alters the money supply to shift the LM curve in the same direction so as to prevent interest rates from changing.

KEY TERMS

Use the space below to record your notes on the following key terms.

Monetary policy _____

_____

_____

Fiscal policy _____

_____

_____

REVIEW QUESTIONS

Problem 10: Suppose that you are a government official in charge of your country's fiscal policy. The country maintains a flexible exchange rate system. You are asked by your country's "Grand Poobah for Life" to use fiscal policy alone to expand the country's output and to reduce its trade deficit simultaneously.

10a. Is it possible for you to obtain these two goals using only fiscal policy? Use the following diagram in your explanation.

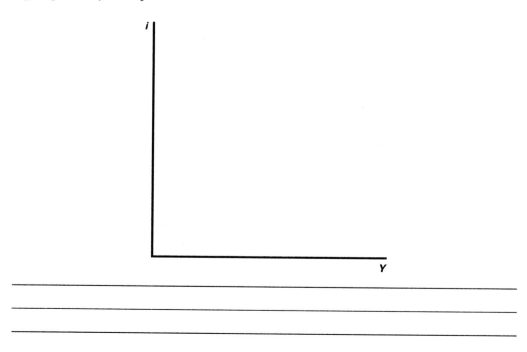

_____

_____

_____

10b. Now suppose instead that you were in charge of the country's money supply. Is it possible for you to obtain these two goals using only monetary policy? Use the following diagram in your explanation.

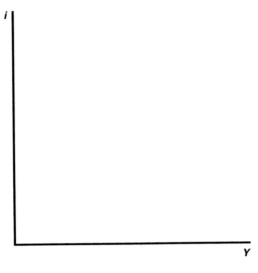

_____

_____

_____

10c. Now suppose that the country has a fixed exchange rate system. Is it possible to use either monetary or fiscal policy to lower the trade deficit and expand national output simultaneously? Use the following diagram in your explanation.

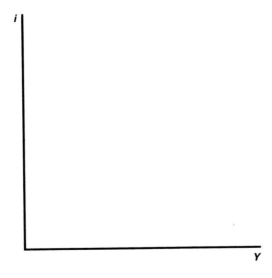

_____

_____

_____

Problem 11: True or False. Please explain your answer. A policy of fixing the nominal interest rate at a set level has the same consequences as a policy of fixing the exchange rate.

_____

_____

6 Stabilization Policy

ESSENTIAL CONCEPTS

Economic shocks are those that shift either the IS curve or the LM curve so that output is not at its natural, long-run level. When used correctly, fiscal and monetary policy can be used to "shock" the economy back to its long-run level by offsetting the effects of other shocks in the economy. When the government acts in this manner, it is following a *stabilization policy*. The ease with which one can shift curves around on paper makes stabilization policy appear to be easy. In practice, however, there are two major problems facing policymakers. First, policymakers generally have incomplete information about the state of the economy. Measuring economic aggregates is an immense undertaking and subject to error. The difficulty of formulating policy due to the slow collection of data is called the inside lag. Second, even after government policies are formulated and implemented, it takes time for their effects to take hold. The effects of fiscal or monetary policy may not be felt until after the adverse temporary shock to the economy has already receded. The slow response of the economy to government policies is called the outside lag.

One area in which the effects of economic policy are likely to take time is in the effect of changes in the exchange rate on the trade balance. Firms may not pass-through exchange rate changes to local currency prices in order to avoid alienating their hard-won local clientele, especially if they know that the movement in the exchange rate is only temporary. Further, to the extent that international contracts for exports and imports are set in advance, changes in the real exchange rate may fail to have a stimulating effect through the trade balance until long after the adverse shock has faded.

KEY TERMS

Use the space below to record your notes on the following key term.

Stabilization policy _____

_____

_____

REVIEW QUESTIONS

Problem 12: Suppose that all investors simultaneously have midlife crises. They are so distracted by the loss of their youth that they invest less at every given interest rate.

12a. What is the impact on the economy if the country has a flexible exchange rate system? Use the following diagram in your explanation.

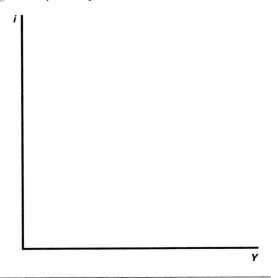

_____

_____

_____

12b. How might the government combat the effects of the investment shock under a flexible exchange rate system?

_____

_____

12c. What is the impact on the economy if the country has a fixed exchange rate system? Use the following diagram in your explanation.

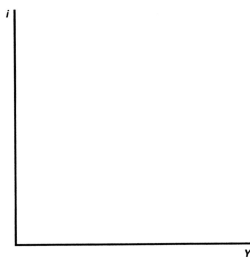

_____

_____

_____

12d. How might the government combat the effects of the investment shock under a fixed exchange rate system?

_____

_____

TIPS

Problem 12 makes the point that any shock to a component of aggregate demand has a similar effect to a change in a government's fiscal policy. A reduction in investment demand has the same impact as a sudden cut in government expenditure in the short run.

Problem 13: Compare and contrast the effect of an increase in Foreign interest rates on Home's economy under fixed and floating exchange rate regimes. Use the following two diagrams in your answer. The top panel corresponds to a flexible system, and the bottom corresponds to a fixed system. Explain your answers below.

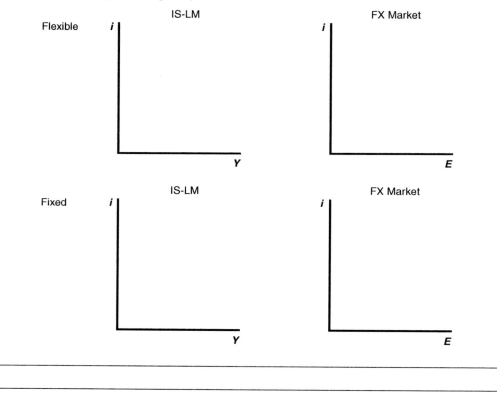

_____

_____

_____

Problem 14: (Multiple Choice) Which of the following complicates the use of stabilization policy?

  a. lag in information collection

  b. slow response of investors to changes in interest rates

  c. J curve effects

  d. all of the above

  e. none of the above

15

Fixed versus Floating: International Monetary Experience

Overview

This chapter discusses the benefits and costs of a fixed exchange rate system relative to a flexible exchange rate system. The primary benefit of the fixed exchange rate system is that it lowers the cost of international transactions by reducing exchange rate volatility. Hence, the benefits for Country A of fixing its exchange rate to the currency of Country B are likely to be large when Country A and Country B engage in a high volume of transactions. The primary cost of a fixed exchange rate system is that a country that pegs the value of its currency to the currency of another has to adopt the monetary policy of that country. Thus, the costs facing Country A to fix its exchange rate to the currency of Country B will be low when the two countries are exposed to similar economic shocks, so the monetary policy appropriate for Country B is also appropriate for Country A. For developing countries, there may be additional benefits to a fixed exchange rate system. First, a country whose external wealth is very sensitive to currency movements may shield itself from wealth shocks by fixing its exchange rate. Second, a country that lacks a credible monetary anchor (a poor reputation for inflation) may see the loss of monetary policy autonomy as a partial blessing.

In practice, many exchange rate systems can be quite large and complex. The Bretton Woods system, for instance, included most of the world's developed countries. This system had formal arrangements that were designed to discourage competitive devaluations and other beggar-thy-neighbor policies that had plagued earlier monetary systems. The level of international cooperation necessary to maintain exchange rate systems is often lacking, however, and a system may therefore eventually collapse.

1 Exchange Rate Regime Choice: Key Issues

ESSENTIAL CONCEPTS

Some countries fix the value of their currency in terms of another, whereas others allow their currency to float freely. A country that has chosen a fixed or floating exchange rate one year might change its mind the next. Differences across time and across countries in countries' choices of exchange rate regimes reflect differences in the magnitude of the costs and benefits of fixing an exchange rate. The benefits of fixing the value of one country's in terms of another country's currency (the *base* or *center currency*) is that the peg reduces the degree of uncertainty in cross-border transactions, by eliminating exchange rate volatility. Empirical studies have shown that a reduction in exchange rate volatility allows the volume of trade in goods, services, and assets between the countries to expand. The cost of a fixed exchange rate system is that the country fixing finds that it cannot follow a monetary policy that is independent of the base country. Because a fixed exchange rate eliminates a country's ability to pursue an independent monetary policy, countries that fix their exchange rate tend to be less stable than those with floating exchange rate systems.

Two countries should be part of a fixed exchange rate system if they are sufficiently similar in terms of the economic shocks (common stabilization priorities) and if their markets are sufficiently integrated. This idea is captured in the *symmetry-integration diagram* shown in Figure 15-1. Above the fix line at a point like *B*, the two countries are either sufficiently integrated or experience sufficiently similar shocks (or shocks that are not too asymmetric) to make a fixed exchange rate system viable. Below the fix line at a point like *A*, the two countries would be better not to be part of the same fixed exchange rate system.

FIGURE 15-1

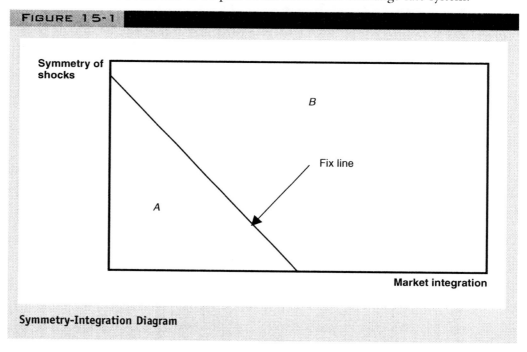

Symmetry of shocks

B

Fix line

A

Market integration

Symmetry-Integration Diagram

Over time, two countries could become more appropriate partners for a fixed exchange rate system moving from *A* toward *B,* or they could grow less appropriate, moving from *B* to *A*. It is therefore not surprising that fixed exchange rate systems come and go.

KEY TERMS

Use the space below to record your notes on the following key terms.

Gold standard _____

_____

_____

Base currency _____

_____

_____

Center currency _____

_____

_____

Asymmetric shock _____

_____

_____

Symmetry-integration diagram _____

_____

_____

REVIEW QUESTIONS

Problem 1: Home fixes its exchange rate relative to Foreign (the center country). Suppose that Home is hit by a negative shock to investment that lowers Home's output but has no effect on Foreign's output. Assume that Foreign does not adjust its policies. Must Home remove its fixed exchange rate in order to stabilize its economy?

_____

_____

....

Problem 1 reminds us that adopting a fixed exchange rate does not prevent a country from using fiscal policy to stabilize the economy.   **TIPS**

....

Problem 2: Why might a country that had previously pegged its exchange rate to one currency begin to peg its currency to another? _____

_____

_____

Problem 3: Suppose that Texas and Massachusetts were countries with their own currencies (the steer and the bean, respectively). Is it obvious that Texas would benefit from fixing the steer to the bean? _____

_____

_____

Problem 4: Why might a country with a fixed exchange rate contemplate capital controls?

_____

_____

_____

2   Other Benefits of Fixing

ESSENTIAL CONCEPTS

A fixed exchange rate system may benefit developing countries through additional mechanisms. First, for a country with a poor history of managing inflation, a fixed exchange rate system may be the only credible nominal anchor. Second, a fixed exchange rate may benefit countries whose external liabilities are denominated in major foreign currencies like the dollar, whereas their assets tend to be primarily in domestic currency. Countries exhibiting liability dollarization find that their total wealth is highly sensitive to exchange rate movements: A depreciation of the country's currency can swell the value of its liabilities relative to its assets. Developing countries are more likely to exhibit such a currency mismatch because foreigners are reluctant to expose themselves to the exchange risk associated with buying local currency assets. Countries with poor institutional histories are said to suffer from original sin: A country cannot borrow abroad in its own currency, because of its reputation.

When a country's foreign exchange liabilities outweigh its foreign exchange assets, a depreciation of its currency makes its citizens poorer by raising the value of its liabilities relative to its assets. If this loss of wealth suppresses consumption and investment, then depreciation can actually depress rather than stimulate output. This possibility is supported by empirical evidence: Countries experiencing losses of wealth due to dramatic depreciations experience large reductions in output. Given the problems associated with exchange rate movements that occur under a flexible exchange rate system, many developed countries are said to have a *fear of floating*.

These additional benefits of a fixed exchange rate lower the threshold tradeoff between symmetry of shocks and degree of economic integration necessary to induce a country to adopt a fixed exchange rate system. It is therefore not surprising that fixed exchange rate systems are relatively common among small, developing countries.

KEY TERMS

Use the space below to record your notes on the following key term.

Fear of floating _____

_____

_____

REVIEW QUESTIONS

Problem 5: The Republic of Inflationstan announces that it will fix its currency to the U.S. dollar in order to control inflation, a perennial problem in the country. Why might you be skeptical about the likelihood that the country will tame inflation? _____

_____

_____

Problem 6: Home's currency, the blott, is fixed in terms of the U.S. dollar. Home has external assets of \$100 million and external liabilities of €100 million. Suppose the dollar depreciates against the euro from $E_{\$/€} = 1$ to $E_{\$/€} = 1.5$.

6a. What is the impact of the currency movements on Home's net external wealth?

_____

_____

_____

6b. What is the impact of the currency movement on Home's national output if the behavior of consumers and investors is sensitive to total wealth? _____

_____

_____

Problem 7: Most of Home's trade is with the European Union, but most of Home's net foreign liabilities are denominated in U.S. dollars. Discuss the challenge facing Home in determining its foreign exchange regime. _____

_____

_____

....

Problem 7 sheds some light on why countries sometimes fix their currency relative to a basket of other currencies.

TIPS

....

Problem 8: Why might a country have a difficult time borrowing in its own currency?

_____

_____

3 Fixed Exchange Rate Systems

ESSENTIAL CONCEPTS

Fixed exchange rate systems can involve many countries. Examples of complex fixed exchange rate systems include the Bretton Woods System, developed after World War II, and the European Exchange Rate Mechanism (ERM). These systems are based on a *reserve currency* system in which the member countries fix the value of their currency relative to a single reserve currency, such as the U.S. dollar, or in terms of a commodity, such as the gold standard. A key feature of these systems, with the exception of the gold standard, is that only the country of the reserve currency is able to pursue an independent monetary policy. However, each country within the exchange rate system might be hit by an economic shock that is special to that country. The key question addressed in this section, therefore, is what kinds of *cooperative arrangements* can be established in order to facilitate burden-sharing across countries.

Suppose that one country within a reserve currency system is hit by an adverse shock so that its output falls below its full employment level. Because the country's interest rates must be fixed to maintain the fixed exchange rate, the country cannot unilaterally ease its monetary policy to combat this shock. There are two mechanisms that could be used to maintain the fixed exchange rate system while simultaneously maintaining the fix. First, all countries within the system could agree to lower their interest rates a little, but not as much as the country receiving the adverse shock would like. In this way the adverse shock is partially stabilized in the directly affected country, whereas the other countries find their economies slightly overstimulated. Alternatively, the adversely affected country could *devalue* its currency by changing the rate at which its currency trades for the reserve currency. In this case, the phenomenon of expenditure switching steers some aggregate demand away from other countries in the reserve system to the devaluing country. In this case, the devaluing country stabilizes its economy at the expense of other reserve currency system countries. Non-cooperative devaluations are a *beggar-thy-neighbor* policy that raises frictions among system members.

KEY TERMS

Use the space below to record your notes on the following key terms.

Fixed exchange rate systems _____

_____

_____

Reserve currency system _____

_____

_____

Cooperative arrangements _____

_____

_____

Devaluation _____

_____

_____

Revaluation _____

_____

_____

Beggar-thy-neighbor policy _____

_____

_____

REVIEW QUESTIONS

Problem 9: Suppose that Home and Foreign are two countries that are (non-center) members of a reserve currency system. Both countries are initially in full employment.

9a. Suppose that Foreign cuts its taxes. If Home's government takes no action, what happens to Home's output?

_____

_____

9b. Now suppose that Foreign revalues its currency. If Home's government takes no action, what happens to Home's output?

_____

_____

Problem 10: Why might it be desirable to fix the value of your currency to gold rather than to fix it to the currency of another country?

_____

_____

Problem 11: Suppose that Home fixes the value of its currency relative to Foreign. Foreign complains that Home's currency is now "undervalued."

11a. If Foreign takes no action, what is the impact of Home's action on Foreign's national output?

_____

_____

11b. Can Foreign use monetary policy to offset the effect of Home's action on Foreign's national output? If so, what is the impact on Foreign's trade balance?

_____

_____

···

Problem 9 points out that there are all kinds of interconnections between countries, even in the presence of a fixed exchange rate system.

Problem 11 captures some of the flavor of the recent economic history of relations between China and the United States.

TIPS

···

4 International Monetary Experience

ESSENTIAL CONCEPTS

This section uses the conceptual framework developed in this chapter to interpret the modern history of the exchange rate systems. A key tenet of this framework is that one of the most important benefits of fixing the exchange rate is to facilitate international trade and other transactions. The rapid growth of such transactions during the period 1870 to 1914 explains in part why the number of countries pegging their currency to gold increased from 15% to 70%. Moreover, as more countries pegged their currency to gold, the integration benefit increased to other countries doing the same. This is an example of a network externality.

The collapse of the gold standard can also be understood through the framework. The collapse of world trade during World War I and the subsequent increase in protectionism after the war reduced the benefit of a fixed exchange rate system. Further, the rising political activism in countries previously controlled by a handful of elites made the instability costs of a fixed exchange rate system more relevant. Finally, during the interwar period, countries were buffeted by asymmetric economic shocks, and the practice of beggar-thy-neighbor–type devaluations increased the cost of pegging to gold.

World War II ushered out the gold standard from the international stage permanently. The Bretton Woods System designed by the United States and the United Kingdom in the waning years of the war was a reserve currency system in which all participating countries pegged their currencies to the dollar while the United States in turn pegged its currency to gold. Initially most countries participating in the system imposed capital controls in order to allow themselves some monetary policy autonomy. Over time, however, these capital controls became hard to enforce. The subsequent decline in monetary policy autonomy combined with growing concerns that the United States would remove the peg on gold led to the demise of this fixed exchange rate system in 1971. Since then, countries have chosen their exchange rate regime based on narrow, individual needs, with substantial variation across countries in the choice of regime and with substantial variation over time.

REVIEW QUESTIONS

Problem 12: Under the Bretton Woods System, the United States was accused of exporting its inflation. If the center country in an exchange rate system increases its money supply, what is the impact on the price levels in the other countries in the system? _____

_____

_____

Problem 13: Why does it become more attractive to fix your currency to the same currency to which other countries are fixing their currency? _____

_____

_____

Problem 14: Why do capital controls make a fixed exchange rate system easier to manage?

_____

_____

_____

Answers to Study Guide Problems

The Global Economy

1. In the example given in the book, the United States has a large trade deficit with China. But this does not mean that the goods are built entirely in China. In fact, China imports a lot of inputs from other countries, which in turn are part of the value of the good. In a sense, then, these imports contain value added from many countries.

2. Small countries that have many nearby trading partners have higher ratios of trade to GDP. Because the internal market is so large in a country like the United States, its international trade is a relatively small portion of its total output.

3. Hong Kong and Malaysia import a lot of goods, add a little value to these goods, and then re-export them to the rest of the world. The trade volumes are "gross" in the sense that they include value added from abroad, but GDP is "net" in the sense that it includes only local value added.

4. There have been two "golden eras" of globalization interrupted by a very long period when countries were more inward looking. The extent of outward orientation of an economy (the degree of globalization) depends in large part on government policies. A big increase in trade barriers can stop globalization.

5. False. There are substantial volumes of migration between countries at similar levels of development. It is important to remember that restrictions on immigration have a strong impact on who can move where.

6. A country may produce the same good in many different countries if the cost of shipping the good is high or if there are high tariffs. Either trade barrier makes local production desirable.

7. Vertical FDI is more likely to lead to an expansion of trade. Production of a good is moved overseas with the intention of lowering the cost of production. For instance, a U.S. multinational may produce washing machines in Mexico for the U.S. market. Horizontal FDI is more likely to lead to a contraction of trade because firms are substituting local production for exports from the country in which the multinational originates.

8. The price of all foreign goods, services, and financial assets relative to domestic goods, services, and financial assets changes with the exchange rate.

9. An appreciation of the exporters' currency puts them at a disadvantage relative to foreigners, whereas a depreciation puts them at an advantage.

10. Brazil's country risk is $10\% - 4\% = 6\%$.

11a. It should decline as the country is forced to borrow more.

11b. Capital gains might improve the country's external wealth by enough to offset borrowing.

12. Anything that eases the cost of international transactions, including policy changes and technological improvements, such as improved communication and transport technology.

2

Trade and Technology: The Ricardian Model

1a. There is more than one way to arrive at this answer. The first is to reproduce the method used in the textbook: Calculate how many shirts can be produced if all 100 workers make shirts (100 workers · 2 shirts per worker), plot that on the Y axis, make the same calculation for the X axis (100 workers · 5 apples per worker), and then draw a line between them. The slope is then the rise (200) over the run (−500).

A more complicated (but illuminating) alternative is to formulate an equation for the PPF. Suppose that L_A is the number of workers making apples and L_S is the number of workers making shirts. If all workers are employed (which we assume!), then $100 = L_A + L_S$. The technology means that the amount of apples produced is $Q_A = 5 \cdot L_A$ and the amount of shirts produced is $Q_S = 2 \cdot L_S$. Combining this information we have

$$100 = \frac{Q_S}{2} + \frac{Q_A}{5} \Rightarrow Q_S = 200 - \frac{2}{5}Q_A.$$

This is the equation that is graphed in Figure 2-2.

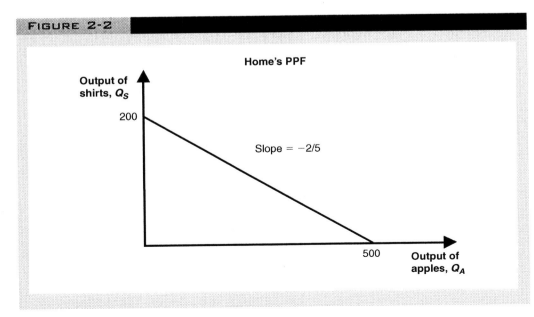

FIGURE 2-2

Home's PPF

Output of shirts, Q_S

200

Slope = −2/5

500

Output of apples, Q_A

1b. We have assumed that the technology features no *diminishing returns*. No matter how many apples or shirts are being made, one worker can produces two shirts, or five apples. Thus, if one more worker is taken out of making shirts, the output of shirts always falls by 2 and the amount of apples always goes up by 5.

1c. The opportunity cost of apples is 2/5 shirts. This is the absolute value of the slope of the PPF drawn in problem 1a but only because apples are on the X axis and shirts are on the Y axis. To produce one more apple, 1/5 of a worker is required because $MPL_A = 5$. The 1/5 of a worker could produce 2/5 of a shirt (1/5 workers · 2 shirts per worker).

1d. The opportunity cost of shirts is 5/2 apples. This is *not* the slope of the PPF drawn in problem 1 because apples are on the X axis and shirts are on the Y axis. To produce one more shirt, 1/2 of a worker is required because $MPL_S = 2$. The 1/2 of a worker could produce 5/2 of a shirt (1/2 workers · 5 apples per worker).

1e. This is illustrated in Figure 2-3.

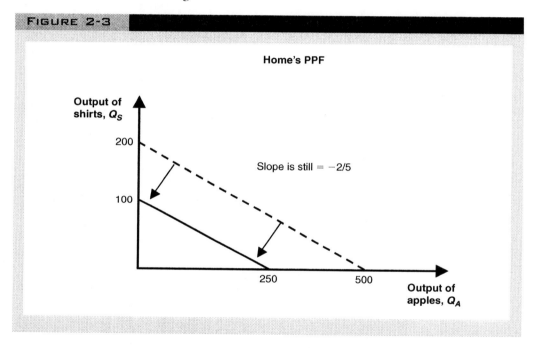

FIGURE 2-3

Home's PPF

1f. Changing a country's size just changes the X and Y intercepts, but it does not change the slope of the PPF and so does not affect the opportunity of cost of one good in terms of the other.

1g. In exactly the same way as it did in problem 1e, the PPF shifts inward so that the intercepts are half of what they had been before. See Figure 2-3.

1h. See Figure 2-4.

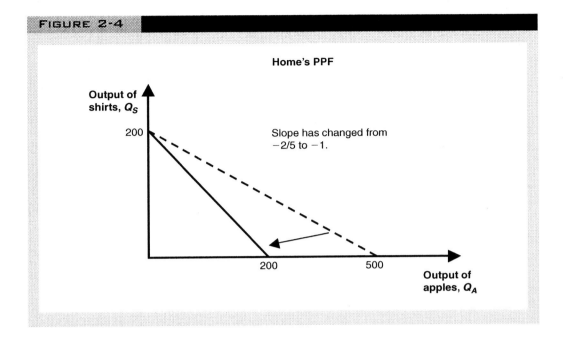

FIGURE 2-4

Home's PPF

Output of shirts, Q_S

200

Slope has changed from −2/5 to −1.

200   500

Output of apples, Q_A

1i. This change alters the opportunity cost of apples in terms of shirts because it has changed Home's "technology" in only one of the two goods. Now to make one apple, 1/2 of a worker is needed. Moving a worker out of the shirt industry reduces shirt production by 1/2 worker · 2 shirts per worker = 1 shirt.

2a. Firms are willing to supply any mixture of goods on the PPF (see Figure 2-2). A firm that makes shirts is willing to hire a worker if the cost of doing so is no greater than the value of sales generated by hiring that worker. A shirt-making firm will then hire a worker if the wage is no more than

$$MPL_S \cdot P_S = 2 \, \frac{\text{shirts}}{\text{worker}} \cdot \frac{\$5}{\text{shirt}} = \frac{\$10}{\text{worker}}.$$

An apple-making firm will hire a worker if the wage is no more than

$$MPL_A \cdot P_A = 5 \, \frac{\text{apples}}{\text{worker}} \cdot \frac{\$2}{\text{apple}} = \frac{\$10}{\text{worker}}.$$

A worker creates $10 worth of output making either good. Perfect competition and the fact that workers are free to move between industries mean that the wage must equal $10. Because firms make zero profits whatever level of output they produce (at the prices given), they are willing to make as much as consumers want of either good as long as the PPF allows it.

2b. The firms will produce 500 apples. Plugging the information into the equations in the previous answer, it should be clear that one worker will create $20 of sales making apples and only $10 of sales making shirts. The wage of workers will then be bid up to $20 and so make it impossible for a shirt-making firm to break even. All workers then make apples, and the maximum number of apples they can make is 500.

3a. The budget constraint is

$$D_S = \frac{\$100}{\$1/2} - \frac{\$1/5}{\$1/2} \cdot D_A = 200 - 2/5 \cdot D_A.$$

This equation is graphed in Figure 2-5. If you did problem 1, this graph should look familiar. If the prices charged by firms reflect the opportunity costs in production, then the consumer's budget constraint is the same as the PPF in the Ricardian model.

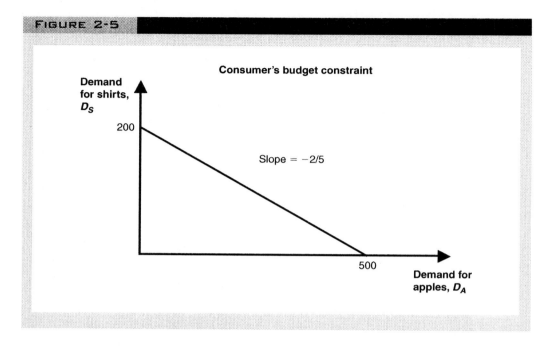

FIGURE 2-5

Consumer's budget constraint

Demand for shirts, D_S

200

Slope = $-2/5$

500

Demand for apples, D_A

3b. There would be no change in the graph. Plugging the information into the budget constraint equation gives you exactly the same equation as for the last question. Equivalently, if the consumer were to spend all her income on shirts, she could buy $200/($1 per shirt) = 200 shirts. If the consumer were to spend all her income on apples she could buy $200/($0.40 per apple) = 500 apples. A straight line drawn between these two points on the graph will have a slope of $-2/5$ (see Figure 2-5).

3c. See Figure 2-6. The opportunity cost of an apple for the consumer has gone up even though the dollar price of an apple stays the same! Now, it costs the consumer 4/5 of a shirt to purchase one additional apple.

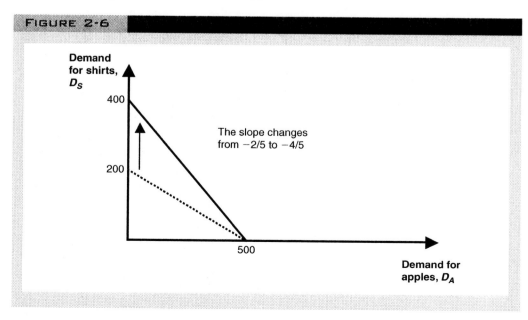

FIGURE 2-6

Demand for shirts, D_S

400

200

The slope changes from $-2/5$ to $-4/5$

500

Demand for apples, D_A

3d. See Figure 2-7. The opportunity cost of an apple has fallen by half. To obtain one more apple one needs only give up 1/5 of a shirt rather than 2/5 of a shirt.

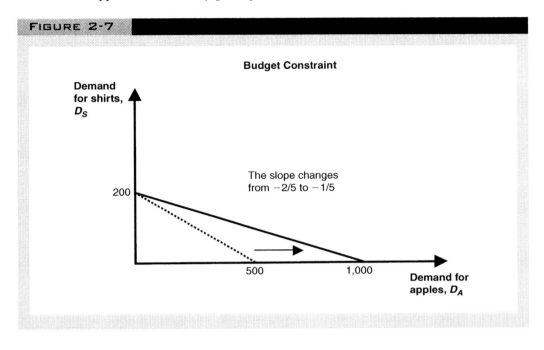

FIGURE 2-7

Budget Constraint

Demand for shirts, D_S

The slope changes from $-2/5$ to $-1/5$

200

500   1,000

Demand for apples, D_A

4a. Because consumers like more of both goods, when given a choice between A, B, and C, the consumer would always choose C.

4b. If given a choice between A and B, there is no way of knowing which will be chosen because the consumer gets the same amount of satisfaction out of both A and B.

4c. See Figure 2-8.

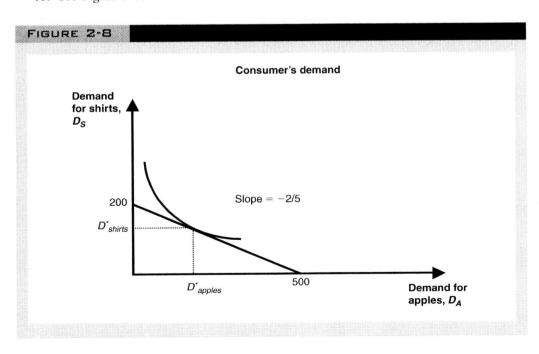

FIGURE 2-8

Consumer's demand

Demand for shirts, D_S

200

D^*_{shirts}

Slope $= -2/5$

D^*_{apples} 500

Demand for apples, D_A

4d. See Figure 2-9.

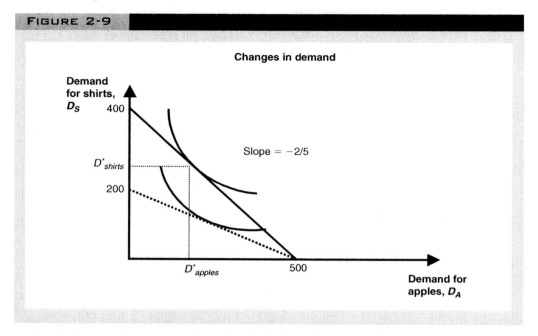

FIGURE 2-9

Changes in demand

5a. As long as the relative price of apples is 2/5, firms are willing to produce anywhere along the PPF. Whatever firms produce, workers' wages will equal the value of the sales of those firms because of perfect competition (and the fact that they are the only factor). Given this income and relative prices, workers' budget constraint is the same as the PPF. Whatever bundle they choose (where the indifference curve is tangent to the budget constraint), firms will supply. An example of an equilibrium is shown in Figure 2-10.

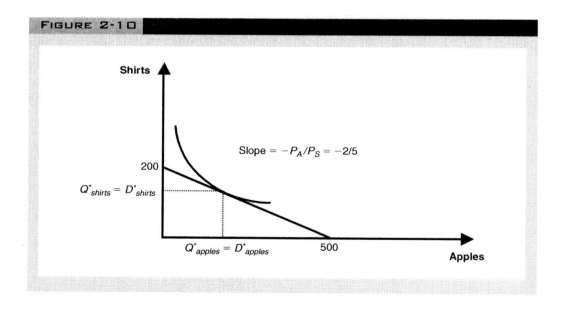

FIGURE 2-10

5b. In Figure 2-11, the quantity of apples demanded and supplied rises and the quantity of shirts demanded and supplied falls as the technology for producing apples improves. Note, however, that given the outward shift in the budget constraint, the consumer is free to consume more of both goods. The consumer purchases fewer shirts because apples have become relatively cheaper. Notice that the indifference curves will *not* cross.

FIGURE 2-11

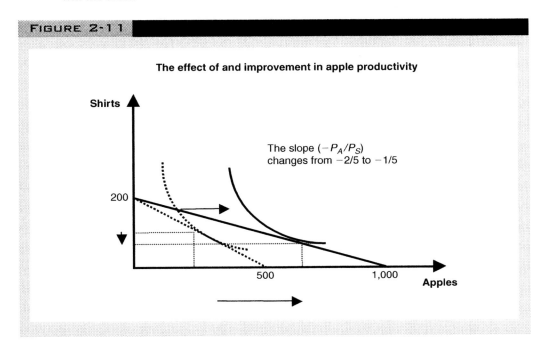

The effect of and improvement in apple productivity

The slope $(-P_A/P_S)$ changes from $-2/5$ to $-1/5$

5c. The higher relative price of apples on world markets induces apple firms to expand, driving up the wage and driving shirt producers out of business. Hence, the economy produces only apples. The income of workers is then 500 apples, which are worth P_A, so that their budget constraint is

$$P_A 500 = P_A D_A + P_S D_S.$$

After some algebra, the country's budget constraint (or consumption possibilities frontier (CPF) becomes

$$D_S = \frac{P_A}{P_S} 500 - \frac{P_A}{P_S} D_A = 500 - D_A,$$

which is graphed in Figure 2-12.

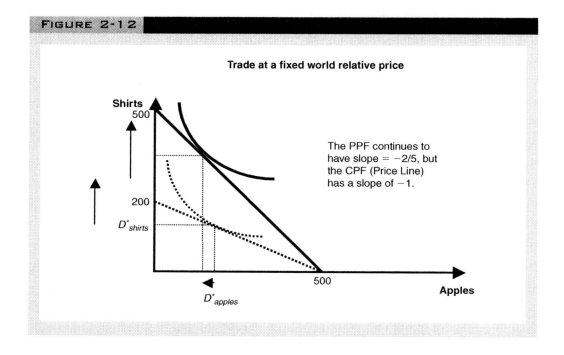

FIGURE 2-12

Trade at a fixed world relative price

The PPF continues to have slope = −2/5, but the CPF (Price Line) has a slope of −1.

6a. For Foreign to have a comparative advantage in apples, the opportunity cost in production for apples in Foreign must be less than one. Hence, a marginal product of labor in shirts in Foreign can be any number less than 6. If it were less than 4, then Home would also have an absolute advantage in shirts.

6b. There are no gains from trade if the opportunity cost of producing each good is the same in both countries. Because the opportunity cost of apples is one shirt in Home, any numbers for which the marginal product of labor was the same in both goods would create a situation in which there was no comparative advantage and so no gains from trade. For the wage to be twice as high in Foreign, Foreign labor must be twice as productive (in both goods in this case), so MPL for apples and shirts in Foreign must be 8.

7. The good in which a country has a comparative advantage will have a lower relative price than in the other country, and the opposite will be true of the good in which it has a comparative disadvantage. Firms in the industry of comparative advantage will find that their lower-priced good is demanded in the foreign market, where the price of the good is higher, so these firms will expand into the foreign market, creating exports. Firms in the industry of comparative disadvantage will find that their higher-priced good is uncompetitive with the foreign market, where the price of the good is lower, so the foreign firms will expand into the home market, creating imports. A trade equilibrium occurs where the value of exports equals the value of imports at new world prices

8a. The price of apples in terms of shirts P_A / P_S must lie between the autarky (no-trade equilibrium) relative prices in Foreign and Home, respectively. For if $P_A / P_S > 1$, then both countries would produce exclusively apples, and if $P_A / P_S < 3/4$, both countries would produce exclusively shirts. Hence, for both goods to be produced it must

be the case that $3/4 \leq \dfrac{P_A}{P_S} \leq 1$.

8b. Foreign has a comparative advantage in apples because the opportunity cost of producing apples is lower than in Home. Hence, Foreign will export apples and import shirts. Because the question assumes that the world relative price is halfway between the no-trade equilibrium prices in each country, it must be true that $P_A / P_S = 7/8$ (halfway between 8/8 and 6/8). Because the price of apples in a trading equilibrium is higher than in the no-trade equilibrium, producers in Foreign specialize in apples. Given world prices, if the consumers in Foreign traded all their apples for shirts, they could afford 700 of them $(7/8 \cdot 800)$. The tangency of the indifference curve with the consumption possibilities frontier gives the actual amount demanded. The country exports $800 - D^*_{apples}$ units of apples and imports D^*_{shirts}. Foreign is illustrated in panel (a) of Figure 2-13, and Home is shown in panel (b).

FIGURE 2-13

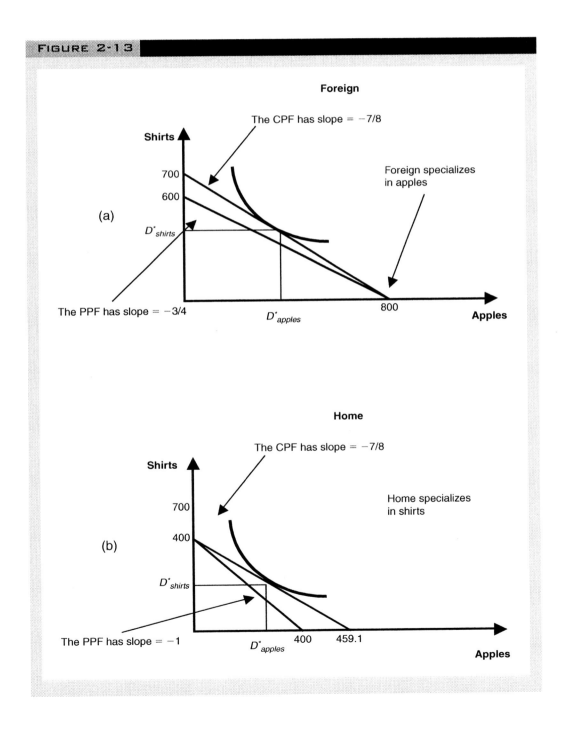

9a. The first step is to identify which good Home exports. Because the opportunity cost of shirts is lower in Home than in Foreign, Home will export shirts. Producers in Home are willing to make up to 400 units of shirts as long as the relative price of shirts is 1 and at this relative price consumers buy 225 shirts ($400 - 175 = 225$). This means that if Home is fully specialized in shirts and consumers buy 225 of them, there are 175 shirts available to export. This explains the flat portion of the export supply function shown in Figure 2-14. To get any more shirts available for export, Home consumers have to cut back their demand, which they will do if the relative price of shirts rises. The supply curve is getting steeper because consumers become less willing to substitute shirts for apples. Note also that Home can never export more than 400 shirts because this is the maximum amount of shirts that Home is capable of making!

FIGURE 2-14

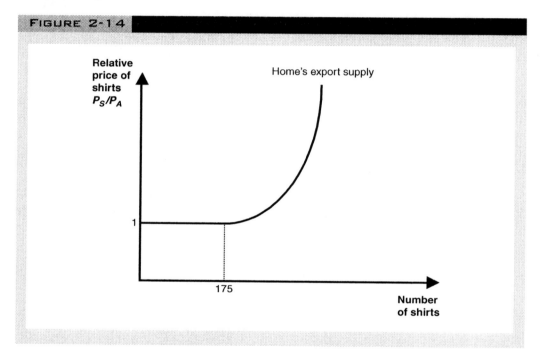

9b. Home export supply and foreign import demand is shown in Figure 2-15. If the world relative price of shirts in Foreign is 4/3, the foreign producers are willing to produce both goods. In this situation, Foreign shirt firms will produce some of the domestic consumption of 300 and import the rest on the flat portion of Foreign's import demand. If the world relative price of shirts falls below 4/3, then there is no production of shirts in Foreign and Foreign consumers start to buy more of the now cheaper good. Hence Foreign's imports begin to rise. This explains the downward-sloping part of Foreign's import demand.

FIGURE 2-15

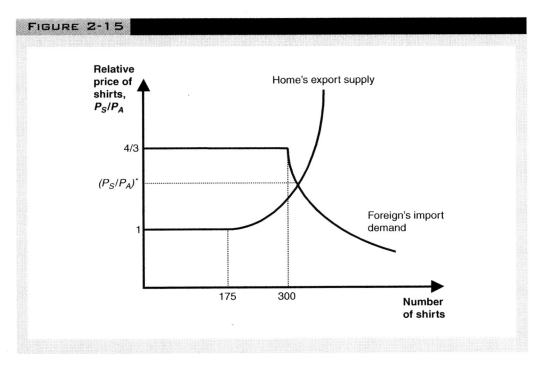

9c. Doubling the size of Home's economy doubles both its ability to produce and its desire to consume. Hence, as shown in Figure 2-16, when Home is completely specialized in producing shirts but the relative price of shirts is still 1, its consumers will produce 800 shirts, of which it will consume 450 shirts, leaving 350 for export. The shift in the export supply curve will reduce Home's *terms of trade,* that is, the value of what it exports in terms of the price of what it imports. The case shown here has Home not fully specialized in its export good; that is, it continues to produce some, but not all, of its import good. The reduction in Home's terms of trade could have been less extreme if the foreign import demand curve for shirts was not so sharply sloped downward.

FIGURE 2-16

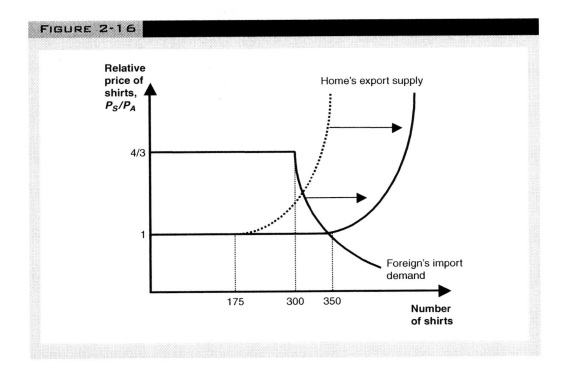

3

Gains and Losses from Trade in the Specific-Factors Model

1a. If the use of both inputs is doubled, then the volume of output is doubled as well. This is an example of a "constant returns to scale" technology.

1b. If the use of only one input is increased, then output will rise but at a decreasing rate. If labor is increased by a factor of 2, then output will increase by a factor of $\sqrt{2}$. Note that it is the same constant returns to scale technology, but there are diminishing returns if only one factor is increased.

1c. Suppose that there are 100 units of capital, so that $Q_M = 10\sqrt{L_M}$. A reduction of employment by 1 lowers output by $\Delta Q_M = 10\left(\sqrt{L_M} - \sqrt{L_M - 1}\right)$. Plugging in the numbers and using a calculator to solve it, reducing employment by one unit lowers output more when $L_M = 10$ than when $L_M = 100$. This highlights the implications of diminishing marginal product of labor.

2a. The opportunity cost of M in terms of A is given by the absolute value of the slope of the PPF. This is higher at point 2 than point 1. Figure 3-1 shows an example of an "increasing opportunity cost PPF."

2b. When all labor is put into Agriculture, the marginal product of labor in Agriculture (MPL_A) is very low (little land per laborer) and the marginal product of labor in Manufacturing (MPL_M) is high (lots of unused machines). Hence, as labor is moved out of Agriculture into Manufacturing, initially there is only a very small drop in Agricultural production and a very large increase in Manufacturing output: The opportunity cost of M in terms of A is low. As more labor is moved, the MPL_A is getting larger and MPL_M is getting smaller. Hence, output of agriculture starts falling at a faster rate and output of manufacturing expands at a slower rate: The opportunity cost of M in terms of A is high.

2c. A profit-maximizing firm will choose a labor force that makes the value of the marginal product of labor equal to the wage. In this example, the value of the marginal product is $20 per worker, so in equilibrium it had better be the case that the wage is $20.

2d. Because $P_M MPL_M = W = P_A MPL_A$ in equilibrium, $MPL_A > MPL_M$ because $P_M > P_A$. Since wages equalize across the industries, the industry with the lower price per unit of output must have the higher marginal productivity of labor.

2e. The value of the marginal product of labor is $40, and workers are being paid only $25. This means that revenues could be expanded by more than costs if another worker is hired. Hence, you are employing too few workers.

2f. If P_M / P_A falls (e.g., suppose that P_M drops while P_A is fixed), then workers will be induced to move out of manufacturing into agriculture. As more workers enter agriculture, the land/labor ratio falls. Hence, the marginal product of labor in agriculture falls. This can be seen directly in Figure 3-3. The fall in the price of a unit of manufacturing goods reduces the value of the marginal product of labor in manufacturing from the dotted curve to the solid curve. This reduction in labor demand lowers the nominal wage and so induces the agricultural industry to expand (a movement along the demand curve for labor in agriculture). Because the amount of land is fixed, the land/labor ratio falls and the marginal product of labor in agriculture falls as well.

FIGURE 3-3

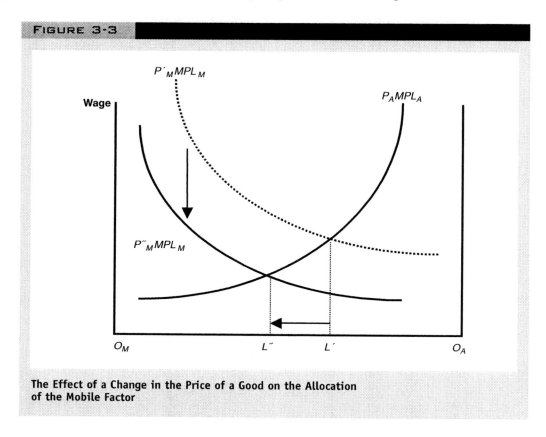

The Effect of a Change in the Price of a Good on the Allocation of the Mobile Factor

3a. See Figure 3-4 on the next page.

FIGURE 3-4

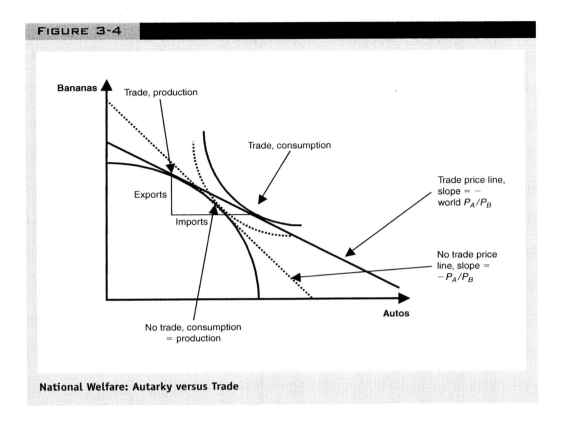

National Welfare: Autarky versus Trade

3b. The country is better off because the opportunity cost of producing a good in autarky is different than the opportunity cost of the good on international markets. By reorganizing production in the country and changing consumption patterns, the country can then expand the production of the good in which its opportunity cost in production is less than the opportunity cost on international markets, thereby obtaining more of both goods. Hence, the country is able to reach a higher indifference curve as shown in Figure 3-4.

3c. Recall that the price of autos in terms of bananas is higher in Foreign than in Home in a no-trade equilibrium. In a trading equilibrium, the relative price of a good must lie between the autarky relative prices of the two countries because if it were not the two countries would like to export the same good. Hence, Foreign adjusts to international trade by cutting back production of autos, expanding production of bananas, and exporting bananas to Home in return for autos. Notice that the law of comparative advantage must hold: A country exports the good in which its autarky relative price is lower and imports the other good.

3d. In a free-trade equilibrium, the two countries face exactly the same relative prices. Producers adjust their production until the ratio of the value of the marginal product of labor is the same in both industries. Hence, the ratio of the marginal product of labor in autos to the marginal product of labor in bananas is the same in both countries. This in turn is equal to the slope of the PPF at the point where production occurs: The opportunity cost of producing autos in terms of bananas must be the same in the two countries.

4a. See Figure 3-5. Note that the diagram already expressed all variables in terms of the price of bananas. So a reduction in the relative price of autos (P_A / P_B) involves the shift in the value of the marginal product of autos when expressed in terms of bananas. This shift induces labor to move from auto production to banana production.

The amount of labor that moves across industries is captured by the distance L_1L_2. The wage expressed in terms of bananas (W / P_B) falls.

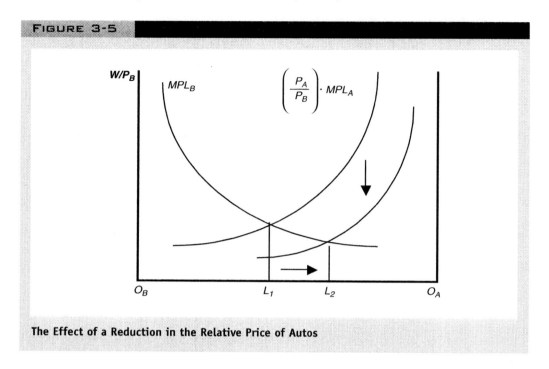

FIGURE 3-5

The Effect of a Reduction in the Relative Price of Autos

4b. Because $P_A MPL_A = W$, it follows that $MPL_A = W / P_A$. MPL_A rises because the amount of labor employed making A declines. Because MPL_A rises, it follows that W / P_A rises. Workers can afford more autos.

4c. Because $P_B MPL_B = W$, it follows that $MPL_B = W / P_B$. Because MPL_B falls (see Figure 3-5), it follows that W / P_B falls. Workers cannot afford as many bananas.

4d. The effect of trade on the well-being of workers is ambiguous if the workers spend their income on both goods.

5a. If labor were truly mobile between industries, then it would move into the higher paid industry until the wages were equalized.

5b. Workers may have skills that they have learned in their industry that cannot be transferred to other industries. Their wages fall when they are displaced because they lack the skills that are valuable to another industry. In some sense, these skills can be thought of as being specific to an industry. This idea helps explain why TAA includes providing retraining to workers displaced by trade.

6a. Because labor is unable to move, the marginal product of labor in computers must stay the same. Hence, the wage must rise by the same amount as the price of computers. This means that the real wage of computer workers in terms of computers is the same. Because the price of tulips has not changed, the real wage of computer workers in terms of tulips has risen.

6b. Because labor is unable to move, the marginal product of labor in tulips must remain the same, so the real wage of tulips in terms of tulips has stayed the same. Because computer prices have risen, however, the real wage of tulip workers in terms of computers has fallen.

7a. See Figure 3-6. (Autarky information is displayed in dotted lines, and trade information is displayed in solid lines.) Home has the higher autarky relative price of autos and so is the exporter of bananas. Home's supply of bananas increases and its supply of autos decreases, whereas the opposite is true in Foreign. Home's consumption of bananas is less than its supply of bananas, and its consumption of autos is greater than its supply of autos. The opposite is true in Foreign.

FIGURE 3-6

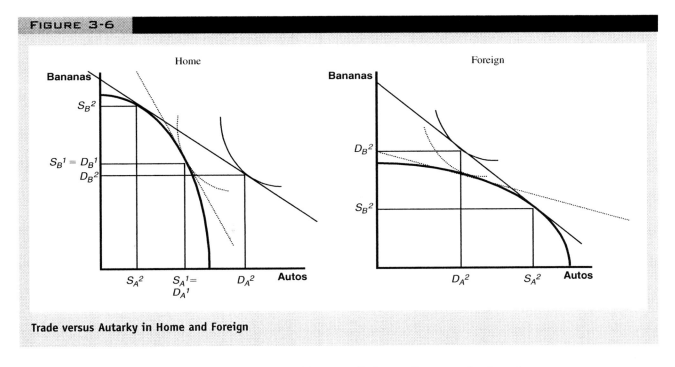

Trade versus Autarky in Home and Foreign

7b. The real rental of capital falls in Home. As labor is pulled out of auto production, the marginal product of capital (*MPK*) falls. Because

$$MPK = \frac{R_K}{P_A},$$

the income of a unit of capital has fallen relative to the price of autos. Now notice that

$$\frac{R_K}{P_B} = \frac{P_A}{P_B} \cdot \frac{R_K}{P_A}.$$

Because P_A / P_B goes down when the country trades, and because R_K / P_A falls as well, the nominal earnings of a unit of capital will buy less of both goods!

7c. Note that the relative price of autos goes up for Foreign, and so the argument for 7b applies here but in reverse. The real rental of capital rises in Foreign.

7d. The demand for land in Home rises as the country increases its production of bananas. The marginal product of land rises as labor is moved from auto production into banana production. The value of the marginal product of land is the demand curve for land.

7e. Because global resources are used more efficiently, both countries can consume more than they did when they were not trading. Because the country gains-from-trade means that winners win more than losers lose, the winners could compensate the losers and everyone could be made better off.

4

Trade and Resources:
The Heckscher-Ohlin Model

1a. The answer is displayed in Figure 4-5. Shoes have a higher labor/capital ratio than computers when the wage/rental ratio is high and have a relatively low labor/capital ratio when the wage/rental ratio is low. Hence, one cannot call either good labor or capital intensive. The Heckscher-Ohlin model explicitly rules out this possibility!

FIGURE 4·5

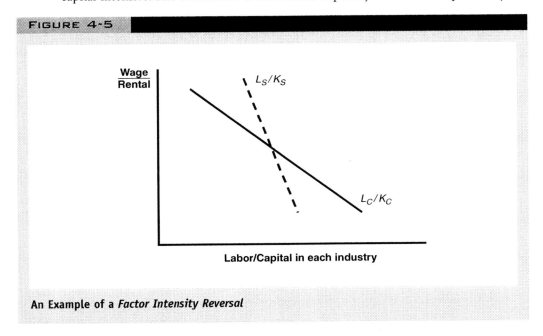

An Example of a *Factor Intensity Reversal*

1b. Factor abundance is measured as the ratio of the endowments of the factors. The capital/labor ratio in Home is 2, and it is 2.5 in Foreign. Foreign is capital-abundant relative to Home even though it has less capital than Home.

2a. Because consumers' tastes are the same in every country, the differences in relative prices in the two countries must stem from differences in the shape of the production possibility frontiers. A situation in which Home has a higher relative price of computers in a no-trade equilibrium is shown in Figure 4-6. The curves relevant to Home are represented by solid lines, and curves relevant to Foreign are in dotted lines. Home's PPF is bowed out toward shoes, and Foreign's PPF is bowed out toward computers. Because tastes are the same in both countries, it is the difference in the shape of the PPFs that give rise to the difference in the no-trade equilibrium prices.

Why is Home's PPF bowed out toward shoes and Foreign's PPF bowed out toward computers? As capital is added to an economy, the PPF tends to bow out toward the capital-intensive good (computers in this example). As labor is added to an economy, the PPF bows out in favor of the labor-intensive good (shoes in this example). Thus, Foreign must have a higher capital/labor ratio than Home, so it is relatively capital-abundant.

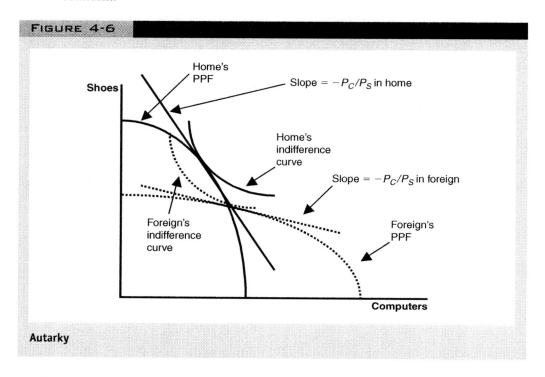

FIGURE 4-6

Autarky

2b. Foreign is producing a higher ratio of computers to shoes in a no-trade equilibrium than Home. The tastes are the same in the two countries, and the relative price of computers is lower in Foreign than in Home. This means that Foreign consumers must be consuming relatively more computers than shoes compared with Home consumers. Because the country must supply its own goods (there is no trade), Foreign must be producing a higher ratio of computers to shoes than Home.

3a. Because Home is labor-abundant relative to Foreign and shirts are labor-intensive relative to airplanes, the *Heckscher-Ohlin theorem* establishes that Home will export shirts.

3b. Assumption six of the Heckscher-Ohlin model is that countries have the same tastes. Because the countries are engaged in free trade, the price of the goods is the same in both countries. Hence, consumers in Foreign consume goods in the same ratio as those in Home.

3c. An increase in the endowment of capital will tend to further skew its PPF toward the capital-intensive good, airplanes. This means that for any relative price of airplanes, Foreign will supply more airplanes and fewer shirts, as shown in the left-hand side of Figure 4-7. As a result, Foreign's export supply curve for airplanes shifts to the right, causing the relative price of airplanes to fall.

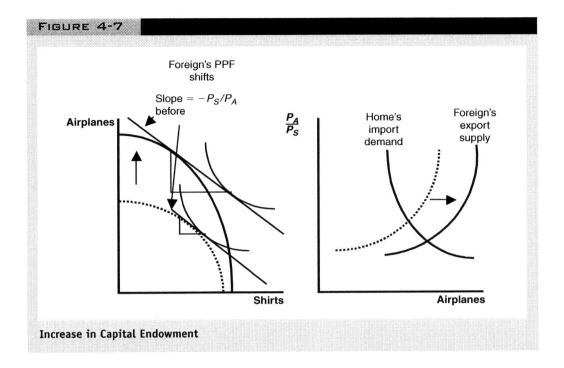

FIGURE 4-7

Increase in Capital Endowment

3d. As established in the last problem, an increase in Foreign's endowment of capital reduces the relative price of airplanes and so increases the relative price of shirts. This is a terms-of-trade improvement for Home, the exporter of shirts. Therefore, Home can get to a higher indifference curve. (See Figure 4-8.) Note that shirt output increases and airplane output falls as a result.

FIGURE 4-8

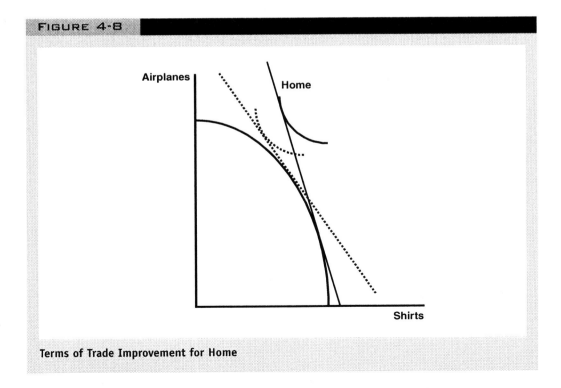

Terms of Trade Improvement for Home

4. Suppose that the capital-abundant country (Foreign) has consumers who have strong preferences for airplanes, whereas the labor-abundant country (Home) has consumers with strong preferences for shirts. Then it is possible that the trade pattern is exactly the opposite of that predicted by the Heckscher-Ohlin theorem, as can be seen in Figure 4-9.

FIGURE 4-9

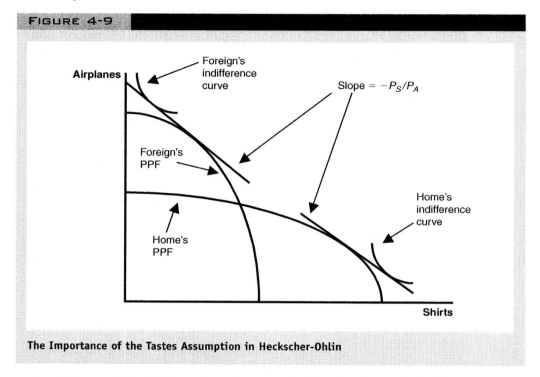

The Importance of the Tastes Assumption in Heckscher-Ohlin

5. There could be (1) factor intensity reversals, (2) technologies that differ across countries, and (3) tastes that differ across countries.

6. If Leontief had found that a bundle of U.S. exports contained a higher ratio of capital to labor than imports, then he would have concluded that the U.S. trade pattern was consistent with Heckscher-Ohlin. There would be no paradox.

7a. Because the country has a larger share of world GDP than it has of labor, it should be a net importer of labor services.

7b. If workers in Home are paid better than in the rest of the world, then they may be more productive than workers elsewhere. In this case, it could be that if effective labor were measured, Home in fact has a share of world effective labor that is greater than its share of GDP.

7c. Yes. A country's relative abundance or scarcity is its share of the world's stock of a type of factor relative to its share of world income. Differences in technologies would show up as differences in shares of the world's income that are not accounted for by differences in factor ownership. A really productive country will appear to be scarce in a larger set of factors and a less productive country will appear to be abundant in a larger set of factors.

8a. The highest relative wage that could occur in this country is 10. The relative demand for the whole economy cannot exceed the relative demand for the shoe industry because it is a weighted average of the relative demands in the two industries.

FIGURE 4-10

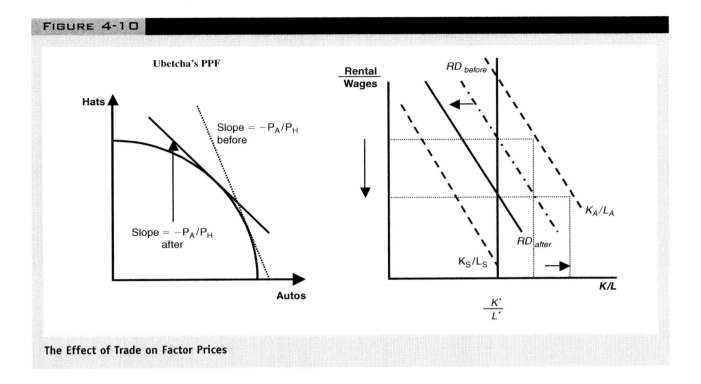

The Effect of Trade on Factor Prices

8b. As resources are moved out of computers and into shoes, the relative demand curve for the economy shifts up. The weights in the weighted average now favor shoes over computers.

8c. An upward shift in the relative demand curve causes the relative wage to rise. Because the industry relative demand curves do not shift, this means that L / K must fall in each industry.

9a. The capital/labor ratio used by Ubetchan producers in both industries would rise. Engaging in free trade would lower the relative price of autos and thereby induce the auto industry to contract and the hat industry to expand. As factors are moved out of autos and into hats, the relative demand for capital would decrease, because autos are relatively more capital-intensive than hats. This is shown as the leftward shift in the relative demand curve in Figure 4-10. The reduction in the relative demand for capital lowers the rental/wage ratio, which induces firms in both the auto and shoe industry to substitute capital for labor. Note that the relative supply of factors in the economy, given by K^* / L^* in Figure 4-10, does not change.

9b. Because the capital/labor ratio used by producers rises, the marginal product of capital should fall, as each machine has fewer workers using it.

9c. A political group that represented the economic interests of capital owners would lobby against free trade. By the Stolper-Samuelson theorem, the decrease in the relative price of the capital-intensive good induced by free trade would lower the real rental and raise the real wage.

10a. By the Heckscher-Ohlin theorem, the United States has a comparative advantage in skill-intensive goods, so free trade raises the price of skill-intensive goods. By the Stolper-Samuelson theorem, trade raises the real income of skilled workers while lowering the real income of unskilled workers. Hence, the Heckscher-Ohlin model is consistent with the survey results.

10b. One would expect exactly the opposite response in a skill-scarce country compared with the response in the skill-abundant country. Trade causes the relative price of goods to move in the opposite direction for this type of country.

11a. Because the two countries are absolutely identical, they should have exactly the same relative price of goods and factors in a no-trade equilibrium. Hence, there is no motive for migration.

11b. Moving capital from Foreign to Home will skew Foreign's PPF (it shrinks but in a skewed way) toward doughnuts and Home's PPF outward toward sofas. The relative price of sofas will fall in Home and rise in Foreign. Applying the Stolper-Samuelson theorem, the real earnings of labor will rise in Home and fall in Foreign. Because they were starting at the same level (before the capital moved), Home must now have a higher real wage than Foreign.

11c. Labor would want to move from Foreign to Home.

11d. The migration of labor from Foreign to Home would tend to skew Home's PPF toward doughnuts and Foreign's PPF toward sofas. This has the opposite impact on the relative price of doughnuts and so has the opposite impact on real wages. Real wages tend to converge between the two countries through the response of goods prices.

11e. Yes, migration causes the relative price of doughnuts to fall (and sofas to rise). By the Stolper-Samuelson theorem, this implies an increase in the real rental to capital.

12. According to the Heckscher-Ohlin model, international trade increases the real income (through the Stolper-Samuelson theorem) of the abundant factor and reduces the real income of the scarce factor. In developing countries, labor is the abundant factor and so should gain from trade. If Bob were educated and fast thinking, he could say, "Oh yeah, what about the Leontief paradox?" Then you'd be pretty much sunk.

5

Movement of Labor and Capital between Countries

1a. The expansion of land increases the marginal product of labor in agriculture for every level of possible employment. Because the prices of goods are fixed on world markets, this change raises the value of the marginal product of labor in agriculture from $P_A MPL_A$ to $P_A MPL'_A$ as illustrated in Figure 5-2. At the old level of employment (measured by the distance $L^* O_A$ in the figure) $P_A MPL'_A > W$, so agricultural firms hire additional labor until the labor employed in A is given by $L' O_A$. This drives up the wage and leads to a movement along the curve $P_M MPL_M$ until $P_M MPL_M = P_A MPL'_A = W'$.

FIGURE 5-2

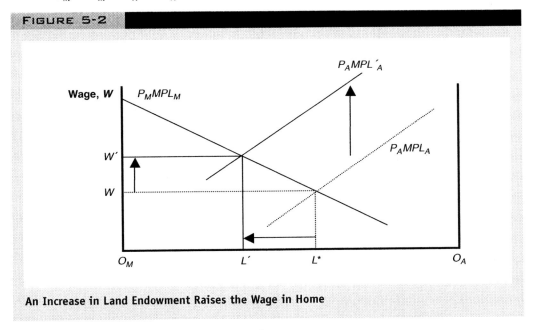

An Increase in Land Endowment Raises the Wage in Home

1b. Immigration leads to an increase in Home's labor endowment and so increases the size of the base of the diagram as illustrated in Figure 5-3. Note that the apparent shift in the $P_A MPL_A$ is not the result of any actual change in the value of the marginal product of labor in agriculture for a given level of employment. It is due to a shift in the origin O_A to the right, reflecting the increase in the labor endowment. The increase in the labor endowment is measured by the distance from O_A to O'_A. The wage will drop as a result of the increase in the endowment of labor. If there are no *moving costs*, then labor will move into Home until its wage level is equal to the world wage level.

FIGURE 5-3

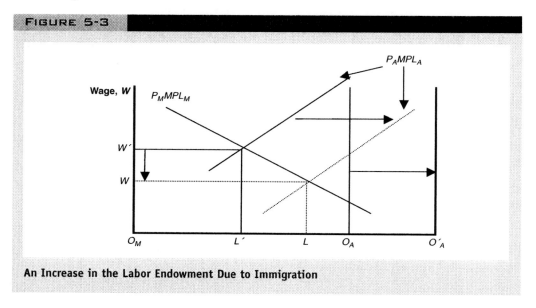

An Increase in the Labor Endowment Due to Immigration

1c. As shown in the answer to 1b, the increase in the endowment of labor reduces the wage. This induces both agriculture and manufacturing to add workers. Hence, the marginal product of capital and the marginal product of land both increase (the capital/labor ratio and the land/labor ratio rise). Because the prices of goods are fixed, this means that the real income of a unit of capital (R_K) and (R_T) both increase. Capitalists and landowners are made better off by immigration.

1d. The PPF shifts outward when more of the mobile factor is available, as shown in Figure 5–4. Because there are more workers employed in both industries after the inflow of workers, the level of output of each good must rise.

FIGURE 5-4

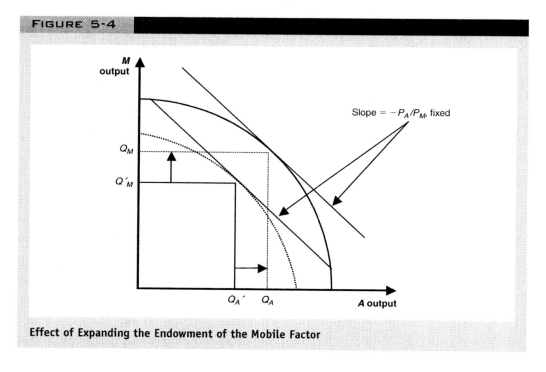

Effect of Expanding the Endowment of the Mobile Factor

2a. Airplanes are capital intensive relative to shirts because the capital/labor ratio is 5/3, which is greater than the capital/labor ratio in shirts, which is 1.

2b. To answer this question, we use the box diagram shown in Figure 5-5. The height of the diagram is the size of the country's endowment of capital, and the length of the base is the original size of the labor endowment. In the diagram, the slope of the line from O_S through point a is equal to 1, which is the capital/labor ratio in shirts, and the slope of the line from a to O_A is equal to 5/3, which is the capital/labor ratio in airplanes. Initially, the amount of capital employed in airplane manufacturing is given by the length of the line from K to O_A and the amount of labor used in making airplanes is given by the length of the line L to O_A. When laborers leave, the box becomes narrower and so we relabel the airplane origin O_A' to reflect this fact. The slope of the line from b to O_A continues to be 5/3. The new intersection at b shows clearly that even though there is less labor available in the country, the amount of labor and capital employed in airplane manufacture has increased!

FIGURE 5-5

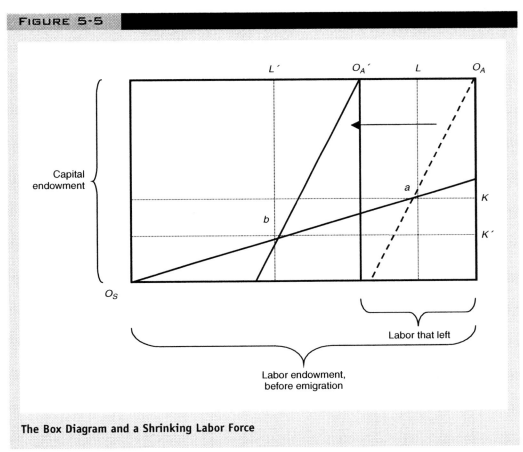

The Box Diagram and a Shrinking Labor Force

2c. Let Q_A be the output of airplanes and Q_S be the output of shirts. Let $\overline{K}$ be the country's endowment of capital, and let $\overline{L}$ be the country's endowment of labor. Using the production information in the question we have

$$\overline{K} = 5 \cdot Q_A + 2 \cdot Q_S$$

and

$$\overline{L} = 3 \cdot Q_A + 2 \cdot Q_S.$$

Doing a little algebra, we find that

$$Q_A = \frac{\overline{K} - \overline{L}}{2} \text{ and } Q_S = \frac{5\overline{L} - 3\overline{K}}{4}.$$

2d. The answer is shown in Figure 5-6. The shift in the PPF is consistent with the Rybczynski theorem in reverse: At fixed relative prices, a decrease in the endowment of labor leads to a reduction in the production of the labor-intensive good and an expansion in the production of the capital-intensive good.

FIGURE 5-6

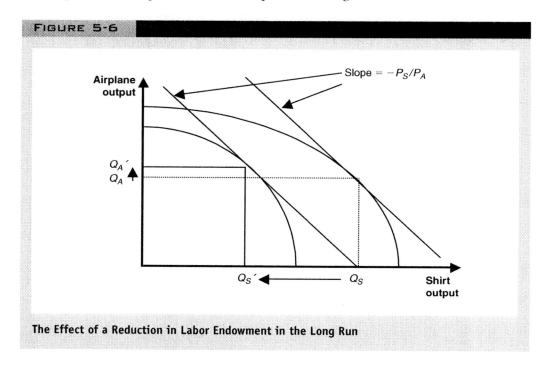

The Effect of a Reduction in Labor Endowment in the Long Run

3a. The entry of computer workers into the country raises the marginal product of capital in the computer industry for any level of capital used in that industry, as shown in Figure 5-7. This induces capital to move into the computer sector, as shown by the shift from K to K'. Because the rental must rise, it must be that the marginal product of capital increases in both industries. This means that marginal product of both computer workers and shirt workers must fall (falling ratio of specific factor to mobile factor in each industry). Hence, both types of workers are hurt.

The fall in real income across computer and shirt workers will not be of the same magnitude, however.

FIGURE 5-7

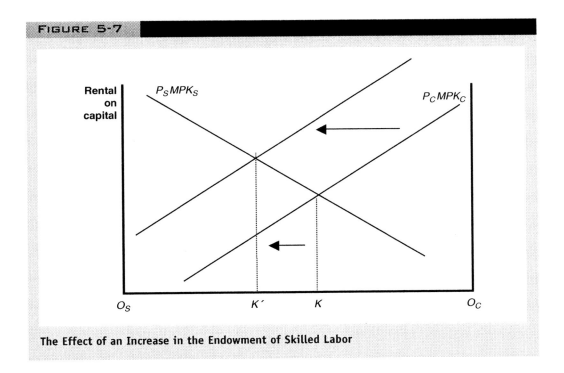

The Effect of an Increase in the Endowment of Skilled Labor

3b. In the long run the factor price insensitivity result must hold: There is no effect on the real wage of either computer or shirt workers. This is because workers can retrain and switch industries in the long run.

3c. In the short run the real rental must rise. Figure 5-7 demonstrates that the rental must rise, and because goods prices are fixed, an increase in the nominal rental is also an increase in the real. In the long run, the factor price insensitivity result must hold so there is no long-run impact on the real rental rate. Output of the labor-intensive good will expand and the capital-to-labor ratios in each industry will return to their normal level.

4a. True. It is estimated that there are 12 million illegal immigrants into the United States, but the number of legal immigrants is much higher. As a portion of the U.S. population, immigrants are most represented among the least and the most educated.

4b. False. Many immigrants into the United States are unskilled. However, a very substantial portion of the most highly skilled workers in the United States are immigrants. There is a U-shaped relationship between immigrants' share of the population and level of educational attainment.

4c. True. Low-skilled apparel industry output expanded and high-skilled industries contracted relative to other American cities.

5a. The problem involves the specific-factors model. Because Home has more labor than Foreign and everything else is the same, the marginal product of labor in Home must be lower than the marginal product of labor in Foreign in both industries. Hence, wages will be lower in Home. If the marginal product of labor is lower in Home than in Foreign in both industries, it must be true that the marginal product of capital is higher in Home than in Foreign. Hence, the rental rate in Home must be higher as well. This creates the motive for capital to leave Foreign, where the rental on capital is low, and enter Home, where the rental on capital is high.

5b. The increase in capital expands Home's PPF in favor of M as in Figure 5-8. Because labor is drawn out of agriculture into manufacturing, the output of agriculture must fall.

FIGURE 5-8

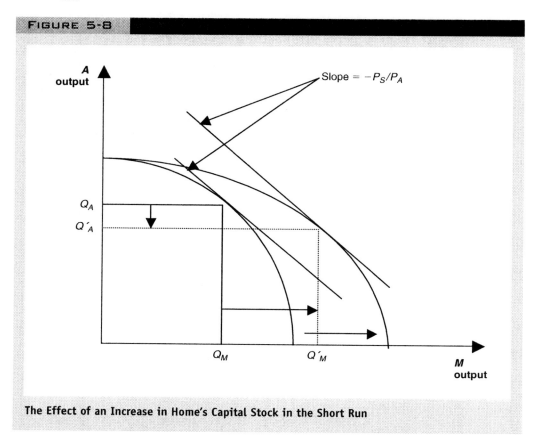

The Effect of an Increase in Home's Capital Stock in the Short Run

5c. The effect of FDI into Home is to raise the real wage. As shown in Figure 5-9, an increase in the capital endowment due to the inflow of capital shifts up the marginal product of labor in manufacturing for every level of manufacturing employment. The new capital increases the demand for labor in manufacturing and so drives up the wage. Because the prices of goods are fixed, this nominal increase in the wage is also a real increase. Because labor is drawn out of agriculture, the land/labor ratio rises so that the marginal product of land falls. Hence the earnings of the owner of a unit of land fall. Note that the capital/labor ratio must rise. To see this, note that the marginal product of labor in manufacturing has risen. For the marginal product of labor to rise in manufacturing, the capital-to-labor ratio must have increased. Hence the marginal product of capital falls, making the earnings of a unit of capital decline in real terms.

FIGURE 5-9

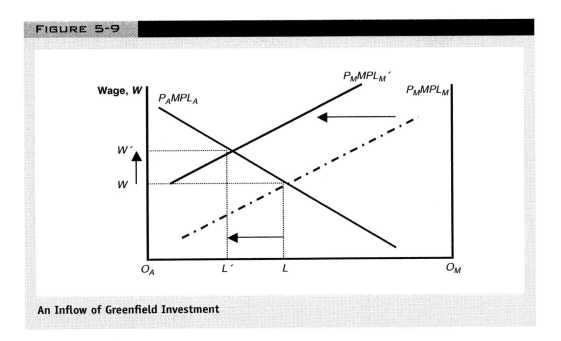

An Inflow of Greenfield Investment

5d. The effect of the outward flow of capital in Foreign is to lower labor demand by shifting down the marginal product of labor in manufacturing. Hence, the nominal and real wage falls in Foreign.

6a. The output of shirts rises! Why is this? Because capital is completely mobile between industries, we can simply apply the Rybczynski theorem. A reduction in the country's stock of capital reduces the output of the good that is intensive in that factor (airplanes) and increases the production of the other good (shirts).

6b. In the long run, the fall in the capital stock has no impact on the real wage because the reallocation of capital and labor between industries leaves the original capital/labor ratios in each industry unchanged. Because marginal products do not change in the long run, the real returns to factors stay the same. This is the factor price insensitivity result.

7a. The value of output is the area under the value of marginal product of labor curve. Given the straight line, this can be calculated as $25 \cdot 50 + (1/2) \cdot (30 \cdot 25) \cdot (150 - 100) = 1375$. Hence, the increase in the value of output is the increase in this total area.

7b. The increase in output was 1375, but of this $25 \cdot 50 = 1250$ is paid to foreigners who have entered the country. Hence, the total gain to the country is 125.

7c. Home-specific factors gain from access to lower-cost labor. They receive the 125 calculated in the previous problem plus the direct effect of paying the same workers less to the tune of $5 \cdot 100 = 500$, so the total gain to specific factors is 625.

8. There are big upfront moving costs to immigration. It may take years for immigrants to earn enough additional income to pay off these moving costs. Older workers expect to work for fewer years than younger workers and so may not be able to pay off these moving costs.

Increasing Returns to Scale
and Monopolistic Competition

1a. See the following table.

Quantity Sold	Price	Revenue	Marginal Revenue
1	7	7	7
2	6	12	5
3	5	15	3
4	4	16	1
5	3	15	−1
6	2	12	−3
7	1	7	−5

1b. The firm should make 3 units. The marginal revenue associated with selling the third unit is $3, which is greater than the marginal cost of $2.5, so selling the third unit increases revenue by more than it increases costs. For the fourth unit, the marginal revenue is $1, so the increase in sales revenue is less than the increase in cost.

1c. The firm's profit is (price − marginal cost) · quantity sold. If the firm makes 3 units, profit is ($5 − $2.5) · 3 = $7.5. Notice that the firm's profits fall to $6 if it sells one more unit.

2. The optimal price and quantity and the associated profits are shown in Figure 6-1.

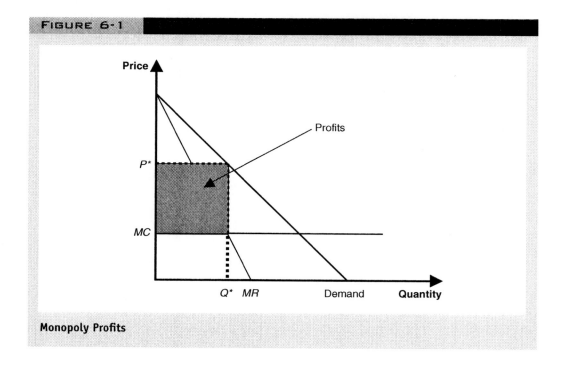

FIGURE 6-1

Monopoly Profits

3. The demand curve, $D / 2$, shows how industry demand is split across two firms that charge identical prices for their own differentiated product. The demand curve d shows how much demand there will be for a firm's product if it should deviate from the typical industry behavior and charge a different price. If it lowers its price, it steals some customers from its competitor's variety, but if both firms lowered their price, then no firm steals customers from its competitors.

4. The firm's average total cost is $(\$2 \cdot Q + \$100)/Q$. When $Q = 10$, $AC = \$12$. A firm selling 10 units must be getting a price of $12 to break even.

5a. The effect of increasing the number of products in the market is shown in Figure 6-2. The solid curve in D / N is demand per firm when each firm charges the same price before the increase in the number of products, and the dotted line labeled D / N' is the curve after the increase in products. The solid line labeled d is demand before the increase, and the broken curve labeled d' is demand after the increase.

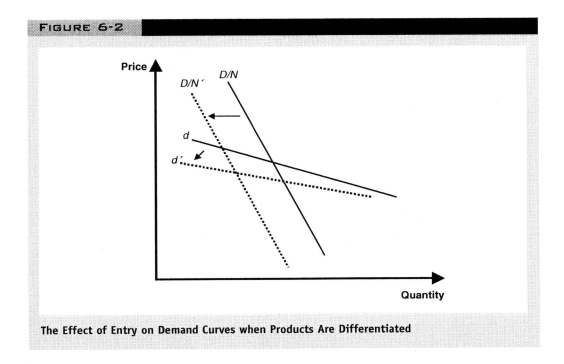

FIGURE 6-2

The Effect of Entry on Demand Curves when Products Are Differentiated

5b. The shift in the D/N curve is simple: The same amount of demand is split over a larger number of firms. The shift in the d curve is more complicated. The curve shifts down because the more products in the market, the less demand there is for any given product. It also becomes flatter because with increased product choice consumers become more sensitive to price differences across products.

6a. See the left-hand panel of Figure 6-3.

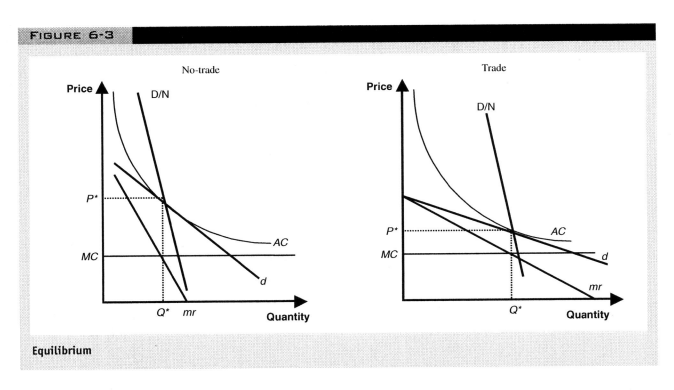

FIGURE 6-3

Equilibrium

6b. See the right-hand panel of Figure 6-3.

6c. The D / N curve has shifted to the right. The demand curve d has had its P intercept fall but has also become flatter. The associated marginal revenue curve has moved in a similar fashion. Finally, the price charged by the typical firm has fallen and the quantity sold has increased. In both cases, zero profits are being made.

6d. When international trade is allowed between the two identical countries, the size of the total market doubles, but the number of operating firms in this market, although larger than in each individual country in autarky, is less than twice the number of firms in each market in autarky. Hence, the D / N curve shifts to the right. Because more firms are operating in the integrated world market than in each country in autarky, the demand curve d has shifted down while also becoming flatter. Firms that stay in the market compensate for the lower price they can charge by selling a larger quantity of output so that price continues to be equal to average cost.

6e. The gains from trade include the availability of increased product variety, and these goods have become cheaper. Trade expands the product range available to consumers. This can be seen in the change in the demand curve d. (It is flatter or more elastic because there are more competing varieties.) Demand per firm has increased, however, as can be seen by the shift in the demand curve D / N to the right. Higher demand per firm allows firms to move down their average cost curve and therefore charge lower prices.

6f. The adjustment costs are associated with the closing of some firms and the subsequent dislocation of the employees at those plants. The fact that the D / N curve has shifted to the right indicates that some of the firms in each country must close and so lay off workers.

7a. The larger a market is, the more variety that market will support. The more variety in a market, the flatter the demand curve d and the lower the price charged for each variety. Hence, the real wage should be higher in the large country in a no-trade equilibrium.

7b. The small country gains more from trade because it gets access to the larger number of varieties that are produced in the larger market.

8. No, the monopolistic competition model would not be appropriate for this industry because with so few firms in the industry, the firms are likely to behave strategically. The monopolistic competition model dispenses with strategic behavior among firms by assuming that there are many of them.

9. The gains from trade in the monopolistic competition model arise from combining small individual markets into large markets that support greater variety and competition. As the economy of the United States is so much larger than the economies of Canada or Mexico, we would expect that most of the gains from trade would go to the smaller markets.

10. Mexico experienced a financial crisis at precisely the same time that NAFTA was implemented, making it difficult to disentangle the effect of NAFTA from the deep recession caused by the financial crisis.

11. The assistance provided to workers under the trade adjustment assistance program was expanded for those workers whose jobs were eliminated by NAFTA.

12. As shown in the textbook, the number of goods being exported from Mexico can be used as the smallest reasonable estimate of the expansion of variety available in the United States. Doing the same for Canada would give a crude measure of the expansion in variety due to NAFTA.

13. Yes. Wine is differentiated to some extent merely by where it is produced. In principle, this is enough to generate intra-industry trade: People may consume both wine from California and from France merely for variety.

14. If workers move across industries, then trade between countries is probably motivated by comparative advantage rather than product differentiation, increasing returns, and imperfect information. Trade causes firms to reallocate resources across industries in comparative advantage models and across firms within industries in the monopolistic competition model.

15. Because the Heckscher-Ohlin model does not give rise to a gravity equation, a gravity equation is more likely to fit the data between countries that have similar endowments.

16. Because product differentiation gives rise to intra-industry trade, the index of intra-industry trade is likely to be closer to 100 when goods in that industry are highly differentiated and closer to 0 when goods are homogeneous.

17. As shown in the textbook, the gravity equation can be made to distinguish between trade between regions within a country and between regions in different countries. The difference in the constant across borders from the constant within borders can be used to gauge the size of the "border effect."

Import Tariffs and Quotas under Perfect Competition

1a. The firm would be selling its product in your market at less than the normal price. Normal price would mean the price in the exporting country's market, the price in a third country, or the average cost of production.

1b. This is an example of a free-trade agreement, which is allowed under Article XXIV of the GATT.

1c. "Normal trade relations" perhaps better conveys the actual meaning of "most favored nation status," which is the principle of nondiscrimination.

2. Anne's consumer surplus is $1, the difference between the $3 that she was willing to pay for the first tomato and the price of the tomato, $2.

3. Producer surplus is the payment to the fixed factor of production. Hence, the producer surplus in this case is revenue minus the wage bill, or $40.

4a. The autarky price is the price at which the country would not want to import any of the product, or $10.

4b. The triangle in Figure 7-2, with area $\frac{1}{2} \cdot (\$10/\text{unit} - \$6/\text{unit}) \cdot 15 \text{ units} = \$30$, is the gains from trade. This is equal to the difference between the gain in consumer surplus and the loss of producer surplus, which is also a triangle, with a height of $10/unit − $6/unit and a base of 15 units. See triangle D in Figure 7-2 in the textbook.

4c. See Figure 7-5.

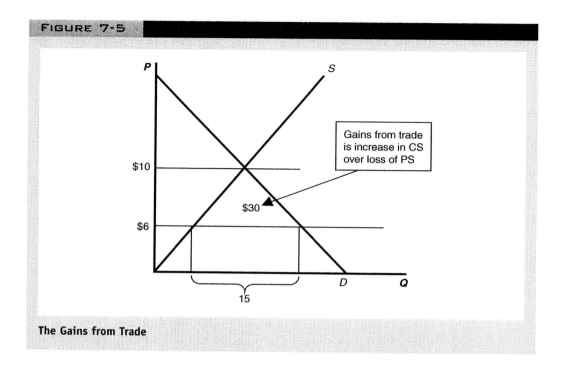

FIGURE 7-5

The Gains from Trade

5a. The price at Home rises to $8 (which is $P_W + t$).

5b. The tariff is $2 per unit and 7.5 units are imported, so the total tariff revenue is $15.

5c. The deadweight loss of the tariff is equal to the reduction in imports (15 units − 7.5 units) multiplied by half the $2 increase in price: 1/2($2/unit)(7.5 units) = $7.5.

5d. The change in producer surplus is equal to the difference between the change in revenue minus the change in payments to variable factors of production, or $5.

5e. Consider Figure 7-6. The figure shows the effect of the tariff on the home country. The labeled geometric figures correspond to components of the welfare change that were calculated earlier in the problem. The total loss of consumer surplus is equal to the area $f + g + h + i$. From 5d, the area f is $5. From 5c, the area $g + i$ is the deadweight loss of $7.5. From 5b, the area h is the size of the tariff revenue, $15 as calculated. Hence, the total loss of consumer surplus is $27.50.

FIGURE 7-6

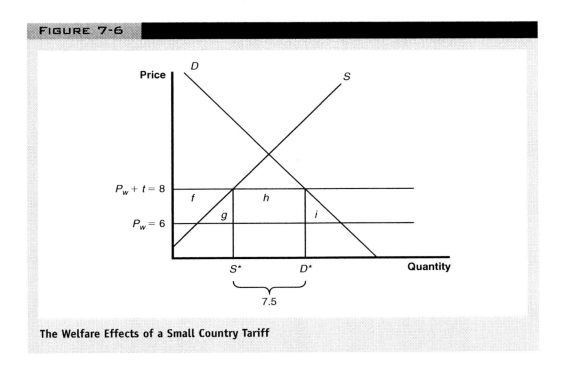

The Welfare Effects of a Small Country Tariff

5f. See Figure 7-6 and the numbers for *f, g, h,* and *i* provided in the answer to 5e.

6a. Producer surplus decreases by $175. This is equal to the reduction in revenue (holding fixed output) of $200 and subtracting the production loss of the tariff 1/2($2)25 = $25.

6b. Consumer surplus increases by $625. Holding fixed the quantity sold, the $2 fall in price raises consumer surplus by $600. Add to this the consumption loss under the tariff 1/2($2)25 = $25.

6c. Tariff revenue falls by $400 = $2(300 − 100).

6d. The deadweight loss of the tariff is equal to $50, and the removal of the tariff gets rid of this deadweight loss, making the country better off.

6e. The information is displayed in Figure 7-7.

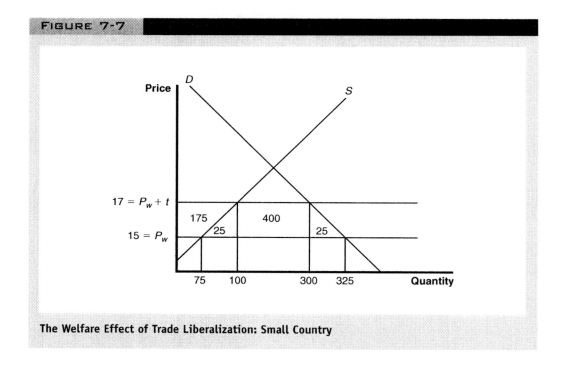

FIGURE 7-7

The Welfare Effect of Trade Liberalization: Small Country

7a. Because the home price is $11 and the tariff is $2, the world price with the tariff must be $9.

7b. The revenue raised by the tariff is $2/unit multiplied by 50 units or $100.

7c. Using the deadweight loss formula we have $(1/2)(\$11/\text{unit} - \$10/\text{unit})(100 \text{ units} - 50 \text{ units}) = \$25$.

7d. The total effect on national welfare is the terms–of–trade gain minus the deadweight loss. The terms–of–trade gain is $(\$10/\text{unit} - \$9/\text{unit})50 \text{ units} = \$50$. This is greater than the deadweight loss by $25. Hence, Home gains from this tariff.

7e. The welfare effect on foreign is its terms–of–trade loss (Home's gain) plus its deadweight loss. The deadweight loss is $(1/2)(\$10/\text{unit} - \$9/\text{unit})(100 \text{ units} - 50 \text{ units}) = \$25$. Hence, the total welfare loss to Foreign is $75.

7f. The effect on world welfare is the sum of the deadweight losses in both Home and Foreign, or $50.

7g. See Figure 7-8.

FIGURE 7-8

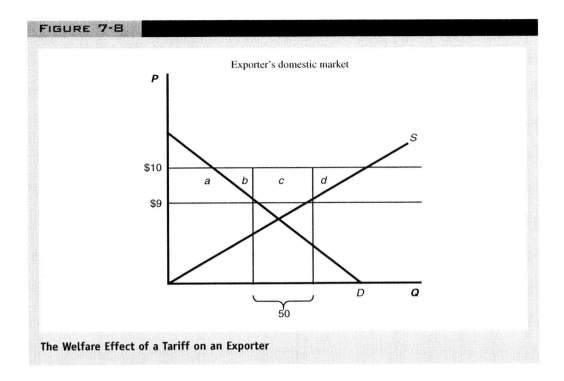

The Welfare Effect of a Tariff on an Exporter

The diagram shows consumer surplus gain *a*, producer surplus loss of *a* + *b* + *c* + *d*, and net loss of exporting country welfare of *b* + *c* + *d*, which is equal in value to the sum of deadweight loss of *b* + *d* = $25 and terms-of-trade loss of *c* = $50.

8. The elasticity of the supply curve is related to its steepness. The steeper the supply curve, the lower the elasticity. When the supply curve is very steep, the more the incidence of the tariff falls on the exporting country. The more of the tariff borne by the foreigners, the larger the optimal tariff.

9a. In the case of perfect competition and quota licenses that are distributed via a perfectly competitive auction, the welfare effect of tariffs and quotas are equivalent. Both raise the domestic price of the good above the world price (and so alter producer and consumer surplus in the same way), and both raise exactly the same amount of revenue for the government.

9b. A producer would rather be protected by a quota than a tariff in this case. In the case of the quota, the domestic price is determined solely by domestic demand, domestic supply, and the size of the quota. Changes in the world price then have no effect on producer surplus. In the case of the tariff, the price at home is equal to the price on world markets plus the tariff. A reduction in the world price would then reduce the home price as well, thereby lowering producer surplus.

10a. The value of the quota rent is the difference between the domestic and world price of the good ($5/units) multiplied by the size of the quota (50 units). Hence, the value of the quota rent is $250.

10b. The deadweight loss to the exporting country is equal to (1/2)($10/unit − $8/unit)(100 units − 50 units) = $50. In addition, the exporting country suffers the terms-of-trade loss of ($10/unit − $8/unit)(50 units) = $100. Hence, the total welfare loss to the exporting country is $150.

10c. The importing country enjoys the terms of trade gain of $100 and a deadweight loss equal to $(1/2)(\$13/\text{unit} - \$10/\text{unit})(100 \text{ units} - 50 \text{ units}) = \$75$. Hence, Home enjoys an increase in national welfare of $25.

10d. See Figure 7-9. The box of size $100 is the terms-of-trade loss (gain) for the exporter (importer), the triangle with size $50 is the deadweight loss in the exporting country, and the triangle with size $75 is the deadweight loss in the importing country.

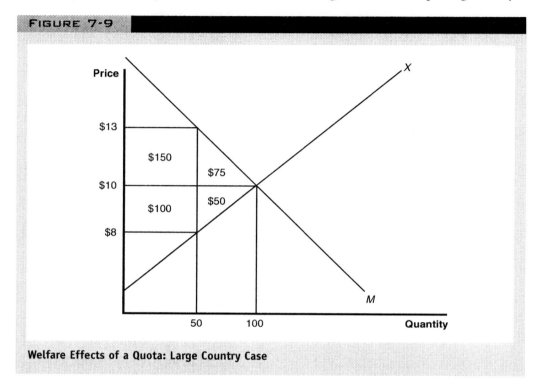

FIGURE 7-9

Welfare Effects of a Quota: Large Country Case

10e. If the importing country were to give the quota rents to the exporting country, then the exporter would see the quota raise its welfare by $100 = $150 − $50, whereas the importing country would see its welfare fall by $225 = $150 + $75.

11. By giving the quota rents to the exporting country, the importing country reduces the incentive for the exporting country to retaliate or seek redress from the WTO. As we found in the last question, the exporting country can actually be made better off.

8

Import Tariffs and Quotas under Imperfect Competition

1a. See Figure 8-2. When international trade is not allowed, the firm is a monopoly and therefore chooses its quantity so that marginal cost is equal to marginal revenue (Q_1). This level of output implies a monopoly price of P^M.

FIGURE 8-2

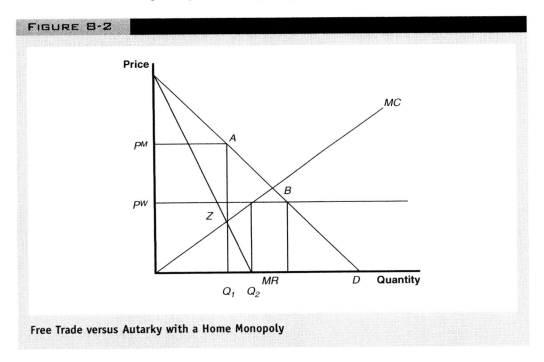

Free Trade versus Autarky with a Home Monopoly

1b. International trade forces the firm to lower its price to P^W.

1c. When the firm is exposed to international trade, the best it can do is choose the quantity that sets the world price (its new marginal revenue curve) equal to its marginal cost (Q_2). Given the way that the diagram is drawn, this actually implies an increase in output.

1d. The international market constrains the monopoly power of the firm and so lowers its producer surplus.

1e. The price charged by the monopolist in autarky (P^M) exceeds the world price, so free trade improves consumer surplus.

1f. Consumers gain the trapezoid, $P^M A B P^W$. This gain in consumer surplus contains within it the lost monopoly profits (the rectangle $P^M A Z P^W$). Hence the country is better off with trade.

1g. If the world price were below the intersection between the marginal revenue and marginal cost curve, then the monopolists' output would fall rather than rise.

2. Yes. Consider Figure 8-2. Suppose that P^W were above the intersection between the demand curve and the marginal cost curve but below P^M. In this case the monopolist would be willing to satisfy all domestic demand at that price. The fact that the country could import at that price is all that is needed to force the domestic price down.

3a. See Figure 8-3. Note that the marginal revenue curve has been omitted to avoid cluttering up the diagram. The result is very similar to the perfect competition small-country case. The tariff increases the price, expanding the producer surplus by the area *a*, and decreasing consumer surplus by ($a + b + c + d$). The tariff collects revenue *c*, so the total impact on national welfare is $-(b + d)$.

FIGURE 8-3

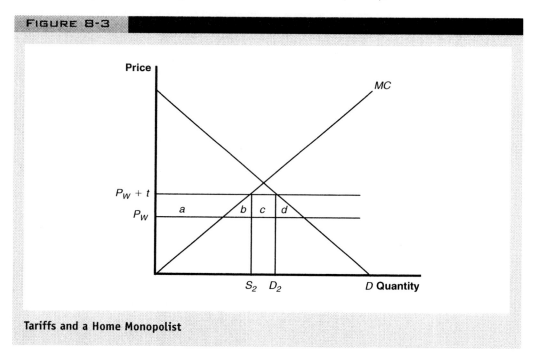

Tariffs and a Home Monopolist

3b. Because the quota does not allow imports to expand above the size of the quota when the price on the domestic market rises, the Home firm has monopoly power. As shown in Figure 8-4, the quota that under perfect competition would lower imports by the same amount as a tariff of size *t* has the effect of shifting the demand curve and marginal revenue curve facing the monopolist to the left. The firm charges a markup over its marginal cost that exceeds the size of the tariff *t*. As a result the domestic price with a quota P^Q exceeds the domestic price with a tariff $P^W + t$, so consumer surplus is lower under a quota than it is under a tariff.

3c. Suppose a tariff *t* resulted in *M* units imported. The tariff revenue would be $t \cdot M$. A quota of size *M* would imply quota rents of ($P^Q - P^W) \cdot M$ because each quota license allows the owner to buy at the low world price of P^W and to sell at the high domestic price of P^Q. Because $P^Q - P^W > t$, it follows that the quota rent associ-

FIGURE 8-4

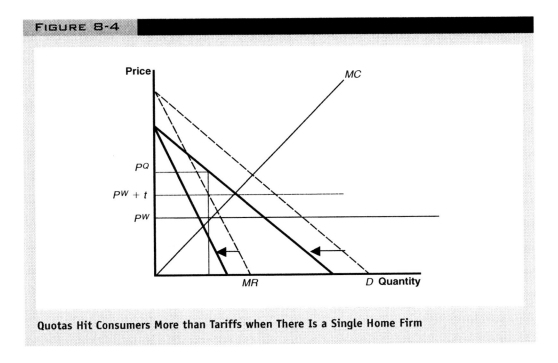

Quotas Hit Consumers More than Tariffs when There Is a Single Home Firm

ated with imports of M exceeds the tariff revenue associated with import with imports of M.

4a. See Figure 8-5. If there is no tariff, then the marginal cost of serving the market is $10. Setting marginal cost equal to marginal revenue $(10 = 100 - 2Q)$ and solving, we find that the optimal quantity to sell is 45 units. Plugging this number into the demand function $(P = 100 - 45)$ gives us a price of $55.

4b. See Figure 8-5. The tariff raises the marginal cost of serving the market to $20. Setting marginal cost equal to marginal revenue $(20 = 100 - 2Q)$, we find that the op-

FIGURE 8-5

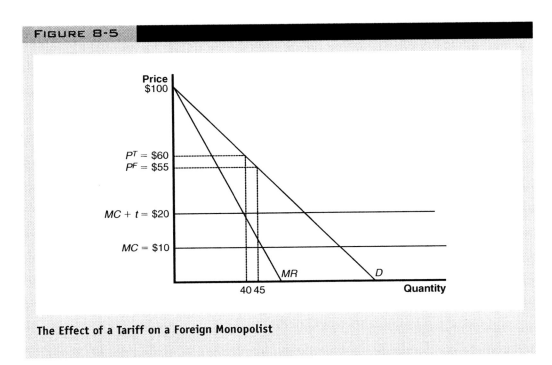

The Effect of a Tariff on a Foreign Monopolist

timal quantity to sell is now 40 units. Plugging this number into the demand function ($P = 100 - 40$) gives us a price of $60. Here is an example of a tariff that is not fully passed on to consumers. A $10 tariff increased the price by only $5.

4c. Using the formula for the area of a triangle, consumer surplus is equal to $1,012.50 with free trade ($1/2 \cdot [100 - 55] \cdot 45$) and $800 with the tariff ($1/2 \cdot [100 - 60] \cdot 40$). Tariff revenue collected by the government is equal to 0 without the tariff and $400 with the tariff ($10 \cdot 40$). National welfare is the sum of consumer surplus plus tariff revenue, so the tariff made the country better off.

5a. See Figure 8-6. The key point is that the marginal revenue curve is not as steep as the demand curve and so the domestic price rises by more than the tariff. Before the tariff is applied, the foreign monopolist sells quantity Q_1 where the marginal cost (MC) of serving the market is equal to the marginal revenue (MR). This quantity implies a home market price of P_1. The tariff increases the marginal cost by t per unit ($MC + t$) and so induces the monopolist to cut back supply to Q_2, which implies a price of P_2. Because the demand curve is steeper than the marginal revenue curve, the price increase $P_2 - P_1$ is larger than the size of the tariff t.

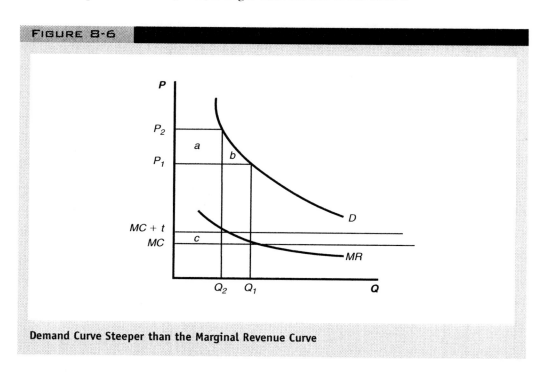

FIGURE 8-6

Demand Curve Steeper than the Marginal Revenue Curve

5b. No, in this case the loss in consumer surplus (area $a + b$ in Figure 8-6) must exceed the increase in government revenue, which is equal to $t \cdot Q_2$ (area c in Figure 8-6). This must be so because $P_2 - P_1 > t$.

6a. At home, $MR = 10 - 2Q$. In Foreign, $MR = 6 - 2Q$.

6b. Setting marginal revenue equal to marginal cost in each market, we find that the amount sold in Home is 4 units and the amount sold in Foreign is 2 units. This translates into a price in Home of 6 and a price in Foreign of 4.

6c. See Figure 8-7. The key feature of the diagram is that the demand curve in the exporter's home market has been drawn steeper than the importing country. The higher price charged by the firm in the exporter's home country is evidence of dumping.

FIGURE 8-7

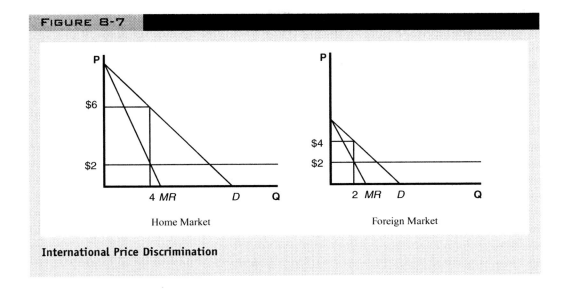

International Price Discrimination

7. Yes, the firm could be accused of dumping if the average cost is greater than $10 (as might happen during a recession) or if the price being charged in the foreign market is not increased above the Home price by the amount of any shipping cost incurred.

8a. See Figure 8-8. (Note that the actual level of demand in Foreign has been assumed to be large relative to the amount sold by the firm).

FIGURE 8-8

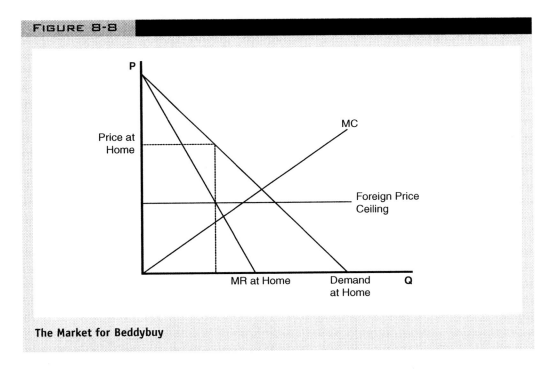

The Market for Beddybuy

8b. If the drug company finds that consumers at Home are buying its product abroad, it may cease to sell their product in Foreign if the profits to being able to charge them monopoly price at Home are large relative to the profits of supplying both markets when consumers are paying the regulated price.

9. As pointed out in the text, the mere threat of antidumping tariffs can induce foreign firms to raise their price in the importing country. Hence, the government official's statement is potentially misleading because foreign producers may have been induced to change their behavior even if no antidumping cases are filed.

10. It is relatively easy to file a dumping case, and there is a good chance that the government will find in favor of a dumping claim. Even when a dumping case is not fully prosecuted, the threat of dumping duties is often enough to induce foreign firms to increase their price.

11. For antidumping tariffs to be applied, there must be evidence of "material injury" to domestic producers. If there are no domestic producers, then there can be no evidence of material injury.

12a. By raising the price of cucumbers above the world price, the tariff would lower consumer surplus in every year that the domestic price is above the world price.

12b. In order for infant industry protection to be appropriate, P must be below the average cost of production for the home cucumber firm now but must be no less than the average cost of product for the home cucumber firm in 5 years.

12c. If capital markets were perfect in Home, then one argument for infant industry protection would not be valid. A firm that will eventually be competitive should be able to borrow against future earnings if these earnings are to materialize. An argument might still be made if there were positive externalities in the cucumber industry.

12d. The existence of positive externalities, such as knowledge spillovers, could justify infant industry protection, but in the cucumber industry that might be a hard sell.

13a. If the reason for infant industry protection were purely that capital markets were imperfect, then it would make no sense to offer the protection. This is because the producer surplus accrues to the foreign multinational rather than to a domestic firm.

13b. If the argument were that this is an industry with knowledge spillovers, then domestic entrepreneurs might benefit from having the foreign multinational. These spillovers would lower the cost of domestic firms and so might justify the tariff. The application to China's auto industry suggests that multinationals may have played a role in getting the auto industry started in China.

14. From the application in the textbook, it appears that Harley-Davidson could not get a loan from the banking system in the absence of the temporary protection. There is no suggestion that it had to do with any positive externalities.

9

International Agreements:
Trade, Labor, and the Environment

1. The multilateral agreement will only work if there are mutual gains to the parties involved. If only one country is large, then that country may have no incentive to agree to tariff reduction.

2. If many small countries join a customs union, they may collectively become large on international markets. Because large countries are better off with restrictions on imports and small countries are better off with free trade, these countries may raise the tariff on outsiders.

3. This odd possibility is possible. Suppose that marginal costs of production are constant in Home and outside the free-trade area. It could be that Home's external tariff is low enough that countries outside the free-trade area have a lower marginal cost than Home and so supply the Home market. Now suppose that another country (Foreign) in the free-trade area has very high tariffs. Because there are rules of origin, Home producers get better access to Foreign's market than countries outside the area and so are the lowest-cost producer for the Foreign market while being a high-cost producer for their own market.

4. See Figure 9-2. Let the marginal cost of production for a country within the free-trade agreement be C. The free-trade agreement lowers the cost for this country to supply the domestic market and so trade rises. This is nothing different from we saw in Chapter 7.

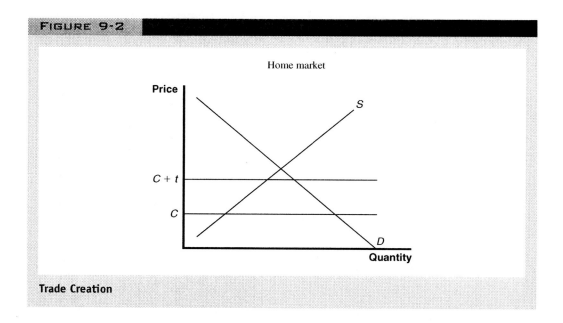

FIGURE 9-2

Home market

Trade Creation

5a. There can be no trade diversion in this example because country A has the lowest marginal cost of the three countries. It would be the supplier before and after the agreement.

5b. An RTA with country B could lead to trade creation if the initial tariff was high enough that home did not import the good from either country A or B.

5c. See Figure 9-3. Before the regional trade agreement, a tariff t is applied to imports of both A and B so that the marginal cost of A serving Home is $C_A + t$ and the marginal cost of B serving Home is $C_B + t$. Because $C_A + t < C_B + t$, the low-cost country A is the sole supplier when the tariff is equally applied to each country. Now suppose that country B joins a regional trade agreement with Home and the tariff is sufficiently large that country B is now the lowest-cost supplier. Because $C_B < C_A + t$, trade is diverted from the low-cost producer A to the high-cost producer B.

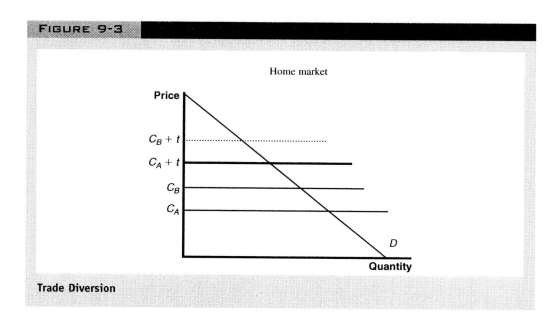

FIGURE 9-3

Home market

Trade Diversion

5d. Yes. Before the RTA, the price in Home was $C_A + t$. After the RTA, the price fell to C_B. It is true that tariff revenue has been lost, but it is also true that consumer surplus has risen because the price does fall.

6. Fair Trade Coffee, which is discussed in Chapter 3, is an example of an NGO that has had some success raising living standards. Consumers pay extra for coffee made under appropriate circumstances.

7. They worry that this is a form of disguised protectionism intended to raise the cost of production in low-wage countries.

8a. This question describes a specific-factors–type framework. If the wage rises in the formal sector, then the value of the marginal product of labor must rise as well. This means that employment in the formal sector must fall.

8b. Labor pushed out of the formal sector finds employment in the unregulated, informal sector. As labor employed in that sector rises, the value of the marginal product of labor falls and so too does the wage paid in the informal sector.

9a. As in the tuna-dolphin case, there is a strong chance that the WTO will rule against Home because it is imposing a production process method on Foreign.

9b. No. As long as the reporting is nondiscriminatory, this would be fine with the WTO.

10. Rich countries will have tighter regulations on pollution than poorer countries. If these regulations raise the cost of highly polluting industries more than less-polluting industries, then tariff reduction could cause highly polluting industries to move to poorer countries. Pollution could increase as a result.

11a. If the pollution is primarily local, then an international prisoner's dilemma is less likely to arise because one country's pollution does not affect another.

11b. If the marginal costs of all producers rise, then the global supply curve for these goods shifts inward, resulting in a higher price for sneeds. The exact amount of the price increase depends on the shape of the demand and supply curves.

11c. Your country's sneed industry benefits from the higher price for sneeds on world markets while its marginal cost curve stays the same. Therefore your country's producer surplus rises.

11d. There is a free rider problem. If all other countries sign on to the agreement, your country gets the benefit of less global pollution from its actions and it benefits in terms of producer surplus because the price of sneeds has risen.

10

Introduction to Exchange Rates and the Foreign Exchange Market

1a. $E_{\$/\mathrm{€}} = 1.2$ (American terms), $E_{\mathrm{€}/\$} = 1 / 1.2 = 0.833$ (European terms).

1b. The dollar depreciated by 20% against the euro: $(1.2 - 1) / 1$.

1c. The euro appreciated by 16.7% against the dollar: $(0.833 - 1) / 1$.

1d. $E_{\$/¥} = 1 / 120 = 0.0833$ (American terms), $E_{¥/\$} = 120 / 1 = 120$ (Japanese terms).

1e. The dollar appreciated by 16.667% against the yen: $(.0833 - .01) / 01$.

1f. The percent change in the effective exchange rate is equal to the trade-weighted average of bilateral exchange rates.

$$\frac{\Delta E_{\mathit{eff}}}{E_{\mathit{eff}}} = \left(\frac{1.2 - 1}{1}\right)\left(\frac{\$200bil.}{\$200bil. + \$400bil.}\right) + \left(\frac{0.0833 - 0.1}{0.1}\right)\left(\frac{\$400bil.}{\$200bil. + \$400bil.}\right)$$

The first term on the right side of the equals sign is the percentage depreciation of the dollar against the euro multiplied by Europe's trade weight. The second term is the percentage appreciation of the dollar against the yen multiplied by Japan's trade weight. Doing the calculation, we find that

$$\frac{\Delta E_{\mathit{eff}}}{E_{\mathit{eff}}} = -0.044 = -4.4\%.$$

So the dollar appreciated against this basket of currencies.

2a. The dollar price of the ale in Munich is $3\mathrm{€}\cdot E_{\$/\mathrm{€}}$ which is equal to $2 when $E_{\$/\mathrm{€}} = 2/3$.

2b. If $E_{\$/\mathrm{€}} = 1$, then the ale is cheaper in Boston. Party on, Volker!

3a. No, Home cannot fix its exchange rate vis-à-vis multiple currencies if those currencies float. To see this, suppose that there are two countries, A and B, and Home fixes its exchange rate vis-à-vis at one. For simplicity assume that one unit of currency A buys one unit of currency B initially. Now suppose that A's currency appreciates vis-à-vis B so that one unit of A's currency buys 2 units of B's currency. One unit of Home's currency buys one unit of A's currency, which buys 2 units of B's currency, but one unit of B's currency buys one unit of Home's currency because of the fixed exchange rate! The exchange rates are not consistent!

3b. Home could fix its currency vis-à-vis its largest trading partner. Alternatively, Home could dollarize by using the currency of its largest trading partner or agreeing to a currency union with its largest trading partner.

4. Spreads are higher for individuals (small players) because there are more middlemen between the final transaction and the underlying foreign exchange market than there are for the large interbank traders who directly transact on the interbank market.

5a. If you buy euros forward at this rate, then the dollar cost in 30 days will be (1.25$/€·€10 million) or $12.5 million. Since you have contracted to sell the wine for $13 million, you will make $500,000.

5b. If the spot rate for the euro rises above 1.3$/€, then your dollar cost will exceed your dollar income, and you will lose money.

5c. If you were to own this call option, then in 30 days you are guaranteed a positive dollar return on the wine. If the spot rate exceeds 1.27, then you will exercise the option, buy the wine, and come away with $300,000. On the other hand, if the spot rate were less than 1.27, you would not use the option and buy euros on the spot market. The benefit of owning the option relative to the forward contract is that if the spot rate is less than 1.25, you will get a better price for the euros and make more money. If the spot rate is more than 1.25, you would have been better off using the forward market.

5d. Your $1 million will buy $1 million / 1.25 $/€ = €800,000 at the forward rate. If the spot rate is 1.3, then this amount of euros converts into (1.3 $/€)·(€800,000) = $1.04 million. Hence, you would make $40,000 in the transaction.

5e. In this scenario, the €800,000 that you bought forward would only be worth $960,000, so you would have lost $40,000.

6. The answer is c. $E_{\$/€} \div E_{\$/£} = E_{£/€} = 3/2 \div 2 = 3/4$.

7. The answer is d, all of the above. Answer a is true: $E_{¥/\$} = 100$, $E_{\$/€} = 2$, so $E_{€/\$} = 0.5$ and $E_{€/¥} = E_{€/\$} \div E_{¥/\$}$. Answer b is true: $E_{\$/¥} = 1 / E_{¥/\$}$. And answer c is true: $E_{¥/€} = E_{¥/\$} \times E_{\$/€}$.

8. The cross rates are not consistent, so there is a triangular arbitrage opportunity. First, trade your $1 million for £500,000. Second, trade your £500,000 for yen 110 million. Third, trade your yen 110 million for $1.1 million. Realize profits of $100,000.

9. Yes, arbitrage prevents the price of the same thing from being different in different locations. For arbitrage to occur, it must be possible to transact across these locations. Capital controls by their very nature prevent arbitrage.

10. The answer is d, depreciate by 2%. According to UIP, the interest rate differential is equal to the expected change in the exchange rate.

11a. The amount of euros that $1 million buys is ($1 million) / (1.25$/€) = €800,000.

11b. At the end of the year you would have (€800,000)(1+0.03) = €824,000. This is the principal plus the interest.

11c. At the end of the year you would have ($1 million)(1.05) = $1,050,000.

11d. To make the amounts identical, the forward exchange rate would have to satisfy the equation $1,050,000 = $F_{\$/€}$(€824,000), where the left side is the amount of dollars you would get from the U.S. deposit, whereas the right side is the amount of dollars you would get from the German deposit if the forward rate were $F_{\$/€}$. Solving for this we find that $F_{\$/€} = 1.274272$.

11e. If investors were risk neutral (i.e., they do not care about risk), then uncovered interest parity ought to hold as well. This means that the expected future spot rate would have to be equal to the forward exchange rate.

11f. The expected rate of depreciation of the dollar is equal to (1.274272 − 1.25) / 1.25 = 1.94%. Note that this is approximately equal to the difference in the interest rates between the United States and Germany.

11g. If U.S. deposits were more liquid and less risky than German deposits, then the rate of return on U.S. deposits might be somewhat less than that on German deposits. (Put another way, investors would have to be compensated to hold German deposits.) This means the expected rate of depreciation of the dollar might be somewhat larger to boost German returns.

12a. To answer these questions, we use the uncovered interest parity equation. Holding fixed U.S. interest rates *and the expected future spot rate,* it is clear that the spot rate must increase. That is, the dollar must depreciate.

12b. If U.S. interest rates rise, it must be that the expected dollar return on British deposits rises as well. Otherwise, the no-arbitrage condition would not hold. There is more than one way for this return to rise: either the expected rate of depreciation of the dollar must rise, or the interest rate on British deposits must rise.

12c. Assuming that capital controls have not been imposed so that the no-arbitrage condition holds, it must be that the expected future spot rate has risen (i.e., depreciated).

11

Exchange Rates I: The Monetary Approach in the Long Run

1. Using the law of one price equation, we find that the price in Germany must be €0.80.

2a. No. For the law of one price to hold for guns, the exchange rate would have to be 2/3. For the law of one price to hold for doctor's visits, the exchange rate would have to be 3.

2b. The cost of an American basket is $175 (the average of the $200 and $150).

2c. The cost of a French basket is €175 (the average of €300 and €50).

2d. Yes, at that exchange rate the cost of the French basket is $175, the same as in the United States..

2e. This would be a real depreciation of the dollar because it would imply that it takes more U.S. baskets of goods to buy a French basket.

2f. For any $E_{\$/€} < 1$, the dollar is overvalued because it takes less than one U.S. basket to buy a French basket.

2g. No, with the different weights placed on guns, the prices of these baskets would be different. The U.S. basket would cost $180, whereas the French basket would cost €150. The dollar would appear to be overvalued if these two differently calculated baskets were compared.

3. The real exchange rate must be appreciating at a rate of 1%, because $\Delta q_{F/H} / q_{F/H} = \Delta E_{\$/blot} / E_{\$/blot} + \pi_F - \pi_H = 5\% + 2\% - 8\%$.

4. The answer is b, a straightforward application of the RPPP formula.

5. True. The percent change in the nominal exchange rate is equal to the percent change in the real exchange rate plus the differences in the inflation rates of the two countries. RPPP holds when changes in the real exchange rate are zero, and it fits better when changes in the real exchange rate are small relative to differences in inflation rates.

6. The answer is d, the law of one price implies both PPP concepts, but the reverse is not true.

7. All three choices are correct, so the answer is d.

8. The rate of inflation should be equal to the rate of money growth, so inflation in Home should be 3% and inflation in Foreign should be 5%. Now apply RPPP to find that Home's currency ought to appreciate at a rate of 2%. Hence the answer is a.

9a. We plug the information into the money market equilibrium equation for the United States \$25 = (1/2)(100 units)P, so $P = 0.5\$/unit$.

9b. Using the APPP equation, we have $(0.1\$/¥)P_{Japan} = 0.5\$/unit$, so $P_{Japan} = 5¥/unit$.

9c. Using the money market equilibrium equation for Japan, we have $M_{Japan} = (5¥/unit)(80 \text{ units})(3/4) = 300$ yen.

10a. The inflation rate in the United States is the difference between the rate of growth of money and the rate of growth of the economy, or 2%.

10b. The inflation rate in Canada is 9%.

10c. The Canadian dollar is increasing (depreciating) at a rate of 7%.

11. During hyperinflations nominal money balances held are rapidly losing value, imposing a severe cost on the holders of that money. People become anxious to exchange their money for things that will hold their value, like goods.

12. A decrease in money demand would tend to increase the price level in Home. To maintain PPP, Home's exchange rate would have to depreciate.

13a. From the Fisher effect we know that Country A has the higher inflation rate.

13b. Assuming arbitrage in financial and goods markets, the real interest rate is the same. Real interest parity arises.

13c. According to the monetary theory, the rate of inflation should be the difference between the rate of money growth minus the rate of growth in real output. Hence, the inflation rate in Country B is 4%.

13d. The real interest rate must be 3% because the interest rate in Country B is 7% and the inflation rate is 4%. Because the real interest rate is the same in Country A, the inflation rate there must be $10 - 3 = 7\%$. Because the inflation rate in A is equal to the money growth rate in A minus the growth in real output, the money growth rate in A must be 9%.

13e. A decrease in the growth of money from 6% to 2% eliminates inflation in Country B in the long run. Hence, the interest rate falls to 3%, which is equal to the real interest rate.

13f. By assumption the liquidity ratio must rise.

13g. The increase in the liquidity ratio increases money demand at time T. Because the money supply is fixed at time T, the sudden increase in the money demand must lead to an immediate decrease in the price level.

13h. The sudden decrease in Country B's price level leads to a sudden decrease (appreciation) in Country B's exchange rate. The appreciation is necessary for APPP to hold.

13i. After time T, RPPP requires that Country B's exchange rate appreciate at a rate equal to Country A's inflation rate of 7%.

14. All of the choices are associated with an appreciation so the answer must be e.

15. Money demand must be increasing in Home, which drives down Home's price level, which has two implications. First, Home's currency must be appreciating because prices are falling. The Fisher effect implies that interest rates in Home are less than in Foreign. Hence, c is the only true response.

16a. With a constant money growth rate of 10% in Home, the inflation rate in Home would be 10%. With a constant money growth rate of 5% in Foreign, the inflation rate in Foreign would be 5%. (Y is constant, and the nominal interest rate is constant at the real interest rate plus the rate of expected inflation). By RPPP the dollar must lose value at a rate equal to the difference in inflation rates, or 5%.

16b. By the Fisher effect, the interest rate differential between Home and Foreign is equal to the inflation rate differential between Home and Foreign. Hence, Home's interest rate is higher than Foreign's interest rate by 5%.

16c. With a lower expected rate of money growth, there is now a lower expected rate of inflation (5% instead of 10%). By the Fisher effect, the interest rate should fall by 5% at time t.

16d. The fall in the interest rate leads to an increase in money demand: $L(i, Y)$ jumps. Because $P = M^S / L(i, Y)$ and M^S is fixed at the moment of t, the price level should fall. By APPP, the dollar should strengthen, that is, E should drop to keep foreign prices measured in dollars equal to domestic prices.

16e. Because the rate of money growth is now the same in the two countries, there should be no difference in inflation rates, and hence by RPPP the exchange rate should be constant over time.

17a. Home's exchange rate would have to appreciate at a rate of 3%.

17b. Home's money supply would need to grow at a rate of 5%.

17c. By the Fisher effect and the difference between Foreign's nominal interest rate and inflation, the world real interest rate must be 3%. Because Home wishes to the inflation rate to be 2%, Home must target a nominal interest rate of 5% (2 + 3).

17d. A fall in the growth rate of real output would alter the relationship between inflation and the rate of growth of the money supply. Hence, it would alter the government's money supply anchor. Neither the interest rate target nor the exchange rate target would have to change.

12

Exchange Rates II: The Asset Approach in the Short Run

1. The answer is d. Applying UIP, the dollar must be expected to depreciate by 2% in order for the expected returns to be the same in both currencies.

2a. UIP requires the dollar to depreciate by 2% in order to make the expected dollar return on foreign assets equal to the dollar return on domestic assets.

2b. The expected change in the exchange rate is 2%, and the current spot is 1, so the future expected spot rate must be 1.02 because $(1.02 - 1) / 1 = 0.02$.

2c. It has increased. There is now a greater gap between interest rates on deposits in the United States and Europe that must be accounted for by a faster rate of expected dollar depreciation.

2d. It must appreciate so as to allow for a greater depreciation in the future.

2e. See Figure 12-1. The increase in domestic interest rates results in a need for a faster rate of dollar depreciation. Because the expected level of the exchange rate has not changed, the downward sloping curve does not move.

FIGURE 12-1

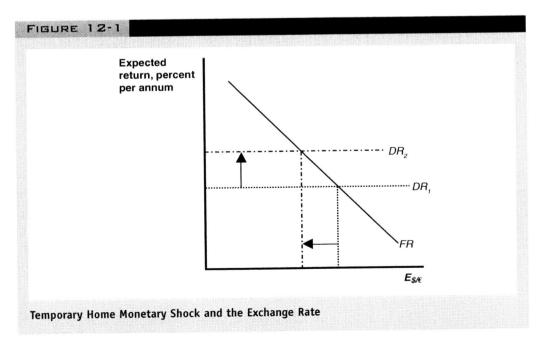

Temporary Home Monetary Shock and the Exchange Rate

2f. Because the interest rate gap has become smaller, uncovered interest parity implies that the expected rate of dollar depreciation has become smaller.

2g. The dollar would have to depreciate at time T because the expected future depreciation has has become smaller.

2h. See Figure 12-2. An increase in the foreign interest rate means that the expected rate of home currency depreciation does not have to be as large to equalize expected returns.

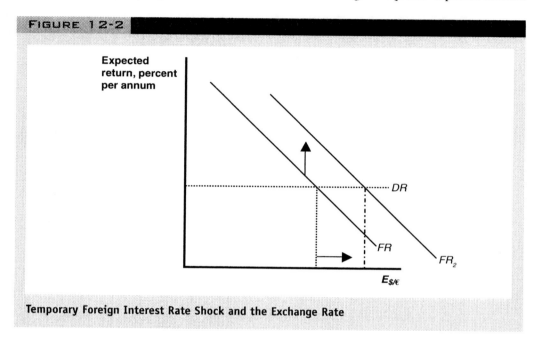

FIGURE 12-2

Temporary Foreign Interest Rate Shock and the Exchange Rate

3a. There is no effect on prices at time T because prices are assumed to be sticky.

3b. To get people to hold the increased real balances, the interest rate must drop. This is shown in Figure 12-3 as a rightward shift in the real money supply leading to a movement along real money demand.

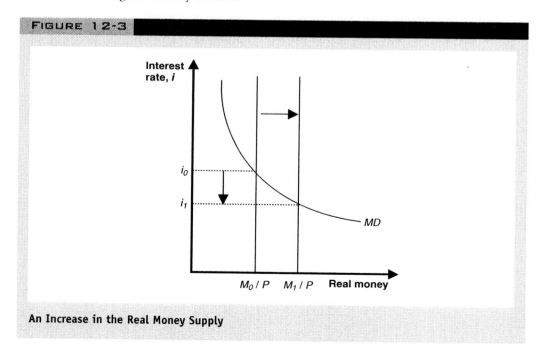

FIGURE 12-3

An Increase in the Real Money Supply

3c. In the long run, the price level must also rise by 10%.

3d. There is no long-run effect of the increase in M on the interest rate because inflation in the long run will be driven back to zero after prices have jumped 10%. When prices rise from P to P_1, it must be that $M_1 / P_1 = M_0 / P$.

4a. There is no effect on prices at time T because prices are assumed to be sticky.

4b. The interest rate must rise at time T because the increase in real output raises the demand for real balances shown in Figure 12-4 as the upward shift in the $L(i, Y)$ curve. To get people to be willing to keep their demand constant, the cost of real balances must rise.

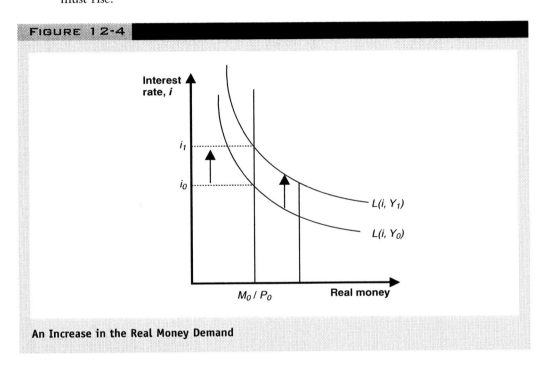

FIGURE 12-4

An Increase in the Real Money Demand

4c. In the long run the price level must fall to increase the quantity of real balances.

4d. There is no long-run effect on the interest rate because prices are flexible in the long run. That is, the price level falls so that the real money supply expands until the interest rate returns to i_0.

5. See Figure 12-5. A temporary increase in Home's money supply lowers its interest rate (left-hand panel) and so leads to a depreciation in the Home currency (right-hand panel).

FIGURE 12-5

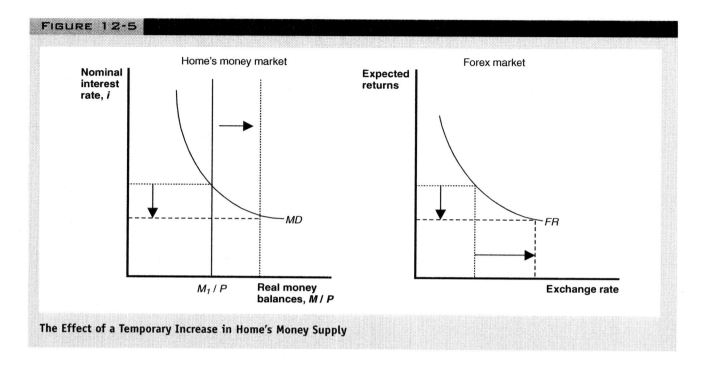

The Effect of a Temporary Increase in Home's Money Supply

6. See Figure 12-6. A temporary increase in Home's real output increases its demand for money (left-hand panel), thereby increasing Home's interest rate. The increase in the interest rate has the effect of causing an appreciation in the exchange rate in order to give Home's currency more room to depreciate in the future (right-hand panel) due to the higher current interest rate.

FIGURE 12-6

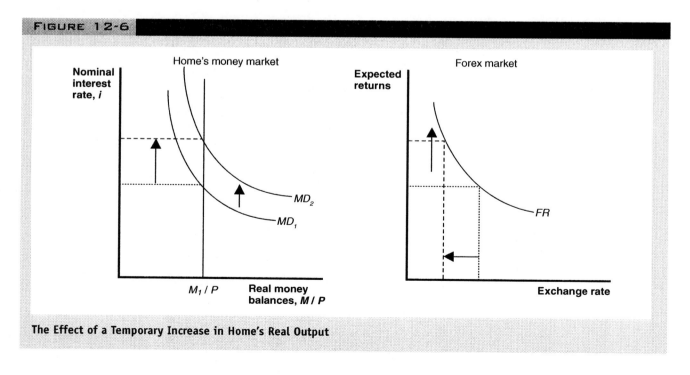

The Effect of a Temporary Increase in Home's Real Output

7. See Figure 12-7. An increase in Foreign's real output increases its money demand and so drives up Foreign's interest rate. This results in an increase in the return on foreign assets, which is represented in the right-hand panel of Figure 12-7 as a rightward shift in the curve. Home's currency depreciates relative to Foreign's currency.

FIGURE 12-7

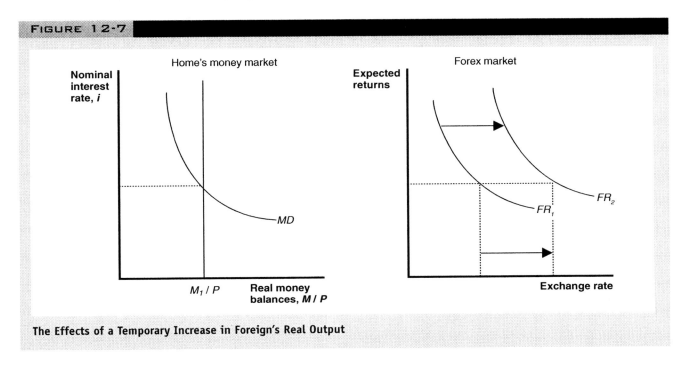

The Effects of a Temporary Increase in Foreign's Real Output

8a. True. If prices were perfectly flexible, then there would be no short-run effect on interest rates that cause overshooting.

8b. Uncertain. Although a sharp drop in the dollar could be consistent with a permanent increase in the money supply and a jump in inflation, it could also be consistent with other possibilities. For instance, there could be a large but temporary increase in the money supply in the United States. Alternatively, a foreign country could have tightened its monetary policy.

8c. Uncertain. Interest rates could increase because of a reduction in the money supply combined with sticky prices, or they could increase because inflation expectations have risen combined with the Fisher effect. The connection between interest rates and exchange rate movements depends on the context.

9a. Because we are in a long-run equilibrium, we can use the monetary approach developed in Chapter 11. Because $L(i)$ is the same in both countries, the exchange rate is equal to the ratio of money supplies ($\$1,000/€500$) multiplied by the ratio of real outputs ($5,000/10,000$) or $1\$/€$.

9b. Using the same approach as 9a, we find that the expected future spot rate is $1.5\$/€$.

9c. They are 5%. Recall that the expected rate of depreciation prior to time T was zero, so by UIP the interest rates must have been the same in the two countries. There is no monetary shock in Europe, so interest rates must have stayed the same after time T.

9d. By UIP, the dollar must be expected to appreciate by 3% at time T because interest rates in the United States are below those of Europe by 3%.

9e. At time T the expected rate of depreciation in the dollar is equal to -0.03 (the dollar is expected to appreciate), which is the gap between interest rates in the United States and Europe. The expected future spot rate is $1.5\$/€$, so if x is the current spot rate, then $(1.5\$/€ - x) / x = -0.03$. Hence, $x = 1.546\$/€$.

10a. See Figure 12-8. The increase in output from Y_0 to Y_1 shifts up money demand and raises the interest rate. People expect prices to fall in the future when they cease to be sticky. By absolute purchasing power parity (APPP) this implies an appreciated future spot rate. Hence, the expected return curve shifts down in the foreign exchange market. The two effects reinforce one another and the exchange rate falls.

FIGURE 12-8

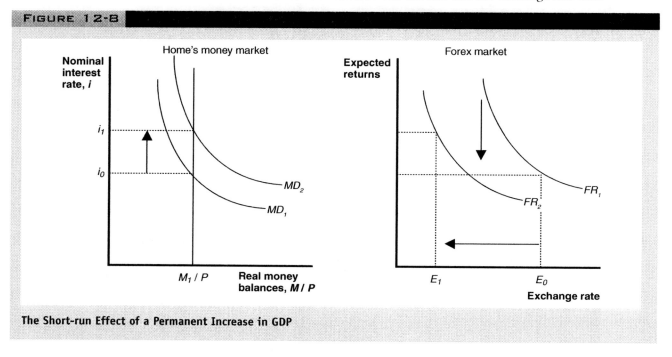

The Short-run Effect of a Permanent Increase in GDP

10b. See Figure 12-9. In the long-run prices fall from P_0 to P_1, and this expands the supply of real money. This lowers the interest rate and leads to a depreciation of the currency to E_2. Notice that the currency has depreciated from its short-run level, E_1, but has appreciated relative to its initial value, E_0. This means that the short-run exchange rate E_1 overshoots its long-run level E_2.

FIGURE 12-9

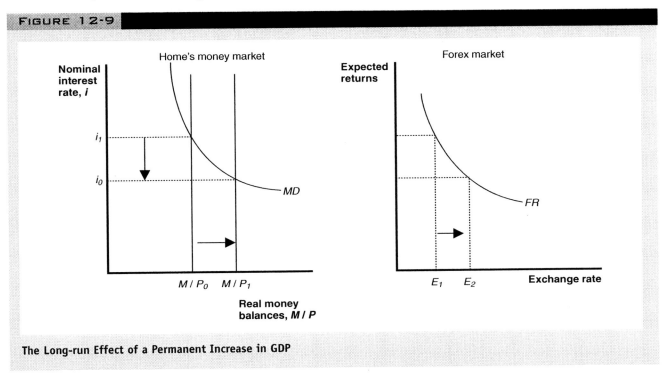

The Long-run Effect of a Permanent Increase in GDP

11. No, as long as PPP holds in the long run, monetary policy ultimately affects the price level, which in turn affects the exchange rate in the long run.

12a. Because Home has pegged its currency to Foreign, it must have the same interest rate as Foreign, so Home's interest rate rises.

12b. Home's real money demand rises, and this would tend to raise interest rates. Because interest rates cannot rise, Home's money supply must rise.

13

National and International Accounts: Income, Wealth, and the Balance of Payments

1a. False. The country may be a net exporter of factor services, or it may be receiving unilateral transfers from abroad.

1b. True. If no goods or services are being contributed to the economy from abroad, then supply-equals-demand dictates that expenditure equals product.

1c. False. A country's GDP includes only sales to final customers. It does not double-count intermediate input production.

1d. True. Consult Figure 13-2 on the next page. Along the circular flow, all the current account items can be found between GNE and GNDI.

2. Domestic citizens working abroad are a source of NFIA or NUT. As a result, GNDI exceeds GDP in countries like Jordan.

3. The current account identity tells us that the current balance is equal to the difference between national savings and investment. Holding fixed the savings rate, an increase in investment ought to lower the current account balance.

4. Yes. If a country has a trade surplus, its GDP will exceed its GNE. If, in addition, it has a deficit on its factor income account, its GNI will be less than its GDP.

5a. $GNE = C + I + G = 100$.

5b. $S = Y - C - G = 95 - 90 = 5$.

5c. $CA = S - I = 5 - 10 = -5$.

5d. A net exporter. A country that runs a current account deficit must export assets to obtain income to fund expenditure.

6. Recall that a country's current account balance is equal to the difference between saving and investment. A country with a high birth rate will tend to have a relatively large number of young citizens relative to other countries. If young people have different savings behaviors from older people, then the country may have very different current account behavior.

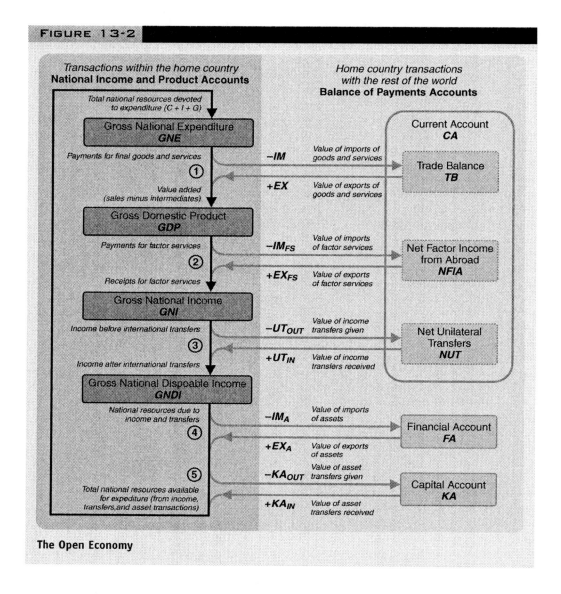

FIGURE 13-2

The Open Economy

7. A country with a very good investment climate will tend to have a higher investment rate. If the country has the same savings rate, then we would expect the country to be running a current account deficit.

8a. True. Government savings increases, and because all other components of savings are held fixed, the current account deficit must shrink.

8b. Uncertain. The chief question is how consumption spending responds. The phenomenon of Ricardian equivalence suggests that consumers will increase their spending in response to lower projected future taxes. If so, this might erode the savings gain.

9. The answer is b. The output of the affiliate is part of GDP, but its earnings will not be counted toward domestic income. Foreign aid does not increase GDP directly, and workers abroad do not affect domestic GDP.

10. The answer is d.

11. Uncertain. A country could use its current account surplus to pay down its existing liabilities to foreigners.

12. A country with a fixed exchange rate system is likely to intervene frequently in the foreign exchange market. As a result, it should have a much larger official settlements balance.

13a. The tractor sale is an $+EX$, and the payment is $-IM^F_A$.

13b. The loan is an import of a foreign asset $-IM^F_A$, and the deposit is an export of a home asset $+EX^H_A$.

13c. The food is exported to Zimbabwe $+EX$, which is balanced by a unilateral transfer $-UT_-$.

13d. The consultant's pay is an export of a factor service $+EX_{FS}$, and the payment is accomplished via a reduction on foreign claims on the American bank, so $-IM^H_A$.

13e. The concert is a service import $-IM$, but it is a gift $+UT_+$.

13f. The Chinese resident is receiving a service $+EX$, and the payment is $-IM^H_A$.

13g. The interest payment is factor service payment $+EX_{FS}$, and the payment method is $-IM^H_A$.

13h. The interest payment is factor service payment $+EX_{FS}$, and the payment method is an import of a foreign asset $-IM^F_A$ because the American bank now has a larger claim on a foreign entity.

14a. Summing over all the current account balances, we find that the external wealth would have been 50.

14b. The difference between the sum of current account balances and the actual external wealth is -7.

14c. The years when external wealth was greater than what was predicted by financial flows are 1991, 1992, 1994, 1995, and 1997.

15. If the current account deficit had been zero, the valuation effect would have increased the country's assets to $25 million, so external wealth would have on net been zero. The current account deficit would have reduced the country's net wealth to $-$5 million.

16. If the rate of return on assets and liabilities were the same and equal to r, then we would expect net income of $r(A - L)$, where A is assets and L is liabilities. Because $A < L$, we would expect these payments to be negative, yet they are positive.

Output, Exchange Rates, and Macroeconomic Policies in the Short Run

14

1a. The marginal propensity to consume is 0.75.

1b. Recall that $S = (Y - T) - C$. Plugging in the equation for C, we obtain $S = 0.25(Y - T) - 5$. Because disposable income $Y - T$ is equal to 100, we have $S = 20$.

1c. A consumption shock could take the form of a change in the intercept or the marginal propensity to consume. A consumption boom could take the form of an increase in either.

1d. A transfer of disposable income from one consumer to another will have no impact on aggregate consumption if both consumers have the same marginal propensity to consume.

1e. False. Although consumption spending will rise by this amount, some of the spending will fall on imports, and these are not part of domestic aggregate demand.

2a. All projects with a rate of return greater than the interest rate will be undertaken. Hence, investment will be 4 units.

2b. All projects with a rate of return greater than the interest rate will be undertaken. Hence, investment will be 2 units.

2c. All projects with a rate of return greater than the interest rate will be undertaken. Hence, investment will be 4 units. This answer is arrived at by doubling the numbers in the table.

3. The answer is illustrated in Figure 14-2. Note that the immediate impact of an appreciation of Home's currency is to reduce the cost of its imports and thereby improve the trade balance. Over time, the real appreciation of the currency induces expenditure switching by Home and Foreign consumers so that exports fall and imports increase. Eventually the trade balance deteriorates.

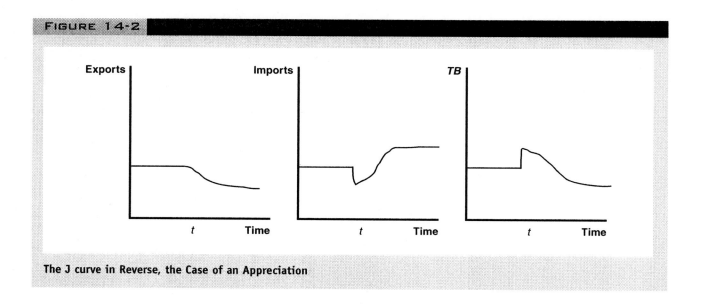

FIGURE 14-2

The J curve in Reverse, the Case of an Appreciation

4. The answer is d because both dollar invoicing and distribution costs reduce the share of the final price that is affected by exchange rate movements. They reduce the link between movements in the nominal exchange rate to movements in the real exchange rate. J-curve effects involve imperfect transmission of changes in the real exchange rate to the trade balance, which is a conceptually different issue.

5. The answer is d, all of the above.

6a. A fall in the interest rate increases investment spending, I, and leads to a depreciation of the exchange rate, which in turn increases the trade balance. Hence, aggregate demand increases and the national output rises.

6b. An appreciation of Home's currency tends to reduce the trade balance, which lowers aggregate demand and national output.

6c. A tax cut raises disposable income and so increases consumer spending. Although some of this spending goes to imports and so does not raise expenditure on domestic goods and services, consumption rises by more than imports. As a result, aggregate demand expands and so does domestic output.

6d. A Foreign tax cut raises consumer expenditure in Foreign, and some of this increased spending falls on Home's goods and services. Hence, aggregate demand in Home expands and so does national output.

6e. A drop in consumer confidence shifts the function $C(Y - T)$ down and so reduces aggregate demand for every level of national output. The downward shift in aggregate demand lowers national output.

6f. This is a sudden drop in the demand for imports. Consumers switch their expenditure away from imports toward domestic goods even with an unchanged nominal exchange rate. As a result, domestic demand increases and national output rises.

7a. A fall in interest rates is associated with a movement along the same IS curve rather than a shift in the IS curve.

7b. An increase in the expected future exchange rate is associated with a rightward shift in the IS curve.

7c. A tax cut is associated with a rightward shift in the IS curve.

7d. A Foreign tax cut is associated with a rightward shift in the IS curve.

7e. A drop in consumer confidence is associated with a leftward shift in the IS curve.

7f. A shift in expenditure toward domestic goods and services is associated with a rightward shift in aggregate demand.

8. The answer is d: a fall in the price level increases the real money supply. None of the other options has any direct effect on the LM curve.

9. True. The LM curve is upward sloping because when prices are sticky, real money demand has to be equal to a constant. An increase in national output raises real money demand, and this increase in money demand has to be offset by an increase in the nominal interest rate. If prices were flexible, then an increase in national output would result in a decrease in the price level and an increase in the real money supply.

10a. No. See Figure 14-3. An increase in the government spending or a reduction in taxes will shift the IS curve to the right, thereby increasing national output. The higher interest rate leads to an appreciation of the currency, however, reducing the trade balance. Moreover, the expansion of disposable income raises demand for imports further reducing the trade balance.

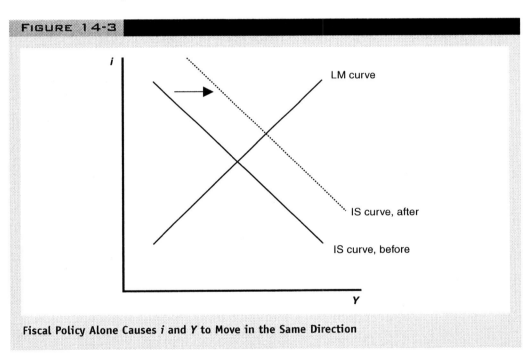

FIGURE 14-3

Fiscal Policy Alone Causes *i* and *Y* to Move in the Same Direction

10b. Yes. See Figure 14-4. An increase in the money supply shifts the LM curve to the right, thereby increasing national output and lowering interest rates. The lower interest rate causes the exchange rate to depreciate and tends to improve the trade balance. Although the increase in national output raises demand for imports, which tends to lower the trade balance, the exchange rate depreciation increases the trade balance. Therefore, it is possible that monetary policy alone could achieve both aims.

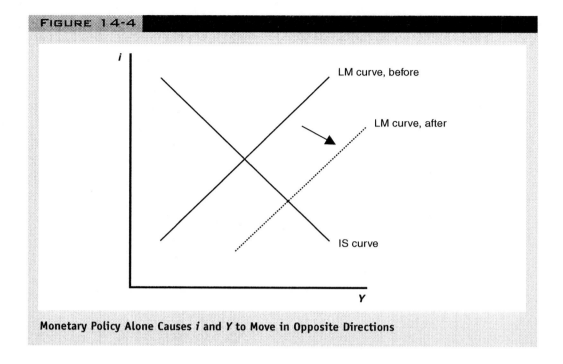

Figure 14-4

Monetary Policy Alone Causes *i* and *Y* to Move in Opposite Directions

10c. No. See Figure 14-5. An increase in the government spending or a reduction in taxes will shift the IS curve to the right, thereby increasing national output and putting upward pressure on interest rates. Because the higher interest rate would tend to appreciate the currency, the government must increase the money supply in order to maintain the fixed exchange rate. While the real exchange rate is unchanged, the increase in disposable income will tend to increase imports and worsen the trade balance.

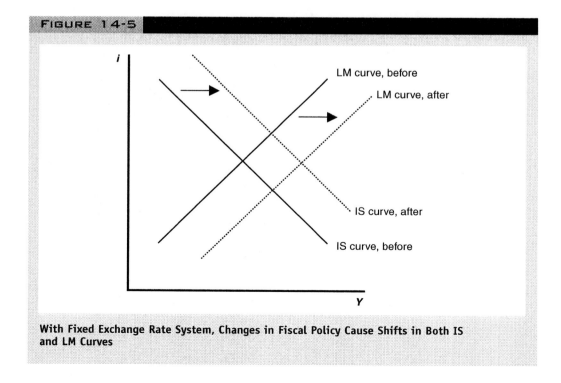

Figure 14-5

With Fixed Exchange Rate System, Changes in Fiscal Policy Cause Shifts in Both IS and LM Curves

11. False. There is some similarity in the sense that the domestic interest rate is fixed and the LM curve must be adjusted to accommodate movements in the IS curve. However, there is no sense in which the interest rates of Home and Foreign must be the same so that changes in the Foreign interest rate can change the exchange rate.

12a. See Figure 14-6. An exogenous drop in investment shifts the IS curve to the left, lowering output and the interest rate. The exchange rate depreciates and the trade balance improves, which offsets some of the recessionary impact of the shift.

FIGURE 14-6

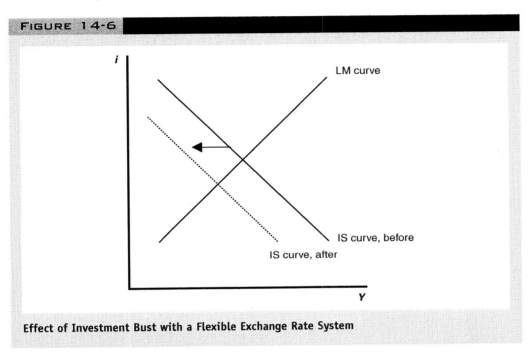

Effect of Investment Bust with a Flexible Exchange Rate System

12b. The most natural thing to do would be to cut taxes or raise government spending in order to shift the IS curve back to its initial level. Alternatively, the government could increase the money supply to shift the LM curve to the right.

12c. See Figure 14-7. Because the fixed exchange rate system requires the interest rate to be fixed, the leftward shift in the IS curve caused by the decline in investment spending induces the LM curve to shift to the left as well as inducing the central bank to lower the money supply. The effects of the shock are therefore magnified under a fixed exchange rate system.

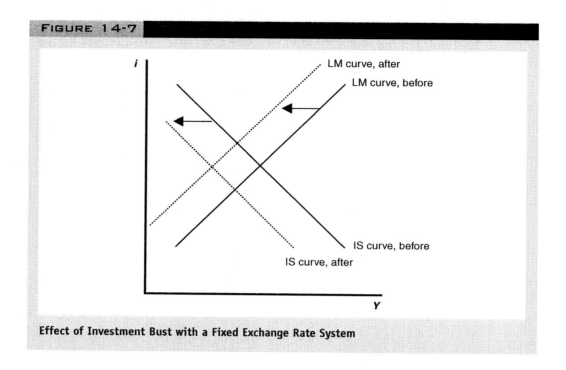

FIGURE 14-7

Effect of Investment Bust with a Fixed Exchange Rate System

12d. Fiscal policy could be used to offset the effect of the investment bust, but monetary policy is not an option.

13. See Figure 14-8. In both cases, the return on Foreign assets rises from FR_0 to FR_1 and the IS curve shifts from IS_0 to IS_1. In the case of a flexible exchange rate system, Home's exchange rate will depreciate, and this will tend to expand exports and contract imports, shifting the IS curve to the right. Output rises, and this drives up the local interest rate but by less than the rise in interest rates in Foreign (note that part of the expected return in Foreign is due to a faster rate of depreciation). In the case of the fixed exchange rate system, Home's exchange rate cannot change, so the interest must go up in Home by exactly as much as in Foreign. Hence, the LM curve must shift to the left. This reduces investment in Home and may result in reduced output.

FIGURE 14-8

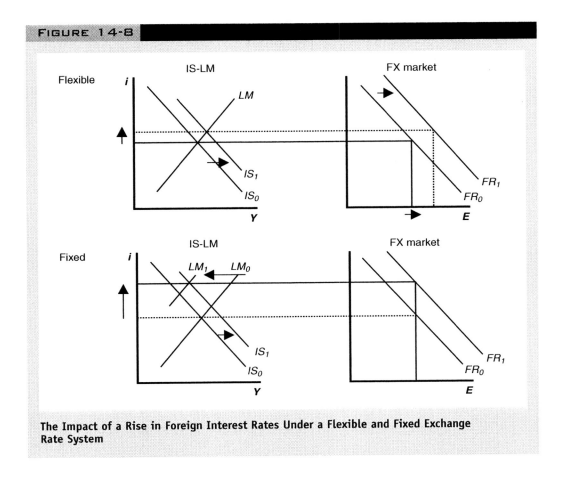

The Impact of a Rise in Foreign Interest Rates Under a Flexible and Fixed Exchange Rate System

14. The answer is d. all of the above.

15

Fixed versus Floating: International Monetary Experience

1. No, a country retains control over its fiscal policy even when it fixes its exchange rate. The decline in investment could be offset by either a tax cut or an increase in government spending.

2. It could be that trading patterns have changed so that the volume of trade with the country to which the currency is pegged has been eclipsed by trade with the other country.

3. Perhaps not. To the extent that the two states do not trade much with each other and may be exposed to asymmetric shocks (a fall in oil prices is good for Massachusetts but bad for Texas), it may be that the states would be better with different currencies.

4. By imposing capital controls the country regains its ability to conduct an independent monetary policy.

5. Countries have many nominal anchors at their disposal. If a country cannot commit to maintain a nominal anchor of a different sort, then it is unclear why it will be any more successful at fixing its nominal exchange rate.

6a. The depreciation of the dollar diminishes Home's assets relative to its liabilities, reducing its total wealth.

6b. If consumption and investment is sufficiently sensitive to changes in total wealth, then it is possible that the depreciation of the dollar will result in a contraction of both investment and consumption and a fall in output. As shown in the textbook, there is evidence that very large depreciations can have this effect on the economy.

7. Ideally, Home's trade in goods and its trade in assets would be with the same trade partner so that the economic integration and the currency mismatch arguments for fixing the exchange rate with a single country would be possible. In this case, however, fixing the currency in terms of the dollar means not fixing it with respect to the euro and vice versa. Thus, Home must choose between fixing its currency with the European Union to gain from market integration or fixing its currency with the United States to avoid the currency mismatch of its assets and liabilities.

8. The problem of original sin. If a country has a reputation of high inflation and an unstable currency, foreign firms may be reluctant to hold assets denominated in the local currency.

9a. If Foreign cuts its taxes, its expenditure rises, and some of the additional expenditure is directed to Home's goods and services. The increase in aggregate demand raises output in Home. Because Home was initially in full employment, its economy begins to overheat.

9b. If Foreign revalues its currency, then its real exchange rate will rise, and some of the expenditure will be shifted toward Home's products. If Home takes no action, its trade balance will rise, and the economy will again begin to overheat.

10. If a country fixes its currency to gold, it does not expose itself to arbitrary policy changes from the base country. Further, if there are enough adherents to the gold standard, it will also benefit from the network externality.

11a. A real devaluation of Home's currency causes expenditure switching away from Foreign toward Home. The reduction in aggregate demand can result in output falling below its full employment level in Foreign.

11b. Foreign could stimulate its economy by lowering the interest rate, thereby expanding investment. The reduction in interest rates in Foreign would have to be matched in Home to prevent Home's currency from appreciating.

12. If the center country increases its money supply, the non-center countries will also have to increase their money supplies in order to prevent their currencies from appreciating. The increase in the money supply in the non-center country could result in inflation if it is permanent.

13. The more countries that are fixed to a given country, the larger the volume of potential transactions that are not subject to exchange rate volatility.

14. Capital controls allow the countries within the system to have a modicum of monetary policy. The extent of policy autonomy is partially disciplined by the strength of the controls.